The Funeral
Encyclopedia

Charles L. Wallis Library, 0-8010-9715-0
1010 Sermon Illustrations from the Bible, 0-8010-9552-2
Speakers' Illustrations for Special Days, 0-8010-9555-7
A Treasury of Story Sermons for Children, 0-8010-9556-5
The Funeral Encyclopedia, 0-8010-9539-5

THE FUNERAL ENCYCLOPEDIA

A SOURCE BOOK

❋ ❋ ❋ ❋ ❋

Edited by Charles L. Wallis

*He hath sent me . . . to comfort
all that mourn.*   ISAIAH 61:2

BAKER BOOK HOUSE
Grand Rapids, Michigan 49516

Special acknowledgment is made to the following publishers and individuals for permission to reprint copyrighted materials:

ABINGTON-COKESBURY PRESS for extract from *Facing Life with Christ* by James Reid, copyright, 1940, by Whitmore & Smith; for poem "To My Father" from *The Glory of God* by Georgia Harkness, copyright, 1943, by Whitmore & Stone; for two quotations from *Poems* by William Alfred Quayle, copyright, 1914, by Methodist Book Concern; for extract from *The Light Shines Through*, copyright, 1930, by The Abingdon Press.

ASSOCIATION PRESS for two prayers from *Prayers for Times Like These* by S. Ralph Harlow, copyright, 1942.

THE BOBBS-MERRILL COMPANY for "Away" from *The Biographical Edition of the Complete Works of James Whitcomb Riley*, copyright, 1913, 1941.

MRS. RICHARD BURTON for "Sealed Orders" by Richard Burton.

THOMAS CURTIS CLARK for his poems "The Journey" and "The Victor"; for "The Kiss of God" by G. A. Studdert-Kennedy from his anthology, *The Golden Book of Faith* and "Turning the Corner" by Arthur B. Rhinow from *Poems for Daily Needs*.

W. B. CONKEY COMPANY for "The Beyond" and "Faith" by Ella Wheeler Wilcox.

MRS. CALVIN COOLIDGE for her poem "The Open Door."

COWARD-MCCANN, INC., for extract from *We Believe in Immortality*, edited by Sydney Strong, copyright, 1929.

THOMAS Y. CROWELL COMPANY for extract from "Faith" from *Poems of Sarah K. Bolton.*

DODD, MEAD & COMPANY for extract from "When All Is Done" from *The Collected Poems of Paul Laurence Dunbar*, copyright, 1895, 1913; for "To My Father" from *Poems* by Iris Tree, copyright, 1919; for "Death Is a Door" from *Star in a Well* by Nancy Byrd Turner, copyright, 1935.

DOUBLEDAY & COMPANY for "L'Envoi" from *The Seven Seas* by Rudyard Kipling, copyright, 1892, 1893, 1894, 1896, 1905, 1933, by Rudyard Kipling. (Permission also from Mrs. George Bambridge, A. P. Watt & Son, London, and the Macmillan Company of Canada.)

E. P. DUTTON & COMPANY for prayer from *The Temple* by W. E. Orchard.

THE EPWORTH PRESS, London, for extract from *The Vigil of God* by P. J. Fisher, copyright, 1943; for "The Unseen Bridge" by Gilbert Thomas.

MRS. ROBERT FREEMAN for "Beyond the Horizon" and "In My Father's House" by Robert Freeman.

HARCOURT, BRACE AND COMPANY for "The Watcher" from *Collected Poems of Margaret Widdemer*, copyright, 1928.

HARPER & BROTHERS for the extracts from *The Bible: A New Translation* by James Moffatt, copyright, 1922, 1935, 1950; for extract from *From Skepticism to Faith* by Charles Fiske, copyright, 1934; for extract from *Greatest Thoughts on Immortality*, edited by Jacob Helder, copyright, 1930; for extract from *If I Had One Sermon to Preach on Immortality*, edited by William L. Stidger, copyright, 1929; for funeral service from *Minister's Service Book* by James Dalton Morrison, copyright, 1937; for "An Epitaph" from *Poems* of Edwin Markham, copyright, 1950, by Virgil Markham; for "After Work," "God's To-

iv

To

James Dalton Morrison

Pastor, Teacher, Friend

By pureness, by knowledge,
by longsuffering, by kindness,
by the Holy Ghost, by love unfeigned.
2 CORINTHIANS 6:6

Introduction

The funeral presents a particularly difficult duty—and privilege—
to every pastor. Funerals frequently come when a pastor is working
under the pressure of an especially crowded schedule. He occasionally
receives a last-minute request to officiate. He may feel sometimes that
he has not the time and energy to prepare an adequate and meaningful service. He will often regret that he does not have at hand the
study and worship resources to offer the words of comfort and consolation which he believes an individual service may require.

This volume is a source book containing an abundance of all of the
materials which are included in the funeral service. The volume is
designed to be immediately useful. To this end special attention has
been given to indexing.

Much of the material is printed here for the first time, although
every effort has been made to include those poems, Scriptures, and
other aids which a pastor should expect to find in a volume of this
nature.

Unless otherwise indicated, all Scriptures come from the Author-
ized Version. In so far as possible, all poems, prayers, sermons, and
other materials have been reproduced from original sources. An
asterisk (*) before sermon titles in the Table of Contents identifies
those sermons which were prepared expressly for this volume or which
are printed here for the first time.

The editor wishes to thank several persons who have generously
aided in the preparation of this volume. Miss Marjorie Taylor of the
Rochester Public Library, Professor Theodore Trost of the Colgate-
Rochester Divinity School Library and Mrs. Frances Wilkens of the
Keuka College Library were helpful in securing source materials.
Dr. Quentin T. Lightner and Dr. James Rodney Branton made valu-
able suggestions.

Contents

* See Introduction, p. ix.

I. The Funeral Service

The order and content of the funeral service will be determined by several factors. The requests of the family of the deceased, if reasonable and consistent with Christian teaching and practice, will be honored. A service held in the home of the deceased or in a mortuary chapel will usually be briefer and less formal than a service in the church. Local custom and practice should seldom be violated.

Brevity and simplicity are the keynotes of the effective and meaningful service. Everything should be done both to ease the burden of the grief-stricken and to emphasize the Christian faith and hope.

A brief, though complete order of worship, may be according to this fashion:

> Opening Scriptural sentences
> Invocational prayer
> Scripture lesson
> Pastoral prayer
> Funeral message
> Benediction

Numerous variations are possible.

In a church funeral the order may follow this pattern:

> Organ Prelude
> Processional Scriptural sentences
> Invocational prayer
> Hymn
> Scripture lesson
> Pastoral lesson
> Hymn or special music
> Obituary
> Funeral sermon
> Hymn
> Benediction
> Organ postlude

The committal consists of

> Scripture
> Committal
> Prayer
> Benediction

Several of the poems in this volume are suitable for use at the committal.

Abundant aids for the preparing of a pastor's own order of worship are included in the succeeding sections of this volume.

When the pastor is called upon to officiate at a funeral of a non-Christian, he will make available his good services as a Christian pastor to do what he can to serve. He will, however, decline to share the Scriptural promises which concern those who "die in the Lord," but will wish his Christian witness to the living to be strong and unhesitant.

The typical services which follow are suggestive of the manner in which a pastor may prepare his own service. They may on occasion serve as texts to be read.

A. TYPICAL SERVICES

General Service—1

OPENING SENTENCE:

1 Our help is in the name of the Lord, who made heaven and earth, and in our Saviour Christ Jesus, who abolished death and brought life and immortality to light through the gospel. (Ps. 124:8; 2 Tim. 1:10, R.S.V.)

INVOCATION, *in the pastor's own words, or the following:*

2 Our Father in Heaven, whose love is infinite and in whose will is our peace: be pleased to look down upon our sorrow, and enable us so to hear Thy Holy Word, that through patience and comfort of the Scriptures we may have hope. And grant us the consolation of Thy Holy Spirit, that we may be raised above the shadows of mortality into the light of Thy countenance and the joy of Thy presence; through Him who died and rose again and ever liveth with Thee, even Jesus Christ our Lord. Amen.

[HYMN, ANTHEM, OR SOLO, *if one be desired*]

SCRIPTURES AND POEMS:

3   Lord, thou hast been our dwelling place
      In all generations.
      Before the mountains were brought forth,
      Or ever thou hadst formed the earth and the world,
      Even from everlasting to everlasting, thou art God.
      For a thousand years in thy sight
      Are but as yesterday when it is past,
      And as a watch in the night. (Ps. 90:1-2, 4)

4 God is our refuge and strength,
   A very present help in trouble.
   Therefore will we not fear, though the earth do change,
   And though the mountains be shaken into the heart of the seas;

Though the waters thereof roar and be troubled,
Though the mountains tremble with the swelling thereof.

(Ps. 46: 1-3, A.S.V.)

5   When thou passest through the waters, I will be with thee; and
    through the rivers, they shall not overflow thee: when thou walkest
through the fire, thou shalt not be burned; neither shall the flame
kindle upon thee. (Isa. 43:2)

6   Who shall separate us from the love of Christ? shall tribulation,
    or anguish, or persecution, or famine, or nakedness, or peril, or
sword? Nay, in all these things we are more than conquerors through
him that loved us. For I am persuaded, that neither death, nor life,
nor angels, nor principalities, nor powers, nor things present, nor
things to come, nor height, nor depth, nor any other creature, shall be
able to separate us from the love of God, which is in Christ Jesus our
Lord. (Rom. 8:35, 37-39, A.S.V.)

7   And I saw a new heaven and a new earth: for the first heaven and
    the first earth are passed away; and the sea is no more. And I saw
the holy city, new Jerusalem, coming down out of heaven from God,
made ready as a bride adorned for her husband. And I heard a great
voice out of the throne saying, Behold, the tabernacle of God is with
men, and he shall dwell with them, and they shall be his peoples, and
God himself shall be with them, and be their God: and he shall wipe
away every tear from their eyes; and death shall be no more; neither
shall there be mourning, nor crying, nor pain, any more: the first
things are passed away. (Rev. 21:1-4, A.S.V.)

8   It singeth low in every heart,
                  We hear it, each and all,—
              A song of those who answer not,
                  However we may call:
              They throng the silence of the breast,
                  We see them as of yore,—
              The kind, the brave, the true, the sweet,
                  Who walk with us no more.

              'Tis hard to take the burden up,
                  When these have laid it down;

They brightened all the joy of life,
They softened every frown;
But oh, 'tis good to think of them,
When we are troubled sore!
Thanks be to God that such have been,
Though they are here no more!

More homelike seems the vast unknown,
Since they have entered there;
To follow them were not so hard,
Wherever they may fare;
They cannot be where God is not,
On any sea or shore;
Whate'er betides, Thy love abides,
Our God, forevermore![1]

9 Let your loins be girded about, and your lamps burning; and be
ye yourselves like unto men looking for their lord . . . ; that, when
he cometh and knocketh, they may straightway open unto him. Blessed
are those servants, whom the lord when he cometh shall find watching.
. . . Be ye also ready: for in an hour that ye think not the Son of Man
cometh. (Luke 12:35-37, 40, A.S.V.)

10　　So live, that when thy summons comes to join
The innumerable caravan, which moves
To that mysterious realm, where each shall take
His chamber in the silent halls of death,
Thou go not, like the quarry slave at night,
Scourged to his dungeon, but, sustained and soothed
By an unfaltering trust, approach thy grave
Like one who wraps the drapery of his couch
About him, and lies down to pleasant dreams.[2]

11 Fear thou not, for I am with thee; be not dismayed, for I am thy
God; I will strengthen thee: yea, I will help thee: yea, I will uphold thee with the right hand of my righteousness. For I, the Lord thy
God, will hold thy right hand, saying unto thee, Fear not; I will help
thee. (Isa. 41:10, 13, A.S.V.)

[1] "Auld Lang Syne" by John White Chadwick.
[2] From "Thanatopsis" by William Cullen Bryant.

12 For as the heavens are high above the earth,
So great is his lovingkindness toward them that fear him.
Like as a father pitieth his children,
So the Lord pitieth·them that fear him.
For he knoweth our frame;
He remembereth that we are dust. (Ps. 103:11, 13-14, A.S.V.)

13 Let not your heart be troubled [said Jesus]: believe in God, believe also in me. In my Father's house are many mansions; if it were not so, I would have told you; for I go to prepare a place for you. And if I go and prepare a place for you, I come again, and will receive you unto myself; that where I am, there ye may be also. (John 14:1-3, A.S.V.)

14 Beloved, now are we children of God, and it is not yet made manifest what we shall be. We know that, if he shall be manifested, we shall be like him; for we shall see him even as he is. Now we see through a glass, darkly; but then face to face: now I know in part; but then shall I know even as also I am known. (1 John 3:2, A.S.V.; 1 Cor. 13:12)

[ADDRESS, *if one be desired*]
PRAYER, *of thanksgiving for the life of the deceased and of comfort for the bereaved, by the pastor in his own words.*
BENEDICTION

THE COMMITTAL SERVICE

SCRIPTURES:

At the grave, the body having been lowered, and the people assembled, the pastor may say:

15 I am the resurrection, and the life: he that believeth in me, though he were dead, yet shall he live: and whosoever liveth and believeth in me shall never die. I am he that liveth, and was dead; and, behold, I am alive for evermore. (John 11:25-26; Rev. 1:18)

ADDRESS:

16 This is the faith of the Christian. We do not sorrow as those who have no hope. It is our confidence that our loved ones move on into the nearer presence of God and abide under His loving care.

Nor do we sorrow as those who have no comfort. Our Master said: "Let not your heart be troubled: believe in God, believe also in me. In my Father's house are many mansions. . . . I go to prepare a place for you. And if I go and prepare a place for you, I come again, and will receive you unto myself; that where I am, there ye may be also."

COMMITTAL, *in the pastor's own words, or one of the following:*

17   O God, our help in ages past, our hope for years to come, into Thy gracious keeping we commit the soul of our beloved *brother,* thanking Thee for all *he* has meant to us and praying that through the grace of our Lord Jesus Christ Thou wilt grant *him* an abundant entrance into Thine eternal kingdom. Comfort, we beseech Thee, the hearts that are heavy with sorrow, and grant that they may find in Thee a Friend who is equal to all their needs. Sanctify to each of us the memories of this solemn hour. Here in this place with its tender associations, may we dedicate ourselves anew to Thy service, that with chastened desires and nobler motives we may return to our homes and to the duties that await us; through Jesus Christ our Lord. Amen.

18   Eternal God, our Father, as in this solemn hour we commit to the ground the body of our beloved friend, and commend to Thy merciful and gracious care *his* spirit, grant that we may so rededicate ourselves to Thee that, finding now the comfort of Thy presence, we may also obtain grace for all that is to come, until the day break, and these shadows flee away; through Jesus Christ our Lord. Amen.

BENEDICTION:

19   The Lord bless you and keep you; the Lord make his face to shine upon you, and be gracious unto you; the Lord lift up his countenance upon you, and give you peace. Amen. (Num. 6:24-26)
Arranged by James Dalton Morrison

General Service—2

OPENING SENTENCES, *one or more of the following may be read:*

20   The Lord is nigh unto all them that call upon him, to all that call upon him in truth. He will fulfil the desire of them that fear him: he also will hear their cry, and will save them. (Ps. 145:18-19)

21 Jesus saith unto her, I am the resurrection, and the life: he that believeth in me, though he were dead, yet shall he live: and whosoever liveth and believeth in me shall never die. (John 11:25-26)

22 I would not have you to be ignorant, brethren, concerning them which are asleep, that ye sorrow not, even as others which have no hope. For if we believe that Jesus died and rose again, even so them also which sleep in Jesus will God bring with him. (1 Thess. 4:13-14)

INVOCATIONAL PRAYERS, *one or more of the following may be read:*

23 Almighty God, our Heavenly Father, who art our Refuge and Strength, and a very present Help in time of trouble: enable us, we pray Thee, to put our trust in Thee, and seeing that we have an High Priest who is touched with the feeling of our infirmities, may we come boldly unto the throne of grace that we may obtain mercy and find grace to help in this our time of need; through Jesus Christ our Lord. Amen.

24 O Lord Jesus Christ, who Thyself didst weep beside the grave, and art touched with the feeling of our sorrows, fulfil now Thy promise that Thou wilt not leave Thy people comfortless, but wilt come to them. Reveal Thyself unto Thine afflicted servants, and cause them to hear Thee saying, "I am the resurrection and the life." Help them, O Lord, to turn to Thee with true discernment, and to abide in Thee through living faith; that, finding now the comfort of Thy presence, they may have also a sure confidence in Thee for all that is to come: until the day break, and these shadows flee away. Hear us for Thy great mercy's sake, O Jesus Christ our Lord. Amen.[1]

25 O Lord, by all Thy dealings with us, whether of joy or pain, of light or darkness, let us be brought to Thee. Let us value no treatment of Thy grace simply because it makes us happy or because it makes us sad, because it gives us or denies us what we want; but may all that Thou sendest us bring us to Thee; that knowing Thy perfectness we may be sure in every disappointment, Thou art still loving us, in every darkness Thou art still enlightening us, and in every enforced idleness Thou art giving us life, as in His death Thou didst give life to Thy Son, our Saviour, Jesus Christ. Amen.[2]

[1] From *Common Worship.*
[2] Phillips Brooks.

HYMN OR SPECIAL MUSIC, *or the pastor may read one of the following:*

26   Servant of God, well done!
            Rest from thy loved employ:
            The battle fought, the victory won,
            Enter thy Master's joy.

            The pains of death are past,
            Labour and sorrow cease,
            And Life's long warfare closed at last,
            Thy soul is found in peace.[1]

27   When Death, the angel of our higher dreams,
            Shall come, far ranging from the hills of light
            He will not catch me unaware; for I
            Shall be as now communing with the dawn.
            For I shall make all haste to follow him
            Along the valley, up the misty slope
            Where life lets go and Life at last is born.
            There I shall find the dreams that I have lost
            On toilsome earth, and they will guide me on,
            Beyond the mists unto the farthest height.
            I shall not grieve except to pity those
            Who cannot hear the songs that I shall hear.[2]

OLD TESTAMENT LESSONS, *one or more may be read:*

28 God is our refuge and strength, a very present help in trouble.
Therefore will not we fear, though the earth be removed, and
though the mountains be carried into the midst of the sea; though the
waters thereof roar and be troubled, though the mountains shake with
the swelling thereof. There is a river, the streams whereof shall make
glad the city of God, the holy place of the tabernacles of the most
High. God is in the midst of her; she shall not be moved: God shall
help her, and that right early. . . . Be still, and know that I am God:
I will be exalted among the heathen, I will be exalted in the earth. The
Lord of hosts is with us; the God of Jacob is our refuge. (Ps. 46:1-5,
10-11)

[1] "Well Done" by James Montgomery.
[2] "The Journey" by Thomas Curtis Clark.

29 I wait for the Lord, my soul doth wait, and in his word do I hope. My soul waiteth for the Lord more than they that watch for the morning: I say, more than they that watch for the morning. Let Israel hope in the Lord: for with the Lord there is mercy, and with him is plenteous redemption. And he shall redeem Israel from all his iniquities. (Ps. 130:5-8)

NEW TESTAMENT LESSONS, *one or more may be read:*

30 Let not your heart be troubled: ye believe in God, believe also in me. In my Father's house are many mansions: if it were not so, I would have told you. I go to prepare a place for you. And if I go and prepare a place for you, I will come again, and receive you unto myself; that where I am, there ye may be also. And whither I go ye know, and the way ye know. Thomas saith unto him, Lord, we know not whither thou goest; and how can we know the way? Jesus saith unto him, I am the way, the truth, and the life: no man cometh unto the Father, but by me. (John 14:1-6)

31 Some man will say, How are the dead raised up? and with what body do they come? Thou fool, that which thou sowest is not quickened, except it die: and that which thou sowest, thou sowest not that body that shall be, but bare grain, it may chance of wheat, or of some other grain: but God giveth it a body as it hath pleased him, and to every seed his own body. All flesh is not the same flesh: but there is one kind of flesh of men, another flesh of beasts, another of fishes, and another of birds. There are also celestial bodies, and bodies terrestrial: but the glory of the celestial is one, and the glory of the terrestrial is another. There is one glory of the sun, and another glory of the moon, and another of the stars: for one star differeth from another star in glory. So also is the resurrection of the dead. It is sown in corruption; it is raised in incorruption; it is sown in dishonour; it is raised in glory: it is sown in weakness; it is raised in power: it is sown a natural body; it is raised a spiritual body. There is a natural body, and there is a spiritual body. And so it is written, the first man Adam was made a living soul; the last Adam was made a quickening spirit. Howbeit that was not first which is spiritual, but that which is natural; and afterward that which is spiritual. The first man is of the earth, earthly: the second man is the Lord from heaven. As is the earthly, such are they also that are earthly: and as is the heavenly, such are they also that are heavenly. And as we have borne the image of the earthly, we shall also bear the image of the heavenly. Now this I say, brethren, that flesh and blood cannot inherit the kingdom of God; neither doth corruption inherit incorruption. Behold, I shew you a mystery; We shall not all sleep, but we shall all be changed, in a moment, in the twinkling of an eye, at the last trump: for the trumpet shall sound, and the dead shall be raised incorruptible, and we shall be changed. For this corruptible must put on incorruption, and this mortal must put on immortality. So when this corruptible shall have put on incorruption, and this mortal shall have put on immortality, then shall be brought to pass the saying that is written, Death is swallowed up in victory. O death, where is thy sting? O grave, where is thy victory? The sting of death is sin; and the strength of sin is the law. But thanks be to God, which giveth us the victory through our Lord Jesus Christ. Therefore, my beloved brethren, be ye stedfast, unmoveable, always abounding in the work of the Lord, forasmuch as ye know that your labour is not in vain in the Lord. (1 Cor. 15:35-58)

32 Wherefore comfort one another with these words. (1 Thess. 4:18)

PRAYER, *in the pastor's own words or the following may be read:*

33 O God, who art the strength of thy saints and who redeemest the souls of Thy servants: we bless Thy name for all those who have died in the Lord, and who now rest from their labours, having received the end of their faith, even the salvation of their souls. Especially we call to remembrance Thy lovingkindness and Thy tender mercies to this Thy servant. For all Thy goodness that withheld not *his* portion in the joys of this earthly life, and for Thy guiding hand along the way of *his* pilgrimage, we give Thee thanks and praise. Especially we bless Thee for Thy grace that kindled in *his* heart the love of Thy dear Name; that enabled *him* to fight the good fight, to endure unto the end, and to obtain the victory; yea, to become more than conqueror, through Him that loveth us. We magnify Thy holy Name that, *his* trials and temptations being ended, sickness and death being passed, with all the dangers and difficulties of this mortal life, *his* spirit is at home in Thy presence, at whose right hand dwelleth eternal peace. And grant, O Lord, we beseech Thee, that we who rejoice in the triumph of Thy saints may profit by their example, thus becoming followers of their faith and patience, we also may enter with them into an inheritance incorruptible and undefiled, and that fadeth not away. Through Jesus Christ our Lord. Amen.[1]

SERMON, *if desirable.*

PRAYER AFTER SERMON, *in the pastor's own words.*

BENEDICTION:

34 The peace of God, which passeth all understanding, keep your hearts and minds through Christ Jesus. Amen. (Phil. 4:7)

THE COMMITTAL SERVICE

SCRIPTURES:

35 Blessed be God, even the Father of our Lord Jesus Christ, the Father of mercies, and the God of all comfort; who comforteth us in all our tribulation, that we may be able to comfort them which are in any trouble, by the comfort wherewith we ourselves are comforted of God. (2 Cor. 1:3-4)

36 And I saw a new heaven and a new earth: for the first heaven and the first earth were passed away; and there was no more sea. And I John saw the holy city, new Jerusalem, coming down from God out of heaven, prepared as a bride adorned for her husband. And I heard a great voice out of heaven saying, Behold, the tabernacle of God is with men, and he will dwell with them, and they shall be his people, and God himself shall be with them, and be their God. And God shall wipe away all tears from their eyes; and there shall be no more death, neither sorrow, nor crying, neither shall there be any more pain: for the former things are passed away. And he that sat upon the throne said, Behold, I make all things new. And he said unto me, Write: for these words are true and faithful. (Rev. 21:1-5)

COMMITTAL SENTENCE:

37 Forasmuch as Almighty God hath received unto Himself the soul of our departed *brother,* we therefore tenderly commit *his* body to the ground in the blessed hope that as *he* has borne the image of the earthly so also *he* shall bear the image of the heavenly.

COMMITTAL PRAYER, *in the pastor's own words or the following may be read:*

[1] From *Presbyterian Common Worship.*

38   Our Heavenly Father, who art waiting to receive and answer
       each sincere and simple prayer, we turn to Thee in our great
need, asking for light in our darkness and deliverance from our doubts
and fears. Thou sendest forth Thy breath, we are created; Thou takest
away our life, we die and return to the dust. Whether we live, then,
or die, we are in Thy compassionate and loving care; and the shadow
that darkens our path is but the close approaching, overbrooding
shadow of Thy nearer presence.

Here, then, we commit to Thy unfailing love the beloved soul now
departed. We thank Thee for the gracious memories which gather
about this life, for kindly deeds and thoughts, for the love freely given
and the love modestly received, for the patient bearing of the heavy
cross of solitude and pain, and now at last for quiet release from the
burden of the flesh and entrance into the peace reserved for those who
love Thee. The Lord gave, and the Lord hath taken away; blessed
be the Name of the Lord. Amen.[1]

THE LORD'S PRAYER.

BENEDICTION:

39   The Lord bless thee, and keep thee: the Lord make his face shine
       upon thee, and be gracious unto thee: the Lord lift up his
countenance upon thee, and give thee peace. (Num. 6:24-26)

A Brief Service

OPENING SENTENCES:

40   Lord, thou hast been our dwelling place in all generations. Be-
       fore the mountains were brought forth, or ever thou hadst formed
the earth and the world, even from everlasting to everlasting, thou
art God. (Ps. 90:1-2)

41   The Lord is nigh unto all them that call upon him, to all that
       call upon him in truth. He will fulfil the desire of them that fear
him: he also will hear their cry, and will save them. (Ps. 145:18-19)

PRAYER:

42   O God, the Lord of life, the Conqueror over death, our help in
       every time of trouble, who dost not willingly grieve nor afflict
the children of men: comfort us who mourn, and give us grace, in

[1] Frances Greenwood Peabody (abbreviated).

the presence of death, to worship Thee the everlasting and eternal God, that, while we accompany the soul departed with the prayer of faith, we may have sure hope of eternal life, and be enabled to put our whole trust in Thy wonderful goodness and mercy; through Jesus Christ our Lord. Amen.[1]

SCRIPTURE LESSON:

43 The Lord is my light and my salvation; whom shall I fear? the Lord is the strength of my life; of whom shall I be afraid? Though an host should encamp against me, my heart shall not fear: though war should rise against me, in this will I be confident. For in the time of trouble he shall hide me in his pavilion: in the secret of his tabernacle shall he hide me; he shall set me up upon a rock. Teach me thy way, O Lord, and lead me in a plain path. I had fainted, unless I had believed to see the goodness of the Lord in the land of the living. (Ps. 27:1, 3, 5, 11, 13)

44 Wherefore seeing we also are compassed about with so great a cloud of witnesses, let us lay aside every weight, and the sin which doth so easily beset us, and let us run with patience the race that is set before us, looking unto Jesus the author and finisher of our faith; who for the joy that was set before him endured the cross, despising the shame, and is set down at the right hand of the throne of God. (Heb. 12:1-2)

45 For as many as are led by the Spirit of God, they are the sons of God. The Spirit itself beareth witness with our spirit, that we are the children of God: and if children, then heirs; heirs of God, and joint-heirs with Christ; if so be that we suffer with him, that we may be also glorified together. For I reckon that the sufferings of this present time are not worthy to be compared with the glory which shall be revealed in us. If God be for us, who can be against us? He that spared not his own Son, but delivered him up for us all, how shall he not with him also freely give us all things? Who shall lay any thing to the charge of God's elect? It is God that justifieth. Who is he that condemneth? It is Christ that died, yea rather, that is risen again, who is even at the right hand of God, who also maketh intercession for us. Who shall separate us from the love of Christ? shall tribulation, or distress, or persecution, or famine, or nakedness, or peril, or

[1] From *Divine Service.*

sword? Nay, in all these things we are more than conquerors through him that loved us. For I am persuaded, that neither death, nor life, nor angels, nor principalities, nor powers, nor things present, nor things to come, nor height, nor depth, nor any other creature, shall be able to separate us from the love of God, which is in Christ Jesus our Lord. (Rom. 8:14, 16-18, 31-35, 37-39)

PRAYERS.

46   O Lord of Life, where e'er they be,
            Safe in Thine own eternity,
         Our dead are living unto Thee.

         All souls are Thine and, here or there,
            They rest within Thy sheltering care;
         One providence alike they share.[1]

47 We seem to give *him* back to Thee, dear Lord, who gavest *him* to us. Yet, as Thou didst not lose *him* in giving, so we have not lost *him* by *his* return. Not as the world giveth, givest Thou, O Lover of Souls! What Thou givest, Thou takest not away. For what is Thine is ours always, if we are Thine. And life is eternal; and love is immortal; and death is only a horizon; and a horizon is nothing save the limit of our sight. Lift us up, strong Son of God, that we may see further; cleanse our eyes that we may see more clearly; draw us closer to Thyself that we may know ourselves nearer to our beloved who are with Thee. And while Thou dost prepare a place for us, prepare us for that happy place, that where they are, and Thou art, we too may be. Amen.[2]

BENEDICTION:

48 Now our Lord Jesus Christ himself, and God, even our Father, which hath loved us, and hath given us everlasting consolation and good hope through grace, comfort your hearts, and stablish you in every good word and work. Amen. (2 Thess. 2:16-17)

THE COMMITTAL SERVICE

49 Let not your heart be troubled: ye believe in God, believe also in me. In my Father's house are many mansions: if it were not so,

[1] "All Souls Are Thine" by Frederick L. Hosmer.
[2] Rossiter W. Raymond.

I would have told you. I go to prepare a place for you. And if I go and prepare a place for you, I will come again, and receive you unto myself; that where I am, there ye may be also. And whither I go ye know, and the way ye know. Thomas saith unto him, Lord, we know not whither thou goest; and how can we know the way? Jesus saith unto him, I am the way, the truth, and the life: no man cometh unto the Father, but by me. (John 14:1-6)

50   Almighty God, the Refuge of the living, the Rest of the dead, and the Hope of all that Thou hast made: we commend unto Thy everlasting mercy the soul of this our *brother*, whom Thou hast summoned from this transitory and uncertain life to the eternal and unseen world, there to appear before the judgment seat of Christ; beseeching Thee to grant unto *him* perfect release from all sin and sorrow, making *him* meet to be a partaker of the inheritance of the saints in light, where in the glory of Thy presence *he* may serve Thee, see Thy face, and be ever satisfied; through the sacrifice and merits of Jesus Christ, our only Saviour and Redeemer. Amen.[1]

51   The Lord bless thee, and keep thee: the Lord make his face shine upon thee, and be gracious unto thee: the Lord lift up his countenance upon thee, and give thee peace. Amen. (Num. 6:24-26)

For a Child

52   The eternal God is thy refuge, and underneath are the everlasting arms. (Deut. 33:27)

53   He shall feed his flock like a shepherd: he shall gather the lambs with his arm, and carry them in his bosom. (Is. 40:11)

54   Jesus said unto them, Suffer the little children to come unto me, and forbid them not: for of such is the kingdom of God. Verily I say unto you, Whosoever shall not receive the kingdom of God as a little child, he shall not enter therein. And he took them up in his arms, put his hands upon them, and blessed them. (Mark 10:14-16)

55   O Thou God of our fathers, we come to Thee as children of Thy loving and watchful care, to pray for those who have loved and

[1] From *Divine Service.*

labored for this little child whom Thou hast called unto Thy eternal
rest. Our minds, O God, are unable to understand the meaning of
Thy purposes for our lives, but we are well-assured that no sorrow
Thou dost ask us to bear is without a Divine meaning. In the name of
Jesus Christ, the good shepherd of the sheep whose love does embrace
us all and especially the little children, we pray that the tears of farewell may one day, as Thou hast promised, become the joy of morning
gladness. Amen.

56 The Lord is my shepherd; I shall not want. He maketh me to lie
down in green pastures: he leadeth me beside the still waters.
He restoreth my soul: he leadeth me in the paths of righteousness for
his name's sake. Yea, though I walk through the valley of the shadow
of death, I will fear no evil: for thou art with me, thy rod and thy
staff they comfort me. Thou preparest a table before me in the presence of mine enemies: thou anointest my head with oil; my cup run-
neth over. Surely goodness and mercy shall follow me all the days of
my life: and I will dwell in the house of the Lord for ever. (Ps. 23)

57 I will lift mine eyes unto the hills, from whence cometh my help.
My help cometh from the Lord, which made heaven and earth.
He will not suffer thy foot to be moved: he that keepeth thee will
not slumber. Behold, he that keepeth Israel shall neither slumber nor
sleep. The Lord is thy keeper: the Lord is thy shade upon thy right
hand. The sun shall not smite thee by day, nor the moon by night.
The Lord shall preserve thee from all evil: he shall preserve thy soul.
The Lord shall preserve thy going out and thy coming in from this
time forth, and even for evermore. (Ps. 121)

58 Blessed be the God and Father of our Lord Jesus Christ, which
according to his abundant mercy hath begotten us again unto a
lively hope by the resurrection of Jesus Christ from the dead, to an
inheritance incorruptible, and undefiled, and that fadeth not away,
reserved in heaven for you, who are kept by the power of God through
faith unto salvation ready to be revealed in the last time. Wherein
ye greatly rejoice, though now for a season, if need be, ye are in heavi-
ness through manifold temptations: that the trial of your faith, being
much more precious than of gold that perisheth, though it be tried
with fire, might be found unto praise and honor and glory at the appearing of Jesus Christ: whom having not seen, ye love; in whom,

though now ye see him not, yet believing, ye rejoice with joy unspeakable and full of glory: receiving the end of your faith, even the
salvation of your souls. (1 Peter 1:3-9)

59   Jesus has called and a child has answered. His arms open to *him*,
and *his* to Him. For one moment we catch a glimpse of them both
together. Jesus draws the child to Himself saying, "Whosoever therefore shall humble himself as this little child, the same is greatest in
the kingdom of heaven." (Matt. 18:4)
   Today every one of us knows that Jesus is right. There can be no
doubt about it. Whatever else remains that is questionable or uncertain, this rings true: "Of such is the kingdom of heaven." Our Lord
says it. We all feel it in our hearts. These words are *true!*
   For we have learned how God can pack Heaven into a small bundle
of life. We have held eternity in our arms. We have recognized something that will never die, a soul radiant with Heaven, lighting up this
child's face. If Heaven is of such life as this—and we have our Lord's
word that it is—then we have good reason to be comforted.
   When a child goes to Heaven, one of the strongest yet most delicate
ties on earth is broken; but in our loss God creates another tie, all the
lovelier and stronger because He has promised that nothing can ever
break it. You have loved your child. Well, Heaven is like that. Your
affections have been environed in heavenly things as you have loved
your child.
   Does not Heaven come nearer now because *his* soul is there?[1]

60   My darling *boy*, so early snatched away
            From arms still seeking thee in empty air,
         That thou shouldst come to me I do not pray,
            Lest, by thy coming, heaven should be less fair.

         Stay, rather, in perennial flower of youth,
            Such as the Master, looking on, must love;
         And send to me the spirit of the truth,
            To teach me of the wisdom from above.

         Beckon to guide my thoughts, as stumblingly
            They seek the kingdom of the undefiled;
         And meet me at its gateway with thy key,
            The unstained spirit of a little child.[2]

[1] James R. Blackwood.
[2] "Of Such Is the Kingdom" by Francis Greenwood Peabody.

61 Almighty God, our Heavenly Father, Thou who hast strengthened Thy children with Thy light and power in all ages, hear us
now as we beseech Thee to give us faith in Thy love that will not let
us go.

Enable us to wait upon Thee in our time of tribulation. We pray
with our Saviour that Thy will be done in our lives. Grant unto us
the privilege of hearing Thy will, the vision to perceive it, and the
courage to fulfill it.

Thy tender mercies remind us that we are not alone in our sorrow
and loss. As we have suffered, so Thou hast suffered in giving of Thine
only begotten Son. As we have loved, so Thou hast loved more and
loved first. If there is pain and death in our lives, so there has been
a cross and a crown of thorns in Thine. O God, Thou art ever near
when we are afflicted, for Thou hast suffered with us.

In our moment of grief guide our steps that we may place our trust
in Thee. Into Thy hands we commit our lives. And having abided in
faith, in hope, and in love, may we yet see the radiance of a new day.
In the name of Him who leads the way out of darkness into light, who
conquered the cross with the resurrection, in the name of Christ, we
turn to Thee. Amen.[1]

62 Now the God of peace, that brought again from the dead our
Lord Jesus, that great shepherd of the sheep, through the blood
of the everlasting covenant, make you perfect in every good work to
do his will, working in you that which is well pleasing in his sight,
through Jesus Christ: to whom be glory for ever and ever. Amen.
(Heb. 13:20-21)

THE COMMITTAL SERVICE

63 Lord, thou hast been our dwelling place in all generations. Before the mountains were brought forth, or ever thou hadst formed
the earth and the world, even from everlasting to everlasting, thou
art God. (Ps. 90:1-2)

64 Blessed be God, even the Father of our Lord Jesus Christ, the
Father of mercies, and the God of all comfort: who comforteth
us in all our tribulation, that we may be able to comfort them which
are in any trouble, by the comfort wherewith we ourselves are comforted of God. (2 Cor. 1:3-4)

[1] Frank R. Snavely.

65   O happy soul, be thankful now, and rest!
            Heaven is a goodly land;
        And God is love; and those he loves are blest;
            Now thou dost understand
        The least thou hast is better than the best
        That thou didst hope for; now upon thine eyes
            The new life opens fair;
        Before thy feet the blessed journey lies
            Through homelands everywhere;
        And heaven to thee is all a sweet surprise.[1]

66 O most compassionate and loving Saviour, who, when on earth
    didst gather the little children into Thine arms and put Thy
holy hands upon them to bless them, we commit to Thee this little
child which our Heavenly Father hath now taken away. Be Thou
the tender Shepherd of this lamb. Carry it in Thy bosom into the
green pastures and beside the still water of Thy paradise among the
happy company of the glorified children, and at the last day restore
it to these yearning hearts, when the mystery of Thy providence shall
be unveiled from all faces. Hear us, O God, for Jesus our dear Redeemer's sake, to whom, with Thee, O Father, and the ever blessed
Spirit, the Comforter, be all praise and glory, world without end.
Amen.

67 The peace of God, which passeth all understanding, keep your
    hearts and minds in the knowledge and love of God, and of His
Son Jesus Christ our Lord. And the blessing of God Almighty, the
Father, the Son, and the Holy Spirit, be amongst you, and remain with
you always. Amen.

For an Aged Person

68 Friends, we are gathered to honor ————. Many of us have
    shared with *him* the companionship and labors of the passing years.
There come to us in these moments many blessed and joyful memories
which will be forever hallowed and cherished in our hearts and minds.
His friendliness, *his* faithfulness, and *his* good works will lose with
the passing days none of their radiance and influence in our homes,
our church, and our community.
    We are met together in the name of Jesus Christ, whom *he* loved

———
[1] "O Happy Soul" by Washington Gladden.

completely and served faithfully, and who has now taken *him* unto
His House of many mansions. We rest our hearts in the promise of
Him who said: "Come unto me, all ye that labor and are heavy laden,
and I will give you rest" (Matt. 11:28).

69 O God, we thank Thee for Thy love revealed in Jesus Christ. In
this hour it comforts us to know that the friendship of our souls
with Thee is an eternal friendship and nothing in life or death is able
to separate us from Thee. Help us so to commit ourselves to Thy
fatherly care that we may be more than conquerors over doubt and
sorrow and may, through the experience of the cross, be able the better to help those who are bowed down with grief. Assured that Thy
love will never let us go, may we face the future with calm confidence,
knowing that whatever comes, Thou art with us and wilt uphold us;
through Jesus Christ our Lord. Amen.[1]

How great is the comfort and promise of the Scriptures in an hour
such as this.

70 Lord, thou hast been our dwelling place in all generations. Before the mountains were brought forth, or ever thou hadst formed
the earth and the world, even from everlasting to everlasting, thou
art God. Thou turnest man to destruction; and sayest, Return, ye
children of men. For a thousand years in thy sight are but as yesterday
when it is past, and as a watch in the night. The days of our years are
threescore years and ten; and if by reason of strength they be fourscore
years, yet is their strength labor and sorrow; for it is soon cut off, and
we fly away. So teach us to number our days, that we may apply our
hearts unto wisdom. O satisfy us early with thy mercy; that we may
rejoice and be glad all our days. Make us glad according to the days
wherein thou hast afflicted us, and the years wherein we have seen
evil. Let thy work appear unto thy servants, and thy glory unto their
children. And let the beauty of the Lord our God be upon us: and
establish thou the work of our hands upon us; yea, the work of our
hands establish thou it. (Ps. 90:1-4, 10, 12, 14-17)

71 The Lord is my light and my salvation; whom shall I fear? the
Lord is the strength of my life; of whom shall I be afraid? One
thing have I desired of the Lord, that will I seek after; that I may

---

[1] James Dalton Morrison.

dwell in the house of the Lord all the days of my life, to behold the beauty of the Lord, and to enquire in his temple. For in the time of trouble he shall hide me in his pavilion: in the secret of his tabernacle shall he hide me; he shall set me up upon a rock. And now shall mine head be lifted up above mine enemies round about me: therefore will I offer in his tabernacle sacrifices of joy; I will sing, yea, I will sing praises unto the Lord. Hear, O Lord, when I cry with my voice: have mercy also upon me, and answer me. When thou saidst, Seck ye my face; my heart said unto thee, Thy face, Lord will I seek. Wait on the Lord: be of good courage, and he shall strengthen thine heart: wait, I say, on the Lord. (Ps. 27:1, 4-8, 14)

72   The time of my departure is at hand. I have fought a good fight, I have finished my course, I have kept the faith: henceforth there is laid up for me a crown of righteousness, which the Lord, the righteous judge, shall give me at that day: and not to me only, but unto all them also that love his appearing. (2 Tim. 4:6-8)

73   After this I beheld, and, lo, a great multitude, which no man could number, of all nations and kindreds, and people, and tongues, stood before the throne, and before the Lamb, clothed with white robes, and palms in their hands; and cried with a loud voice, saying, Salvation to our God which sitteth upon the throne, and unto the Lamb. And all the angels stood round about the throne, and about the elders and the four beasts, and fell before the throne on their faces, and worshipped God, saying, Amen: Blessing, and glory, and wisdom, and thanksgiving, and honor, and power, and might, be unto our God for ever and ever. Amen. And one of the elders answered, saying unto me, What are these which are arrayed in white robes? and whence came they? And I said unto him, Sir, thou knowest. And he said to me, These are they which came out of great tribulation, and have washed their robes, and made them white in the blood of the Lamb. Therefore are they before the throne of God, and serve him day and night in his temple: and he that sitteth on the throne shall dwell among them. They shall hunger no more, neither thirst any more; neither shall the sun light on them, nor any heat. For the Lamb which is in the midst of the throne shall feed them, and shall lead them unto living fountains of waters: and God shall wipe away all tears from their eyes. (Rev. 7:9-17)

*(At this point the funeral message may be given, or one or
both of the following may be read.)*

74 You are not dead—Life has but set you free!
Your years of life were like a lovely song,
The last sweet poignant notes of which, held long,
Passed into silence while we listened, we
Who loved you listened still expectantly!
And we about you whom you moved among
Would feel that grief for you were surely wrong—
You have but passed beyond where we can see.

For us who knew you, dread of age is past!
You took life, tiptoe, to the very last;
It never lost for you its lovely look:
You kept your interest in its thrilling book;
To you Death came no conqueror; in the end—
You merely smiled to greet another friend![1]

75 All the way my Saviour leads me;
What have I to ask beside?
Can I doubt His tender mercy,
Who through life has been my guide?
Heavenly peace, divinest comfort,
Here by faith in Him to dwell;
For I know whate'er befall me,
Jesus doeth all things well.

All the way my Saviour leads me;
O the fulness of His love!
Perfect rest to me is promised
In my Father's house above;
Where my spirit clothed, immortal,
Wings its flight to realms of day,
This my song thro' endless ages
Jesus led me all the way.[2]

76 Father of mercies and God of all comfort, who art the Author of
life on both sides of death: we cast all our cares upon Thee, for
Thou dost care for us. We do not always understand Thy ways, but
Thy ways are higher than our ways and Thy thoughts than our
thoughts, and we trust in Thee. We praise Thee that through the life,
death, and resurrection of Thy Son, our Lord Jesus Christ, Thou hast
brought life and immortality to light.

[1] "On the Death of an Aged Friend" by Roselle Mercier Montgomery.
[2] From "All the Way My Saviour Leads Me" by Fanny J. Crosby.

We thank Thee for the life of the one who has been called away from this earthly existence into Thy eternal home. We praise Thee for *his* years upon earth, for those things in *his* life which made *his* family and friends love *him*. Though *he* has passed through the valley of the shadow of death, there is no evil to fear for Thou art with *him*. We commend *his* spirit to Thee. We trust that Thou who art a great and good God, and our Father, will be with *him* and take care of him where *he* is.

We magnify Thy holy name that, *his* trials being now ended, sickness and death past, *his* spirit is at home in Thy presence, where now *he* knows those heights which never can we fully know on earth. Having fought the good fight, having finished *his* course, and having kept the faith, wilt Thou grant unto *him* the crown of life that fadeth not away.

We pray for those whom *he* leaves behind, for *his* family and friends. Wilt Thou comfort and strengthen their hearts and guide and direct their lives. Help them to know that deeper than the pain and mystery of death are Thine everlasting arms of tender love and mercy. As they continue their lives here on earth, wilt Thou grant to them steadfastness of purpose, faith in Thee, and a willingness to perform the duties and responsibilties which come their way under Thy guidance and direction.

This prayer we make in the name of Jesus our Lord, who Himself conquered death, not for Himself alone, but for His children.[1]

77   Now unto him that is able to keep you from falling and to present
     you faultless before the presence of his glory with exceeding joy, to the only wise God our Saviour, be glory and majesty, dominion and power, both now and ever. Amen. (Jude 24-25)

THE COMMITTAL SERVICE

78   I will lift up mine eyes unto the hills, from whence shall my
     help come. My help cometh from the Lord, which made heaven and earth. He will not suffer thy foot to be moved: he that keepeth thee will not slumber. Behold, he that keepeth Israel will neither slumber nor sleep. (Ps. 121:1-4)

79   I am the resurrection, and the life: he that believeth in me,
     though he were dead, yet shall he live: and whosoever liveth and believeth in me shall never die. (John 11:25-26)

[1] Herman G. McCoy.

80 And I heard a voice from heaven saying, Write, Blessed are the dead who die in the Lord from henceforth: yea, saith the Spirit, that they may rest from their labors; for their works do follow with them. (Rev. 14:13)

81 Sunset and evening star,
   And one clear call for me!
And may there be no moaning of the bar,
   When I put out to sea,

But such a tide as moving seems asleep,
   Too full for sound and foam,
When that which drew from out the boundless deep
   Turns again home.

Twilight and evening bell,
   And after that the dark!
And may there be no sadness of farewell,
   When I embark;

For tho' from out our bourne of Time and Place
   The flood may bear me far,
I hope to see my Pilot face to face
   When I have crost the bar.[1]

82 Dear Heavenly Father, the more helpless we find ourselves in life, the greater Thy power is to help us for we have long since learned that "Thy strength is made perfect in our weakness." We cherish the blessed words of our Saviour, "He that loseth his life shall find it," as we commit this loved one to Thee. Freed at last from all the tensions, confusions, and limitations of this mortal life, we pray that Thou wilt let all the aspirations and prayers of our beloved be multiplied in power by infinity that all the loveliest wishes of our departed one may come to pass in glorious fulfillment for all the loved ones left behind and for the benefit of Thy children everywhere.[2]

83 Our Father which art in heaven, hallowed be thy name. Thy kingdom come. Thy will be done in earth, as it is in heaven. Give us this day our daily bread. And forgive us our debts, as we forgive our debtors. And lead us not into temptation, but deliver us from evil: for thine is the kingdom, and the power, and the glory for ever.

---

[1] "Crossing the Bar" by Alfred Tennyson.
[2] Glenn Clark.

84   Now the God of peace, that brought again from the dead our
     Lord Jesus, that great shepherd of the sheep, through the blood
of the everlasting covenant, make you perfect in every good work to
do his will, working in you that which is well pleasing in his sight,
through Jesus Christ; to whom be glory for ever and ever. Amen.
(Heb. 13:20-21)

B. OPENING SCRIPTURAL SENTENCES

The number of opening sentences from the Bible is inexhaustible. The following are among the more obvious which are especially adaptable for the funeral service and the committal:

85 God is our refuge and strength, a very present help in trouble. (Ps. 46:1)

86 Lord, thou hast been our dwelling place in all generations. Before the mountains were brought forth, or ever thou hadst formed the earth and the world, even from everlasting to everlasting, thou art God. (Ps. 90:1-2)

87 He that dwelleth in the secret place of the most High shall abide under the shadow of the Almighty. I will say of the Lord, He is my refuge and my fortress: my God in him will I trust. (Ps. 91:1-2)

88 For as the heaven is high above the earth, so great is his mercy toward them that fear him. Like as a father pitieth his children, so the Lord pitieth them that fear him. For he knoweth our frame; he remembereth that we are dust. (Ps. 103:11, 13-14)

89 I will lift up mine eyes unto the hills, from whence cometh my help. My help cometh from the Lord, which made heaven and earth. He will not suffer thy foot to be moved: he that keepeth thee will not slumber. Behold, he that keepeth Israel shall neither slumber nor sleep. (Ps. 121:1-4)

90 The Lord is nigh unto all them that call upon him, to all that call upon him in truth. He will fulfil the desire of them that fear him: he also will hear their cry, and will save them. (Ps. 145:18-19)

91 Verily, verily, I say unto you, He that heareth my word, and believeth on him that sent me, hath everlasting life, and shall not come into condemnation; but is passed from death unto life. Verily,

verily, I say unto you, The hour is coming, and now is, when the dead shall hear the voice of the Son of God: and they that hear shall live. For as the Father hath life in himself; so hath he given to the Son to have life in himself. (John 5:24-26)

92 And this is the will of him that sent me, that every one which seeth the Son, and believeth on him, may have everlasting life: and I will raise him up at the last day. (John 6:40)

93 I am the living bread which came down from heaven: if any man eat of this bread, he shall live for ever: and the bread that I will give is my flesh, which I will give for the life of the world. (John 6:51)

94 Jesus saith unto her, I am the resurrection, and the life: he that believeth in me, though he were dead, yet shall he live: and whosoever liveth and believeth in me shall never die. (John 11:25-26)

95 Let not your heart be troubled: ye believe in God, believe also in me. In my Father's house are many mansions: if it were not so, I would have told you. I go to prepare a place for you. And if I go, and prepare a place for you, I will come again, and receive you unto myself; that where I am, there ye may be also. And whither I go ye know, and the way ye know. (John 14:1-4)

96 For none of us liveth to himself, and no man dieth to himself. For whether we live, we live unto the Lord; and whether we die, we die unto the Lord: whether we live therefore, or die, we are the Lord's. For to this end Christ both died, and rose, and revived, that he might be Lord both of the dead and living. (Rom. 14:7-9)

97 But now is Christ risen from the dead, and become the firstfruits of them that slept. For as in Adam all die, even so in Christ shall all be made alive. (1 Cor. 15:20, 22)

98 And as we have borne the image of the earthy, we shall also bear the image of the heavenly. For this corruptible must put on incorruption, and this mortal must put on immortality. (1 Cor. 15:49, 53)

99 Blessed be God, even the Father of our Lord Jesus Christ, the Father of mercies, and the God of all comfort: who comforteth us in all our tribulation, that we may be able to comfort them which are in any trouble, by the comfort wherewith we ourselves are comforted of God. (2 Cor. 1:3-4)

100 For we know that if our earthly house of this tabernacle were dissolved, we have a building of God, an house not made with hands, eternal in the heavens. (2 Cor. 5:1)

101 But I would not have you to be ignorant, brethren, concerning them which are asleep, that ye sorrow not, even as others which have no hope. For if we believe that Jesus died and rose again, even so them also which sleep in Jesus will God bring with him. (1 Thess. 4:13-14)

102 I have fought a good fight, I have finished my course, I have kept the faith: henceforth there is laid up for me a crown of righteousness, which the Lord, the righteous judge, shall give me at that day: and not to me only, but unto all them also that love his appearing. (2 Tim. 4:7-8)

103 And I heard a voice from heaven saying unto me, Write, Blessed are the dead which die in the Lord from henceforth: Yea, saith the Spirit, that they may rest from their labors; and their works do follow them. (Rev. 14:13)

C. THE FUNERAL SCRIPTURES

The voice of God made manifest in the reading of the Scriptures at the funeral service will doubtless do more to comfort the bereaved than any ministration of pastor or friend. Yet many pastors give almost no attention to the preparing of suitable Scriptures for a specific funeral occasion. Not only is the selecting of Scriptures hurried, but the reading of Scripture is often ineffective and uninspirational.

The great breadth of biblical readings especially suitable for funerals makes it unnecessary for the pastor to use the same passages at each successive service. Indeed it is most desirable that he select particular readings for particular needs. The pastor who is conversant with the Bible will have little difficulty in recalling selections which match the requirement of the hour and situation.

Perhaps the most frequent weakness in regard to the use of Scriptures at a funeral is that the pastor will make his readings so lengthy that their message becomes somewhat ineffectual. This represents poor selection.

Custom suggests that readings be taken first from the Old Testament and second from the New Testament. There is, of course, no need to follow consistently such a pattern.

The discerning pastor will realize that while variety of selection is desirable, there should be, nonetheless, a sequence of thought and emphasis in the Scriptures chosen. He will give thought to the choice of passages which will represent the biblical explanation of the mystery of life and death, the gospel of hope and consolation, the promise of resurrection and immortality, and so on.

Four or perhaps five readings seem desirable. These readings should generally console and comfort rather than depress and too obviously admonish. For this reason some passages, e.g., Job 14, long included in prepared services, are not included in the suggested list which follows. While, of course, there is a place for such instruction in the teaching and preaching ministry, such passages do not always seem appropriate in the funeral service.

Frequently a member or friend of the deceased will suggest certain passages which have meaning in terms of the life of the departed or might offer special comfort to the family. The naming of 1 Corinthians 13, for instance, would not, under such circumstances, be inappropriate.

Although some pastors hesitate to read extracts from a particular chapter, the reading of an entire chapter will not necessarily contribute to the service and will require a longer reading period and necessarily make impossible the reading of other passages. The list of Scriptures given in this section illustrates how certain verses may be omitted without robbing a chapter of its inherent message. All extracts, however, should represent complete thoughts or else the danger of incoherence is possible.

The constant practice of reading Scriptures in public makes it possible for most pastors to read from the Bible with ease, clarity, and poise. The funeral, however, sometimes tends to dampen the manner of the pastor and the reading becomes maudlin or lugubrious, displaying what some have called "a liturgical gloom" or a "professional whine." Most of the Scriptures which most adequately meet the needs of those who mourn are anything but gloomy; they radiate the joy of our Christian faith and hope. Faith and hope should, therefore, speak not only through the words themselves but in the interpreter's voice and manner.

No attempt is made here to offer a definitive listing of Scriptural passages:

A. GENERAL READINGS

104   Psalm 23
              Psalm 27:1, 4-9, 13-14
              Psalm 42
              Psalm 46
              Psalm 91
              Psalm 116:1-8, 15-19
              Psalm 121
              Psalm 130
              Psalm 139:1-12, 17-18
              Isaiah 35:3-10
              Isaiah 40:1-11, 28-31
              Matthew 11:25-30
              Matthew 25:31-40
              John 5:19-29

John 11:21-27
John 14:1-6, 15-20, 25-27
Romans 8:14-19, 24-28, 31-35, 37-39
1 Corinthians 15:20-28, 35-38, 42-35, 49-58
2 Corinthians 4:15-5:10
Ephesians 3:14-21
Philippians 3:7-16
1 Thessalonians 4:13-18
1 Peter 1:3-9
Revelation 7:9-17
Revelation 21:1-7, 22-22:7

B. FOR A CHILD OR YOUTH

105
2 Samuel 12:16-23
Psalm 23
Psalm 103:13-18
Psalm 121
Isaiah 40:9-11
Matthew 9:18-19, 23-26
Matthew 18:1-5, 10-14
Mark 5:22-23, 35-42
Mark 10:13-16
Luke 7:11-16

C. FOR A PERSON OF ADVANCED YEARS

106
Job 5:17-26
Psalm 39:4-13
Psalm 90:1-12
Hebrews 11:1-10

D. FOR A FAITHFUL MAN OR WOMAN

107
Psalm 1
Psalm 15
Psalm 103:1-5, 10-18
Proverbs 31:10-12, 20, 25-31

D. THE FUNERAL HYMNS

Throughout the Christian tradition the singing of hymns has been an important—and one is tempted to say, almost an essential—part of the funeral service.

While there are very real difficulties attending the singing of hymns in a service at a home or in a funeral parlor (e.g., the lack of a suitable accompanying instrument), the comfort and promise of the great hymns, and particularly the most familiar hymns, cannot be too greatly overestimated. This, too, is a feature of the service in which all may participate.

Hymns may serve several uses:

a. Congregational hymn singing in a church funeral is made possible by the presence of instruments for accompaniment. A hymn which seems particularly appropriate in terms of the life and work of the deceased, or a hymn which was a particular favorite of the deceased, may become an added blessing to those who mourn.

The talented accompanist will usually sustain the same tempo for the hymn sung at a funeral as in the regular church service.

The use of hymns in the funeral service will generally be determined by local custom and practice.

b. The familiar hymns may be interpreted by a soloist or quartet, and frequently this form of hymn usage will overcome any reticence on the part of the bereaved to express themselves in group singing.

c. A medley of hymn tunes, played skillfully on the organ or piano, will often serve more effectively for the prelude and postlude than less familiar organ melodies.

d. A pastor should not overlook the possibilities offered in the reciting of the words of familiar hymns in the service. The reading of hymns will compensate somewhat when there are poor facilities for congregational singing.

Suggestions for the reading of hymns follow much the same pattern offered in the section of this volume devoted to funeral poems. Of course, the pastor will wish to avoid the "sing-song" manner of recitation which too frequently, and unconsciously at times, accompanies the reading of words which are more generally sung than read.

The following list of hymns, most of them found in the standard hymnals, indicates the priceless treasure which many devout persons have contributed to funeral worship:

108   Abide with Me (Henry F. Lyte)

Beneath the Cross of Jesus (Elizabeth Cecilia Clephane)

Come, Thou Almighty King

Come, Thou Fount of Every Blessing

Come, Ye Disconsolate (Thomas Moore)

Dear Lord and Father of Mankind (John Greenleaf Whittier)

Face to Face (Mrs. Frank A. Breck)

For All the Saints Who from Their Labors Rest (William W. How)

Forever with the Lord (James Montgomery)

Guide Me, O Thou Great Jehovah (William Williams)

Hark, Hark My Soul (Frederick W. Faber)

He Leadeth Me, O Blessed Thought! (Joseph H. Gilmore)

I Heard the Voice of Jesus Say (Horatius Bonar)

I Need Thee Every Hour (Annie S. Hawks)

It Singeth Low in Every Heart (John W. Chadwick)

Jerusalem the Golden (Bernard of Cluny)

Jesus, Lover of My Soul (Charles Wesley)

Jesus, Saviour, Pilot Me (Edward Hopper)

Lead, Kindly Light (John Henry Newman)

My Faith Looks Up to Thee (Ray Palmer)

Nearer, My God, to Thee (Sarah F. Adams)

Now the Day Is Over (Sabine Baring-Gould)

Now the Laborer's Task Is O'er (John Ellerton)

O God, Our Help in Ages Past (Isaac Watts)

O Jesus, I Have Promised (John E. Bode)

O Love, That Wilt Not Let Me Go (George Matheson)

O Mother Dear, Jerusalem

One Sweetly Solemn Thought (Phoebe Cary)

Peace, Perfect Peace (Edward H. Bickersteth)

Rock of Ages (Augustus M. Toplady)

Safe in the Arms of Jesus (Fanny J. Crosby)

Saved by Grace (Fanny J. Crosby)

Servant of God, Well Done (Charles Wesley)

Shall We Meet beyond the River
Still, Still with Thee (Harriet Beecher Stowe)
Sun of My Soul (John Keble)
Ten Thousand Times Ten Thousand (Henry Alford)
The King of Love My Shepherd Is (Henry W. Baker)
There Is a Land of Pure Delight (Isaac Watts)
Unto the Hills Around Do I Lift Up (John Campbell)
What a Friend We Have in Jesus (Joseph Scriven)
When My Life-work Is Ended (Fanny J. Crosby)
When on My Day of Life (John Greenleaf Whittier)

E. BENEDICTIONS

The complete funeral will have two benedictions, one after the service in the home, the funeral parlor, or the church, and the other at the grave. The first service should be concluded with a benediction because many persons may be unable to journey to the grave. The benedictions at each service need not be identical.

Among the Scriptural benedictions, these are most appropriate for the funeral service:

109 The Lord bless thee, and keep thee: the Lord make his face shine upon thee, and be gracious unto thee: the Lord lift up his countenance upon thee, and give thee peace. (Num. 6:24-26)

110 Now the God of hope fill you with all joy and peace in believing, that ye may abound in hope, through the power of the Holy Ghost. (Rom. 15:13)

111 Grace be to you, and peace from God our Father, and from the Lord Jesus Christ. (1 Cor. 1:2)

112 The peace of God, which passeth all understanding, keep your hearts and minds through Christ Jesus. (Phil. 4:7)

113 The God of peace sanctify you wholly; your whole spirit and soul and body be preserved blameless unto the coming of our Lord Jesus Christ. (1 Thess. 5:23, paraphrased)

114 Now our Lord Jesus Christ himself, and God, even our Father, which hath loved us, and hath given us everlasting consolation and good hope through grace, comfort your hearts, and stablish you in every good word and work. (2 Thess. 2:16-17)

115 Grace, mercy, and peace, from God our Father and Jesus Christ our Lord. (1 Tim. 1:2)

116 Now the God of peace, that brought again from the dead our Lord Jesus, that great shepherd of the sheep, through the blood of the everlasting covenant, make you perfect in every good work to do his will, working in you that which is well-pleasing in his sight, through Jesus Christ; to whom be glory for ever and ever. Amen. (Heb. 13:20-21)

117 The God of grace, who hath called us unto the eternal glory by Christ Jesus, after that ye have suffered a while, make you perfect, stablish, strengthen, settle you. To him be glory and domination for ever and ever. Amen. (1 Pet. 5:10-11)

118 Now unto him that is able to keep you from falling, and to present you faultless before the presence of his glory with exceeding joy, to the only wise God our Saviour, be glory and majesty, domination and power, both now and ever. Amen. (Jude 24:25)

119 Unto him that loved us, and washed us from our sins in his own blood, and hath made us kings and priests unto God and his Father; to him be glory and dominion for ever and ever. Amen. (Rev. 1:5-6)

F. THE OBITUARY

The use of an obituary in the funeral service is almost extinct in many quarters. This, perhaps, is to be regretted for there is little in the obituary as such about which one might find objection. The practice, however, has frequently led to profusive statements which sometimes have been more laudatory than factual, more fictional than truthful.

Where custom still calls for an obituary, or when the family of the deceased requests it, the obituary should surely be included.

The obituary may be of two kinds. The first is a brief statement of the pertinent facts of a person's life: his birth, education, affiliations, honors, and so on. This should be prepared in consultation with a dependable source and should usually be worded by the pastor himself.

The second represents more of a tribute. Frequently a representative group in the church or community may wish to express briefly certain sincere sentiments regarding the work and contributions which the deceased has made. The church board may believe that a public commendation is in order; a Sunday School class may wish to pay tribute to one who has taught the group with fidelity for an extended period. The remarks should represent a group rather than an individual.

In either case understatement is preferable and effusive sentiment will not be considered in good taste. In either case, too, the statement should be prepared in advance and in all but the most rare circumstances should be read by the pastor.

Two typical tributes follow:

120   This tribute has been prepared by the members of the church board and is read at their request. *John Doe* has been a member of this church for more than fifty-five years. He has served the church generously and faithfully in many capacities. Never when his services were needed was he unable to find the time to work cheerfully and to lead with fidelity. To know him has been to love him; to work with him has always been encouraging and inspiring. The witness of

his faithfulness will ever be a challenge and a blessing. We believe that each church member shares with us in saying of him, "To live in hearts we leave behind is not to die."

121 The members of the Young Men's Class of the church have prepared this statement and it is read at their request. *John Doe* long ago opened his heart and home to the youth of this church. Twenty-two years ago he organized the Young Men's Class. During the passing years he has given to the youth of the church a generous portion of his time and the unlimited love of his heart. We cannot measure the breadth of his influence, for although his class rolls have through the years totaled more than three hundred youth, these young men have in turn become better teachers and leaders in the church, better parents in the home, and better citizens in the community because of the work he always felt God had particularly called him to perform.

II. A Treasury of Funeral Sermons

Should a sermon form a part of the funeral service? The question is easily answered in many instances. Frequently local custom and practice makes the use of a message almost obligatory. At other times a member of the family of the deceased will request words suitable for the occasion. Usually, however, the decision is left to the discretion of the pastor.

For what reasons may a pastor consider a sermon to be significant at a funeral? First, traditionally a funeral sermon has been a feature of the Christian funeral. Second, at a moment so fraught with discouragement, doubt, and perplexity, a pastor should draw from the Scriptures expositions which will show the Christian witness concerning the meaning of life and death, of immortality and resurrection, and of the love and comfort of God. Third, those who grieve are particularly receptive and eager for the Word of God brought by the shepherd of the flock.

If there be truth in this, why have many pastors in recent years omitted the funeral sermon? Too often an inappropriate funeral message has characterized the funeral. The long and extremely eulogistical or harshly admonitory sermon, so long objectionable, has been generally replaced by the briefly worded sermon of comfort and consolation, of hope and faith, which finds in the everlasting Word of God those thoughts which speak to the grief-stricken of the life and immortality which Christ brought to mankind.

The sermons in this volume indicate how in a few hundred words—in three to six minutes—the great treasures of Scripture may be interpreted to those whose need is particular and acute.

The sermons are somewhat arbitrarily separated according to text and theme into ten divisions.

A. GOD'S GLORY IN THE MORNING

And in the morning, then ye shall see the glory of the Lord.   EXODUS 16:7

I want to take these words and hold them above the darkness of the grave. Is there not a great message here about death and the dawning of eternity? Here in this present human life we are permitted to know something of beauty, truth, and goodness, to read something of the ultimate plan and meaning of the universe, to see something of the splendour of the majesty of God. Yet the very best that we can see and know on earth is but a poor fraction of what must be waiting yonder to be revealed.

We can find a parable of this in modern science. There are whole ranges of color, the scientist tells us, which our physical eyes cannot perceive. True, we can see all the colors of the rainbow, ranging from red at the one end of the spectrum to violet at the other. But now we are assured that this is only a comparatively small fraction of the colors which really exist; that beyond the red rays at one end of the spectrum there are the infra-red, beyond the violet are the ultra-violet, and out beyond these again whole unimaginable reaches of color which we never see at all, because our eyes as at present constituted cannot get hold of them. In short, what we do see is only a tiny segment of the whole.

If this is true of our physical eyes, is it not likely to be true of the inner eye of our soul? Here on earth we do apprehend something of the eternal spiritual realities; we do see, even if through a glass darkly, something of the marvel of the kingdom and the beauty of the King. But our present moral spectrum—how poor a fraction of the whole! And beyond the best insights we can ever hope to have in this dark, shadowed existence of time and sin and limitation, what reaches of glory must be waiting for us yonder in the morning! We are going to find the answers to all questions unanswered here. We are to see the dearest faces we have loved and lost. We are to gaze upon that one Face which has haunted the dreams of humanity since the day when God walked with men in Galilee, the Head that once was crowned with thorns and is crowned with glory now.

There was a December day in Edinburgh in 1666 when Hugh Mackail, youngest and bravest of the Covenanting preachers, was brought before his judges and condemned to the scaffold. They gave him four days to live: then back to the Tolbooth the soldiers led him. Many in the watching crowd were weeping as he went—so young he seemed, so terrible his coming fate. But in his own eyes no tears were seen, no trace of self-pity or regret on the radiant, eager face of this young Galahad of the cross. "Trust in God!" he cried, and his eyes were shining—"Trust in God!" Then, suddenly catching a glimpse of a friend among the crowd, "Good news," he cried, "good news! I am within four days' journey of enjoying the sight of Jesus Christ!"

Death? What is death, if that is beyond it? In the morning, then shall ye see the glory of the Lord.

James S. Stewart

123   *GOOD MORNING!*

Yea, though I walk through the valley of the shadow of death, I will fear no evil: for thou art with me; thy rod and thy staff they comfort me. PSALM 23:4

Always men have greeted friends and loved ones at the beginning of a new day with a cheery greeting, "Good morning!" In these words is the story of the night that is gone and the day which beckons. Fled from us are the lurking shades of night; eagerly we rush to greet the rosy countenance of the dawn. No longer does darkness separate from view those whom we love, but bathed in the light of the new day we rejoice in the presence of those who are our light and our song.

It is fitting that the discovery of the resurrection of our Lord should have been realized in the dawning light of a new day. Behind the disciples was the nightmare of the cross and the tomb. "Very early in the morning" they came to the sepulchre to minister to the dead body of Jesus—only to hear the angels' words: "Why seek ye the living among the dead? He is not here, but is risen" (Luke 24:5-6). It is as if the angels had said, "Good morning!" It was a good morning; there was nothing more to fear. "Forget the fears and dreads of the night; rejoice in the wonders of the day! For He whom ye seek is not dead, but lives!"

In this our bitter night of deep sorrow we, too, hear this joyous "Good morning!" Henry Wadsworth Longfellow said, " 'Tis always morning somewhere."[1] The Psalmist breathed the same hopeful thought when he said, "Yea, though I walk through the valley of the shadow of death, I will fear no evil: for thou art with me; thy rod and thy staff they comfort me." The "valley of deep and dark shadows" may lie before me, but in Thy presence is the light of hope. And hope substantiated by faith brings assurance.

> O welcome pure-ey'd Faith, white-handed Hope,
> Thou hovering angel girt with golden wings.[2]

It is needless that we should spend these precious moments eulogizing one who needs no eulogy. Suffice to say that *he* was a loyal *son*, a devoted *husband* and *father*, a true friend, and a consecrated Christian. Knowing these things we are certain that our loved one is with Christ, which is far better. In reality, therefore, our mourning is not for *him* but for ourselves. *He* has gone from us and we are lonely. In the darkness of our night of sorrow we long for the day, a day which seems strangely far away, but which is wondrously near. Welcomed words to our listening ears would be the cheery "Good morning!" of Him who is the subject and object of our faith. Thus we press our ears of faith against His bosom that we may hear His words, "Peace, be still."

In strange and unexpected places one often finds a beautiful flower growing. Likewise, do we find faith and hope where we least expect them. When the brother of Robert G. Ingersoll died, the famous agnostic delivered his funeral address. In spite of his unbelief, he spoke these words of assurance: "But in the night of death Hope sees a star, and listening Love can hear the rustle of a wing."[3] This star heralds the coming day, and the rustling wing is that of the angel of assurance who comes to bid us "Good morning!"

On the night before the crucifixion of our Lord, when fear and despair had settled about the twelve, Jesus spoke to them of peace in a storm, of light in darkness: "Let not your heart be troubled." Jesus' secret of an untroubled heart is not found in stoic acceptance or rebellious rejection, but in faith: "Believe in God, believe also in me" (John 14:1). In other words, we are to have faith in the love, will, and purpose of God—even in bereavement. God loves us in the night as well as in the day. His will is not that our loved ones should die, but

[1] From "The Birds of Killingworth."
[2] From "Comus" by John Milton.
[3] From "Tribute to Eben C. Ingersoll."

that in our sorrow we should glorify Him. And His purpose is not only to raise them from the dead—out yonder—but to lead us *through* this valley of shadows—here and now.

At one time or another all are called upon to walk through the valley, but note that we walk *through* it. In the thought of Victor Hugo, death is no blind alley or box canyon; it is a thoroughfare, a pass into the beautiful vale of glory. Furthermore, David reminds us that death is but a shadow, a shadow which may frighten but cannot harm us. And when we walk through the vale of shadows we find the light of God's love and grace awaiting us, more beautiful because we have seen it covered by the cloud of our sorrow. When the night seems darkest, remember

> Sad soul, take comfort nor forget
> The sunrise never failed us yet.[1]

The Sun of righteousness with healing in His wings is rising to dispel the darkness of your grief.

In John Bunyan's *Pilgrim's Progress* we find Christian about to cross a narrow path over a deep, dark chasm. Fearing lest he fall he hesitates. Then he hears a voice from out of the darkness: "Keep your ear attuned to my voice. Come straight to me and you will be all right." We, too, falter as we face this valley of dim and dark shadows. But listen! Hear the voice from out the encircling gloom: "Keep your ear attuned to my voice! Come straight to me, and you will be all right." Guided thus by His rod and supported by His staff, we walk unperturbed through this valley of the shadow of death until we walk in the sun once more—and, emerging from the shadows, the first word which we shall hear will be His glad "Good morning!"

Herschel H. Hobbs

124   *WHEN THE SUN BURSTS FORTH*

When mists have hung low over the hills, and the day has been dark with intermittent showers, at length great clouds begin to hurry across the sky, the wind rises, and the rain comes pouring down; then we look out and exclaim: "Why, this is the clearing-up shower." And when the floods have spent themselves, the clouds part to let the blue sky tremble through them, and the west wind bears them away seaward, and, though they are yet black and threatening, we see their silver edges as they pass, and know that just behind them are singing

---

[1] Celia Thaxter.

birds and glittering dewdrops; and, lo! while yet we look, the sun
bursts forth, and lights them up in the eastern heaven with the glory
of the rainbow.

Now, to the Christian whose life has been dark with brooding cares
that would not lift themselves, and on whom chilling rains of sorrow
have fallen at intervals through all his years, death, with its sudden
blast and storm, is but the clearing-up shower; and just behind it are
the songs of angels, and the serenity and glory of heaven.

Henry Ward Beecher

125   *THE LIGHTS OF HOME*

But now they desire a better country, that is, an heavenly: wherefore
God is not ashamed to be called their God: for he hath prepared for them a
city.   HEBREWS 11:16

> Pilot, how far from home?—
>   Not far, not far to-night,
>   A flight of spray, a sea-bird's flight,
> A flight of tossing foam,
>   And then the lights of home.—
>
> And, yet again, how far?
>   And seems the way so brief?
>   Those lights beyond the roaring reef
> Were lights of moon and star,
>   Far, far, none knows how far!
>
> Pilot, how far from home?—
>   The great stars pass away
>   Before Him as a flight of spray,
> Moons as a flight of foam!
>   I see the lights of home![1]

Pilot, how far from home? The question is one that every sea
traveler of long voyage asks. However eager was the embarkation,
however thrilling stages and events of the voyage, the meridian of
expectancy is duly passed, and from then on all one wishes to do is to
get home. We may be strangers and pilgrims on land and ocean, but
nothing is right if we have to stay too long away from the home-nest,
the home-retreat, the place where loved ones are and life bestows its
successive consummations. Joseph Conrad describes the heart's nos-
talgia for the port which is the goal of any sailing; even Tennyson
gets at it in the panting of Enoch Arden to return to Annie and the

---

[1] "The Lights of Home" by Alfred Noyes.

children. So, the question is fairly bursting with its own emotion. "Pilot, how far from home?" The most welcome answer meets it!

> Not far, not far tonight.
> Not far, not far tonight.
> *Just*: A flight of spray—a sea-bird's flight.
> *Just*: A flight of tossing foam.

And then—you will see: "The Lights of Home." You will see them gleam through the mists: the quiet lights that have burned each night until you should come in. O, glory of hope and happiness!

But perhaps it is the very eagerness of the questioner that makes doubt descend upon the pilot's reassuring promise. "How far, really is it, till we're in?" And could the watcher at the crow's nest be mistaken? Instead of home-lights beyond the crashing spray on yonder reef, possibly he has seen only the reflection of moon and star. Perhaps this rolling, creaking ship is yet hundreds of miles from home!

So in the third stanza, the appeal is made to God. And, as the prayer, with its consequent affirmation, lifts above the concerns of any single earth-born voyage, so is the "home" now the Eternal Destination, with its lights beckoning all mortal travelers to its everlasting blessedness.

"Pilot, how far from home?"—with God there is no error of identification! Nor can either stars or moon obstruct the welcome which shines from Him to His children. Hence, the crowning affirmation of certainty. If any one of us has sometime had misgiving that we follow a will-o'-the-wisp in our faith in the future life of the soul, or at any time trembled that our leaders were mistaken in what they believed they saw, it is now dispelled in a triumphal plenitude of praise to God. He is able to the uttermost to keep the lamps forever sure and burning.

> Pilot, how far from home?—
> The great stars pass away
> Before *Him* as a flight of spray,
> Moons as a flight of foam!
> *I see the lights of home!*

'Tis a Christian creed, and a firm saying of Christian worth. It is the Christian doctrine that there is a Home for all earth's weary travelers, nor are the lights of it impossible to see. Jesus' plain statement about His Father's House is packed with sentiment, since these deep matters concerning life and death and the life to come have our heart's avowal. But it has not become a sentimental saying. We have taken it from the sincerity of His lips as David Livingstone on the banks of the Zambezi and facing menacing enemies took another phrase: "Lo, I am with you alway." "And He is a gentleman of the strictest honor. So I'll take Him at His word." That word "House" may be a symbol of what we cannot imagine, because of our finitude. Yet it is enough for anyone that a Home—with the sweetness of fellowship, the invigoration of the faith, and the security of the love, of any earthly home at its best, and then enriched—awaits our coming. "I see the lights of home."

Paul C. Johnston

126   OUR REACH TO HEAVEN

In him was life; and the life was the light of men.   JOHN 1:4

It is true that there may come to many men and women, perhaps to most, a time when they grow physically very weary, and existence in this weakened body seems no longer beautiful. But this does not mean that they have lost the desire for life, and for the horizon of a larger day. Said Marshal Foch to the priest who stood by his side when he was dying: "I have had my span of life. All I want now is Heaven." How right that is! The pathos and simplicity of a little child is in it, and yet the gallantry of a warrior, too. We may recognize that the span of this life is done. But if life has meant anything great and purposeful, we are reaching out to a Heaven which lies beyond.

Granted that this word has been caricatured so that many almost affect to despise it. Granted that religious symbolism has been turned into a mawkish sentimentality, so that people have talked of Heaven as though it means nothing except white robes and palms and harps and a kind of saccharine idleness in general. Yet the Heaven toward which the reality of our souls reaches out is not like that. It is rest, but not the rest of idleness; rather it is the movement of increasing life which has found its center and its rest in God. It is the power of a life released from friction and from limitation. It is the chance to be all that we have just become aware of in ourselves and so to achieve that indomitable desire of which Tennyson sang in *In Memoriam*:

> And, doubtless, unto thee is given
>   A life that bears immortal fruit
>   In those great offices that suit
> The full-grown energies of heaven.[1]

[1] St. XL.

What sense can be made out of the existence if rocks and earth and water and the dust beneath our feet go on enduring and human souls, which seem to be the fruition toward which all the slow forces of evolution have been working, should blindly and stupidly be brought to naught? In the face of such a universe, a man might laugh with contempt before he went to his annihilation. But we cannot believe that contemptuous laughter is the ultimate verdict to be passed upon our world. There must be within it something that has caused our own ideals, something akin to our passion for continuing life, and something upon which eternally we can rely. God must be in it, and God is life, and God is love. Even in the moments when our intellect is baffled, and even in those times when contradictions beset our faith, still we refuse to be put to permanent intellectual and spiritual confusion, and still our deepest souls declare that beyond the shadows there is light, and in the depths of the utmost darkness life goes upon its undefeated way.

Here is the world as it is, with all its stark realities. Here is hate. Here is sin. Here is suffering. And here is death. These things are frightfully real. They seem sometimes invincible. It looks as though life had to be interpreted with these facts as its final key. But here, on the other hand, is Jesus. For those who knew Him in Galilee, He became a center of certainty for mind and heart. Nothing else was as sure as Jesus. They might think this or think that, but there were certain things about Him which to the utmost reaches of their whole selves they knew. They knew there was a goodness in Him which thrilled them with its strength and beauty. They knew His spirit had a mastery over all the conditions of His world. They saw that there was no conceivable circumstance which He did not dominate. And as they pondered these things, they felt the mighty power in them. Through the hard crust of every contradiction, this expanding certainty of the truth that was in Jesus broke.

When they saw Him on Easter morning, they were inwardly prepared for what they saw. They had been hideously frightened and desolated by Good Friday. But the old hope and confidence in their invincible Master was underneath the surface waiting for the touch of His releasing hand. When they saw Him they knew that it was not a mirage, nor any unnatural thing which tomorrow they would begin to doubt because it should seem out of all relation to their normal thought and life. On the contrary, it was only the radiant confirmation, after the days of terrible but temporary eclipse, of what they had known before. It was not possible that Jesus should be defeated. What they had believed and felt as they walked with Him was true—that the spirit is stronger than the body, and that death is only a shadow on the advancing roads of love and life.

Walter Russell Bowie

127   *THE OPEN WAY TO HEAVEN*

In the world ye shall have tribulation, but . . .   JOHN 16:33

Let not your heart be troubled. . . . I go to prepare a place for you.
JOHN 14:1-2

Mark the connection of thought. He did not say, "This is the best world that was ever made: things are growing better and better; there is ten times more happiness than sorrow on the earth. Only live in the sunny side of the house, and keep your window curtains lifted, and you will be all right." No such optimistic vaporing as this. "In the world ye shall have tribulation." "Let not your heart be troubled. . . . I go to prepare a place for you" in another world.

The Scripture says that Christ came to "deliver us from this present evil world" (Gal. 1:4). Sin, sorrow, disappointment, and death are real facts, so real that it took the tremendous anguish of the cross to overcome them. And our Lord came into this world and put Himself beneath these things, in order that He might lead us out of them. Hence the significant words: "I go to prepare," and from henceforth we are to look along the upward track of light which He left behind Him, awaiting His summons to come after Him saying triumphantly: "For our citizenship is in heaven; from whence we look for the Saviour, the Lord Jesus Christ" (Phil. 3:20).

Our hope and succor are not in assimilating ourselves to present conditions or in transforming those conditions, but in following the Lord in the upward path of glory. St. Cuthbert was once driven upon the coast of Fife by a terrific snow-storm, and to his disheartened comrades he said: "The storm bars our way over the sea; the snow has closed our path upon the land, but the way to Heaven lies open." Heroic and most scriptural utterance! Since our Lord ascended into Paradise He has opened the kingdom of heaven to all believers. And He has never allowed the way thither to become blocked and never will. Therefore note the concluding words of the promise: "If I go and prepare a place for you, I will come again and receive you unto myself." No soul is left alone to climb the *scala sancta* of heaven, the holy ladder on which the angels ascend and descend. Our forerunner

Jesus has passed within the veil and He will come forth again and fetch us thither with Him, that where He is we may be also.

A. J. Gordon

128   *WE LOOK FOR A CITY*

For he looked for a city which hath foundations, whose builder and maker is God. HEBREWS 11:10

And I John saw the holy city, new Jerusalem, coming down from God out of heaven, prepared as a bride adorned for her husband. And I heard a great voice out of heaven saying, Behold, the tabernacle of God is with men, and he will dwell with them, and they shall be his people, and God himself shall be with them, and be their God. And God shall wipe away all tears from their eyes; and there shall be no more death, neither sorrow, nor crying, neither shall there be any more pain: for the former things are passed away. And he that sat upon the throne said, Behold, I shall make all things new. And he said unto me, Write: for these words are true and faithful. And he said unto me, It is done. I am Alpha and Omega, the beginning and the end. I will give unto him that is athirst of the fountain of the water of life freely. He that overcometh shall inherit all things; and I will be his God, and he shall be my son. REVELATION 21:2-7

These passages of Scripture come from different authors, yet one seems to have anticipated the other. The writer of the book of Hebrews pictures Abraham traveling toward a city, but not finding it. He seems to be ever traveling, but never arriving. He was a pilgrim, looking for a city which hath foundations whose builder and maker is God. John gives in Revelation a picture of the Holy City, the new Jerusalem, coming down from God out of Heaven, a city without tears, sorrow, or death. So it is with the human family. We never find the city that hath foundations whose builder and maker is God in this world. The one thing all admit about this earth is its incompleteness and the lack of permanence in everything about us. Our knowledge is incomplete, our character is incomplete, and our accomplishments are incomplete.

Our Saviour said the birds of the air have nests and the foxes have dens, but "the Son of man hath not where to lay his head" (Matt. 8:20). The birds of the air have nests and that is all they want. They have not changed the manner of building their nests. They are satisfied. The foxes have dens. They build now as they did centuries and millenniums ago. They are satisfied. But the Son of Man hath not where to lay His head. Was God better to the birds and foxes than He was to the Saviour? No, for Him there is another chapter to be written. So it is with the human family. We have our dissatisfactions in this world because it is an incomplete world. We anticipate another. We are looking forward to a city that hath foundations whose builder and maker is God, and that city will not be found until the Holy City, perfect in all its appointments and complete in all its satisfactions, comes down from God out of Heaven, prepared as a bride adorned for her husband.

God gives us thirst in this world and satisfies our thirst with water. He gives us hunger in this world and satisfies our hunger with food. He would indeed be a tyrant God if He gave us thirst and hunger and did not provide water and food. So He gives us eternal spiritual longings for a perfection not attained in this world. But this life is only anticipatory of the fuller life which is to come. Kipling explains it beautifully in his poem, "L'Envoi":

> When Earth's last picture is painted and the tubes are twisted and dried,
> When the oldest colours have faded, and the youngest critic has died,
> We shall rest, and, faith, we shall need it—lie down for an aeon or two,
> Till the Master of All Good Workmen shall put us to work anew.

> And those that were good shall be happy: they shall sit in a golden chair;
> They shall splash at a ten-league canvas with brushes of comet's hair;
> They shall find real saints to draw from—Magdalene, Peter, and Paul;
> They shall work for an age at a sitting and never be tired at all!

> And only the Master shall praise us, and only the Master shall blame;
> And no one shall work for money, and no one shall work for fame,
> But each for the joy of the working, and each, in his separate star,
> Shall draw the Thing as he sees It for the God of Things as They are!

How do we attain that full and complete life in the world which is to come? We receive that life through Jesus Christ our Lord who came to make all things new. He said He had come to give us life abundant. That abundance begins when we yield our hearts to Him and is completed in the perfect life beyond.

Wallace Bassett

129   *THEN COMETH THE END*

And I saw a great white throne, and him that sat on it, from whose face the earth and the heaven fled away; and there was no place found for them. And I saw the dead, small and great, stand before God; and the books were opened; and another book was opened, which is the book of life: and the dead were judged out of those things which were written in the books, according to their works. REVELATION 20:11-12

One of the most fundamental laws of life is this—that we are not isolated units, dependent wholly on ourselves, and gaining what we need only through our own hard-breathing efforts. Life teaches us the very opposite—the facts of our inter-dependence; of vicarious toil, and of vicarious suffering; that one bears, and another, who was not in the thing at all, receives the benefit. We are born, only through another's pain; we are free, only because numbers have died, and are still dying, for us.

All that we value comes to us as a free gift from others, who lost everything that we might have; or who labored, and we have entered into their labors. Are not innumerable all-important things done for us every day which we could not do for ourselves? And the big things can be received only on the same humbling terms. We can't win Heaven by our own righteousness; we can only take it of pure grace. We can't gain our salvation by our own worthiness. If it is ever to be ours at all, we must accept it from a Saviour.

And there is a Saviour, and a Book of Life. Whether your name or mine is entered in it, it is for Christ to say. Why should it be? how can it be? conscience asks derisively. Well! there is this to give us hope—that Christ's eyes can see, and often do see, what others never saw, and won't believe is there.

Everyone was unanimous about Zacchaeus. There was not one dissentient in the whole outraged city. And all the sordid facts of years and years flocked, hurrying to add to the huge weight of evidence against him. Every one had the same damning opinion—everyone—except Jesus Christ. Not all the facts, He said, not all the possibilities. And in the Book of Life, openly, daringly, confidently, He wrote down that outcast's name. "This day is salvation come to this house" (Luke 19:9).

There was a woman whose life had broken down in open and unblushing infamy, from the contamination of whose pollution decent folk shrank back; whose whole being and character were summed up in one comprehensive blasting phrase. For, when any one thought of her, or named her, the one thing that rose up in people's minds was— that she was a sinner. But Christ did not shrink back. There is more here than sin, He said, far more; and put her in the Book of Life.

And once a wild passionate career was ending in unendurable agony, in open infamy and shame, and in a horror of gross darkness. Yet when the poor throbbing head managed to turn in Christ's direction, and the parched lips to whisper, "Lord, when Thou comest into

Thy kingdom, remember me!" (Luke 23:42). Then, when life was over, when there could be no rubbing out, no emendation, "To day," said Christ, "shalt thou be with me in paradise!" So that name, too, stands, plainly written by our Lord's own hand, in the decisive Book of Life. Where Christ is, there is infinite hope. And, for my part, I mean to trust Him even on the Great White Throne. I have no plea except just this—that He said, "Him that cometh to Me, I will in nowise, for no conceivable reason, for no statable case, cast out." And here is a poor failure coming to give in his account. As Christ decides, so may it be. So it will be. But where Christ is, there is a wild, a wonderful, an infinite hope. And Christ is still Christ even on the Judgment Seat.

And those who saw Him face to face for years have set down this as one of His most certain characteristics—that, having loved His own that were in the world, He loved them unto the end. And to us also He clings in that same unbelievably loyal way; loves on whatever we may do, will not be turned from it. And when at last we reach the other side, and stand there, muddy and ashamed, and very conscious how unlike we are to all these clean and shining spirits round us, eagerly He will come to us, with outstretched hands and happy face, and let us see how much it means to Him that we are there. I know it, because I have proved it; because He has done that very thing to me, time and again, and yet again. And He is the same yesterday, and today, and forever. "I know," says Paul, "in whom I have believed, and am persuaded that He is able to keep that which I have committed unto Him against that day (2 Tim. 1:12). And so do I. And so am I.

> And so beside the Silent Sea
> I wait the muffled oar;
> No harm from Him can come to me
> On ocean or on shore.
>
> I know not where His islands lift
> Their fronded palms in air;
> I only know I cannot drift
> Beyond His love and care.[1]

No. For the grace of our Lord and Saviour Jesus Christ, and the love of God our Father, and the fellowship of the Holy Spirit have been given to us, and are ours, now—and forever.

Arthur John Gossip

[1] From "The Eternal Goodness" by John Greenleaf Whittier.

130   *OUR NEW HOME*

We know that we have passed out of death into life. 1 JOHN 3:14 (R.S.V.)

Two strangers, a small boy and an older man, were fishing from the banks of the Mississippi. As time passed they discovered that, although the fishing was rather poor, conversation was good. And by the time the sun began to sink in the west they had talked of many things. At dusk a large river boat was seen moving slowly in the distance. When the boy saw the boat, he began to shout and to wave his arms that he might attract the attention of those on board. The man watched for some time and then said: "Son, you're foolish if you think that boat is going to stop for you. It's on its way to some unknown place and it surely won't stop for a small boy."

But suddenly the boat began to slow down and then it moved toward the river bank. To the man's amazement, however, the boat came near enough to the shore that a gang-plank could be lowered. The boy entered the boat and, turning to the new friend on shore, said: "I'm not foolish, mister. You see, my father is captain of this boat and we're going to a new home up the river."

Sometimes life is like that. There are times when the ship of death makes an unexpected stop along the river of life and to our surprise picks up a passenger. But I am confident of one thing: "My Father" is captain of that boat and it is headed for a new home. Death is not the end of life; it is the beginning of a new adventure upon the river of life. The boat pushes upstream towards our Father's home.

In the first epistle of John are these precious words: "We know that we have passed out of death into life." Jesus taught his followers that life is eternal and that death is not the end. His followers have always believed that death is only a door through which we must all sometime pass—into eternal life. That is the primary reason why we are here today. We are here to show honor and respect for this our loved one, but we are here also for a much greater reason. We are here to bear witness to the achievement of life eternal. Because of this, we join not in a service of deep mourning but in a service acclaiming a glorious achievement. It is not a time for sadness and uncontrolled grief. As far as the spiritual life is concerned, it is a time for the singing of the Hallelujah Chorus. Our loved one has passed out of death into life. He has moved up the river of life in a boat on which "My Father" is captain.

Many people have been greatly strengthened as God has revealed to them the full meaning of the words of John. Certainly Edwin Markham caught something of their meaning.

> Let us not think of our departed dead
> As caught and cumbered in their graves of earth;
> But think of death as of another birth,
> As a new freedom for the wings outspread,
> A new adventure waiting on ahead,
> As a new joy of more ethereal mirth,
> As a new world with friends of nobler worth,
> Where all may taste a more immortal bread.
> So, comrades, if you pass my grave sometime,
> Pause long enough to breathe this little rhyme:
> "Here now the dust of Edwin Markham lies,
> But lo, he is not here: he is afar
> On life's great errands under mightier skies,
> And pressing on toward some melodious star."[1]

Jesus said: "I am the resurrection, and the life: he that believeth in me, though he were dead, yet shall he live; and whosoever liveth and believeth in me shall never die" (John 11:25-26). As Christians we believe that our loved one has now passed out of death and into life and now continues on the river of life on board the boat whose captain is "My Father."

Harold E. Johnson

131   *THE KEY TO GOD'S SILENCE*

We shall all be changed. 1 CORINTHIANS 15:51

Often have I asked myself, Why is it that the religion of the Son of Man is so silent about the destiny of the sons of men! He has told us of many mansions, but He has not revealed their form. Other masters have been explicit, minute, detailed in their descriptions of the coming heaven, but the verdict even of Christ's most beloved disciple is this: "It doth not yet appear what we shall be" (1 John 3:2). And here is the key to the whole silence: before we reach Heaven "we shall all be changed." It is as if it were said: What is the use of describing the joys of heaven? they would not be joys to you as yet. You would not tell the child of the pleasures he shall have when he becomes a man. And why? because the pleasantness of these pleasures is now beyond him. He would shed bitter tears to be told that in the

[1] "An Epitaph."

time to come he should rejoice in that which is not play—in study, in work, in care, in responsibility, in duty. He shall see the glory of these things when he himself shall be changed.

Thou who art crying for a new revelation of Heaven, art thou ready for thy wish? Would it be to thee a joy if there were revealed to thee the pleasures at God's right hand? What if these pleasures should be what the selfish man calls pain? Knowest thou not that the joys of love are not the joys of lovelessness? Love's joy is the surrender of itself; the joy of lovelessness is the keeping of itself. If Heaven were open to thy vision, the sight might startle thee; thou mightst call for the rocks to hide thee, for the mountains to cover thee from the view. To make the revelation a joy to thee thou thyself must be changed into the same image.

It is not every soul that can rejoice to be a ministering spirit sent forth to minister to the heirs of salvation; to rejoice in it fully we must all be changed. If death were abolished today it would not free thee from that need. It is not death that demands thy change; it is life. It is not death that brings thy change; it is the Spirit of the Christ. Thou needst not wait for death to find thy change, for the Spirit too can transform in a moment, in the twinkling of an eye. Blessed are they who shall not taste of death until they shall see the Kingdom of God.

George Matheson

B. THE HOUSE OF MANY MANSIONS

132   *CHRIST'S CONCEPT OF IMMORTALITY*

In my Father's house are many mansions . . . . I go to prepare a place for you.   JOHN 14:2

We need to go back to the revelation of Christ to gain the true conception of immortality. He revealed God as each man's Father. Now, the highest work of a father is education, and the end of God's education of man is the finished and harmonious development of *all* his powers. If in the future life our intellect or imagination is left undeveloped, it is not education, and we cannot conceive of a perfect fatherhood. If all our powers have not there their work and their opportunities of expansion, the full idea of fatherhood is lost. If any of our true work here on earth is fruitless work, and does not enable us to produce tenfold results in a future life, no matter what that work may be, work of the artist, historian, politician, merchant, then the true conception of education, and therefore of God's fatherhood, is lost.

We rest on this: "I go to prepare a place for you." A place is prepared for each one of us; a place fitted to our distinct character; a separate work fitted to develop that character into perfection, and in the doing of which we shall have the continual delight of feeling that we are growing—a place not only for us, but for all our peculiar powers. Our ideals shall become more beautiful, and minister continually to fresh aspiration, so that stagnation will be impossible. Feelings for which we found no food here shall there be satisfied with work, and exercised by action into exquisite perfection. Faint possibilities of our nature, which came and went before us here like swallows on the wing, shall there be grasped and made realities. The outlines of life shall be filled up, the rough statue of life shall be finished. We shall be not only spiritual men, but men complete in Christ, the perfect flower of humanity.

And this shall be in a father's home, where all the dearest dreams of home-life shall find their happy fulfilment; in a perfect society, where all the charming interchange of thought, and giving and receiving of each other's good, which make our best happiness on earth, shall be easier, freer, purer, more intimate, more spiritual, more intellectual; and, lastly, in a perfect polity, "fellow-citizens with the saints" (Eph. 2:19), where all the interests of large national life shall find room and opportunities for development; and, bind all together, the omnipresent Spirit of love, goodness, truth, and life, whom we call God, and whom we know in Jesus Christ, shall abide in us, and we in him, "for he is not a God of the dead, but of the living: for all live unto him" (Luke 20:38).

Stopford A. Brooke

133   *IN MY FATHER'S HOUSE*

In my Father's house are many mansions: if it were not so, I would have told you. I go to prepare a place for you.   JOHN 14:2

Those of us who look to Jesus for guidance in the great problems have, perhaps, wondered why He had so little to say about immortality. The philosophers have said so much. But Jesus was no philosopher; and, judging by many philosophers, I do not know that we should be sorry. Jesus never argued about any of the great things. To Him they were not problems to be demonstrated, as were those of Euclid, but to be accepted by faith. To Jesus immortality was a necessity for the man into whom God had breathed the breath of life and made more than perishable flesh. Mountains were bigger than man, but they had had no breath of life breathed into them. So they could pass away and be forgotten. But not God-inspired man. To Jesus there was only one question about immortality: What was it like? That He answered in a simple and compelling fashion with the words of the text.

He had chosen with care the time for giving that answer. It was when they who heard it needed it most. It was not on the Temple porch where so often the crowds had gathered, sometimes to learn and sometimes to argue. It was to a little company, men who had left all to follow Him. They were to see, and very shortly, the end of that comradeship at the cross. They had gathered in the good man's guest chamber for the ancient feast of their people. That was over now, and He gave them of the bread and the wine of the new feast of a greater remembrance. And then He turned to the answer, for He knew how they would need it on the morrow—and we need it today. "Let not your heart be troubled: ye believe in God, believe also in me. In my Father's house are many mansions: if it were not so, I would have told you. I go to prepare a place for you. And if I go and prepare a place for you, I will come again, and receive you unto myself; that where I am, there ye may be also." That is what immortality meant for Him. That is what He meant it to mean for them—and for us. Back again to the Father's house. At home!

He could have chosen no livelier word as symbol. What memories the words stir in us! It may have been only a humble house on a little street or a cottage down a country lane. But it held what the heart desires above all else, sympathy and understanding and welcome. To the boy away at school or in the foxhole, or to the man or woman anxious amid the tasks the years have brought, it tells of a place where problems are left behind and wounds are healed. Some day there would come the turning of the last corner, and then the mounting of the steps to the door that opened with the touch. And there would be light beyond the door and a mother's kiss and the warm clasp of a father's hand. Home—at last!

That to Jesus was what immortal life was like. With the simplicity He always used in dealing with the great things of the Gospel He set forth His idea of what awaited the people of God after their days here were done. It brought hope to those who heard Him, and in the strength which the words gave them they did impossible things. For beyond the battles waited something they could understand.

So, today, as we are called upon to face this matter of death, let us think of it as Jesus taught His disciples to think of it, not as something to be feared, but as the turning of the last corner that leads to the Father's house. "If it were not so, I would have told you," He said. And they who have believed that have found life as

A shepherd leading home his flock serenely
Under the planet at the evening's end.[1]

William E. Brooks

134   *IF IT WERE NOT SO*

In my Father's house are many mansions: if it were not so, I would have told you. JOHN 14:2

In an hour such as this our souls are stirred to their very depths, and we face the most difficult task which God assigns: placing to final rest one who is dear to us. With our hearts torn and saddened, I shall

[1] From "The Old Enemy" by Sara Teasdale.

not speak glowing words of praise. There is praise enough in our hearts already. No words of mine could add more.

Let us not then dwell upon the virtues which you and I have lost by *his* passing, but upon the glory which *he* has gained. For mourning the loss which we feel so keenly only makes our hearts heavy, but the realization that *he* has gone into a far more glorious existence should lift a burden from our hearts, even as the burden of earthly life has been lifted from *his* heart.

Speaking of the mansions in Heaven, Jesus said, "If it were not so, I would have told you." For many centuries men have believed that beyond the grave there is a life far more beautiful than this earthly life. Jesus made sure this hope and added, "If it were not so, I would have told you."

God's promises never fail. Let us rest in the assurance of His Word that we shall one day be reunited with those whom we have loved and lost awhile. Do not ask me how we shall appear when God raises us to be with Him; I do not know. But I know that I shall see our lost loved one in His presence. And you will see *him* and be with *him*. This hope Christians through the centuries have held close to their hearts, for Jesus said, "If it were not so, I would have told you."

Do you not see that we weep selfishly? The loss is ours—and it is a bitter loss. But surely *he*, now at the throne of Heaven with *his* Saviour whom *he* loved so well, has not suffered a loss. When God calls a servant who has been devout in worship and regular in study, I do not despair of *his* well-being. *His* faith has secured for *him* a place in the mansions of Heaven. For this purpose Jesus Christ died for us all.

In the fall of the year the countryside is at its loveliest. What makes it so? It is death! When the leaves are dying they achieve their greatest glory. So it is with the Christian: through faith in Jesus Christ *he* comes to his greatest glory as *he* enters the mansions in the presence of the Father.

Out of the world's deepest sorrow came the world's most glorious hope. What appeared to be death, as the world saw the Son of God nailed to a cross, was in reality the birth of eternal life. What appeared to be a victory for Satan was in reality the defeat of Satan's forces, the proof that light is eternally triumphant over darkness and life victorious over death.

This is the faith we need for the sorrow of this hour. It is the faith which can be ours through our blessed Saviour who promised, "If it were not so, I would have told you."

William Goddard Sherman

135   *THE WAY PREPARED*

I go to prepare a place for you.   JOHN 14:2

Christ goes ahead to prepare the way. How characteristic, how in keeping with all we know about Him! "I go to prepare a place for you."

If we could have lived with Jesus in Galilee what about Him would have impressed us the most? With some it would be His eyes, with others His hands, and still others His voice. But I would like to have seen Him walk. I would like to have seen His stride, the poise of His head; for I am sure that His walk would reveal the majesty of His life.

His walk, for instance, would illustrate His passion to prepare the way. His walk would reveal His determination not to ask of another what He would not do Himself. Always Jesus was preparing the way, even as, when going toward Jerusalem for the final test, He walked ahead. And as the shadows were falling, He said, "I go to prepare a place for you."

It is no wonder, therefore, that the New Testament is full of hope of the life beyond. He has prepared the way. It is no wonder that we read, "Let not your heart be troubled . . . neither let it be afraid." Christ has prepared the way. It is no wonder that faith in immortality has become the heart of Christian faith. And we are not surprised that the followers of Christ cast the fear of death and dying aside. Christ prepared the way.

So, out of a time of persecution, suffering, frustration, and death, there rises like a tidal wave a note of triumph, a hymn sung again and again in different ways, but always with the same theme, "Thanks be to God, which giveth us the victory" (1 Cor. 15:57).

Christ has prepared the way. Thus John saw a new Jerusalem, a tabernacle of God, a city foursquare, where men would dwell without tears, without sorrow, crying, or pain, a city with no need of the sun, neither of the moon to shine in it—for the glory of God did lighten it, and the Lamb is the light thereof.

How much easier it is to walk in the valley of the shadow since He has passed therein. How great the confidence in which we lay our dead away, knowing that they have now passed a threshold over which the

Master Himself has crossed. What reassurance and hope is ours as we face the fact of our own death to know that Christ, and those whom we have loved long since and lost awhile, have gone on to prepare a place for us.

Thus John White Chadwick has taught us to sing:

> More homelike seems the vast unknown,
> Since they have entered there;
> To follow them were not so hard,
> Wherever they may fare;
> They cannot be where God is not,
> On any sea or shore;
> Whate'er betides, Thy love abides,
> Our God, forever more.[1]

W. Ralph Ward, Jr.

136 *THE ROOM NAMED HEAVEN*

In my Father's house are many mansions. JOHN 14:2

Up to the time of Christ all men had thought that there were two worlds—one of earth and sea and sky, of clasping hands and loving hearts; and another into which men pass at death, chill, cheerless, robbed, at its best, of much that made life glad. But with Jesus there are not two worlds, but one. Heaven is God's seat. Earth is His footstool. All the universe of created things is His Father's house. "In my Father's house are many rooms." Earth, with its green meadows and steadfast hills and shining stars, is only one room in the Father's house. There may be, and most likely are, many rooms in God's spacious creation. Heaven, with its unseen and unknown and eternal beauty, is another room in the Father's house. There is a life to be lived with the Father here. There is a life to be lived with the Father there.

What, then, was death to Jesus? Dying might mean pain and tears and sorrow and loneliness and loss to those who are left behind. Dying has its torment because of sin, but dying ought to be but the passing from one room to another. When Jesus would die, when He would not pass, as He might have passed, through the gate which was never closed to Him, but through the dreadful avenue of death, He would go to prepare the room for us. Death is not the close of life. It is only the putting off of the garment of that mortality which we wear in the room called earth, and the putting on of that robe of immortality which we shall wear in the room named Heaven.

W. M. Clow

[1] From "Auld Lang Syne."

137   *GRACIOUS INTERPRETATIONS*

Let not your heart be troubled: ye believe in God, believe also in me.
In my Father's house are many mansions: if it were not so, I would have
told you. I go to prepare a place for you. And if I go and prepare a place
for you, I will come again, and receive you unto myself; that where I am,
there ye may be also.   JOHN 14:1-3

We turn again and again to these familiar words and ever with
deepening comfort and enlarging blessing. How striking is the inter-
pretation which Jesus brings of God. The God of Heaven, He suggests, wishes to be our "Father." Through the ages poets, philosophers, evangelists, and teachers have endeavoured to make the Deity
real to us. They have emphasized His holiness, stressed His almightiness, and exalted His wisdom. But the imposing witness of His many
attributes serves only to accentuate our personal defilement and to
multiply our chains.

It was reserved for the Saviour to bring to us this simple, sweet,
attractive picture of the Most High. "When ye pray," Jesus said, "say,
Our Father which art in heaven" (Luke 11:2). Here is a word that
warms the heart and wins our instant confidence. No normal child
fears his normal father. Rather this man is his hero, confidant, pro-
tector, and most intimate companion. Isn't this a thrilling and glorious conception of the Eternal which Jesus brings to us?

Again I am enthralled by the Saviour's thought of death. So many
shrink from any serious consideration of death. They do not speak
of it and they prefer never to be reminded of it. Death seems to be an
unnatural usurper who invades and wrecks man's world. He believes
he was never intended to die. Death outrages man's innate sense of
fundamental rightness. It is the ultimate humiliation when man is
compelled to submit reluctantly to the claim of death.

When Jesus faced death He did not speak of it. There is no mention of the anguish and the horror of the crucifixion. Looking into
the faces of His closest earthly friends He calmly announces: "I am
going to my Father's House. I am going *home!*"

What a winsome picture of death. And Jesus further explains that
in His Father's House there are many dwelling places. I like to think
that this earth is a humble room in the Father's House. Death simply
means that we leave this familiar place and step into another larger
and more beautiful apartment where new lessons await us, richer relationships, and more exciting services. I cannot remember that I was

ever afraid, or even reluctant, to enter into my earthly father's house
—to go home. Home represents everything that is good and splendid
and precious. It is a fortress of love, a holy sanctuary of happiness and
security. And this is death to a believer; it is going home.

Once more I am unspeakably grateful for the assurance which is
here of a happy reunion with our loved ones. "I am going," Jesus
said, "but I will not forget you. Indeed I shall be thinking constantly
of you, for I shall be preparing a place for you. And as surely as I go,
I will come again for you so that where I am there you can be also."

The disciples dared not think of life without their Master. And
reverently I suggest that Heaven would be forever incomplete to
Jesus until these dear and precious friends of His were once more by
His side. And so He leaves with them this priceless, inspiring hope of
a certain meeting again.

I rejoice today in the knowledge that God is indeed my Father.
And, if Jesus tarries and I have to walk down into the valley of the
shadow, I know it is my way home. How many valued friends and
cherished loved ones have gone before. And they will be among the
very first to welcome me into the warmer, brighter room in my Heavenly Father's House.

Benjamin Goodfield

138   *THE HOUSE NOT MADE WITH HANDS*

For we know that if the earthly house of our tabernacle were dissolved,
we have a building from God, a house not made with hands, eternal in the
heavens. 2 CORINTHIANS 5:1

So Death is not the end, but only an epoch in a life which is endless.
The self survives and life goes on forever. The crisis which bears our
loved ones away conducts them into the new home where the corrod-
ing hand of time is stayed. There they shall live the eternity which is
in them, and the building which houses the emancipated soul shall
never know dissolution.

In the Father's house are many mansions and Christ has gone to
prepare a place for those who are His. A place is always ready when
angels come with the soul whom God has called. For those who remain to mourn, the time of departure of some loved one always comes
too soon. But even as the last hour is set, so also the place is prepared
and those who die in the Lord enter into rest. Death takes our dear
ones away and precious ties which have grown stronger with time are
broken, but death cannot separate them nor us from the love of God

which is in Christ Jesus our Lord. The unbreakable tie holds in death and the crisis issues in blessedness.

The permanence of life and the larger blessedness of life after death are not matters of speculation for the Christian. They are among the certainties of Christian faith. The New Testament speaks the language of assured knowledge. We know—*we know*. The last mysterious journey from which no traveler returns has its terminus in the heavens in that ultimate clothing of the immortal spirit with the house not made with hands, a building from God. The last great adventure is complete gain. It fits in with Divine provision and purpose. Without it the best that is to be still tarries. The glorious fruitage of life in Christ is gathered on the other side of death. The garden of the Lord is there.

> I know not, O, I know not,
> What joys await me there,
> What radiancy of glory,
> What bliss beyond compare.

What we do not know is merely the particulars. The fact that it is well with those who have gone is a certainty.

> For glory, glory dwelleth
> In Immanuel's land.

"If the earthly house of our tabernacle be dissolved!" Nature defies the process as long as possible, but it is ever going on. When the last reserves are spent, the earthly house, unable to sustain the occupant, falls in a heap and the forces of dissolution display their hideous triumph. To us it seems to be the end, the heart-rending end of all the love and hope and life which for us centered in that soul. "But at evening time there shall be light" (Zech. 14:7). Our distracted sight is lured away from the crumbled earthly house to mansions in the skies. We are assured that all we hoped and wished for has come to pass. The crisis of the end is the crisis of beginning. The promise of life has its fruition in the paradise of God. God's actual so far exceeds our ideal that even the general revelation of it without detail makes for composure and enduring faith.

Against the dark background of physical decay, the apostle Paul sets up the divine structure which God has prepared for His people. The day of death is moving day when the human soul, unable longer to abide in the worn-out body, is transferred by angel convoy to the perfect home in the heavens. Death is the crisis of exchange when the mortal makes way for the immortal. Death is the soul's ascension day, when the cloud which receives the departed out of our sight, is wafted by heavenly breezes into the presence of Christ. The last humiliation is illumined by the light of revelation. The strong Son of God turns the seeming defeat into supreme triumph. The dark valley of death lies prone against the everlasting hills of God and affords sepulchre to the exhausted earthly house only. The real self is not a partner in the imminent corruption, but wings its flight to eternal heights. If faith has tuned our hearts to the reality of the spiritual transaction, we shall be able to echo the refrain,

> Angels of Jesus, angels of light,
> Singing to welcome the pilgrims of the night.

It is natural to want to know more about the future life than has been revealed. The intimacies of everyday life are the native sphere of love's interest. If the land of fadeless bloom could only be made more real to us by a series of colored photographs! If some inspired pen could only enrich us with the treasures of exact description! If the departed could only send us personal messages, written by their hand and signed with the familiar name or spoken by the voice we loved to hear! Such longings cannot, perhaps, be repressed but they betoken our bondage to the things of sense. It is impossible to overestimate the damage to faith and hope and to the spirit of high adventure which would follow the Divine accommodation to the longings which characterize the frailty of our sensuous nature. The foundations of life's grandeur would be destroyed and the pilgrim spirit would suffer extinction in the absence of the call of the unknown. The source of human refinement would be dried up at the spring. The star of hope would fade from our sky. We can conceive of no greater blow to religious experience and to religious interest and to the cause of religion in general and thus to the dignity and grandeur of human life than the physical satisfaction of earthborn desires with reference to the kingdom of the departed. Think it through and it must become evident how great is our debt to the fact that we walk by faith, not by sight.

It is a question whether Christians generally have exposed their grief in bereavement to the full weight of what has been revealed. Recall again the weighty assurance of the apostle Paul which we are now considering. Does it not establish the certain gain of death to the Christian? Life is not exhausted by death. It experiences the great change spoken of elsewhere by the same inspired writer, but the change is to a better sphere and to a perfect instrument for a deathless life. The frequent affirmations in the New Testament of the believer's destiny are unspeakably consoling. They assure us of the glory of going on and still to be. "Because I live, ye shall live also" (John 14:19). "I am the resurrection and the life, he that believeth on me, though he were dead, yet shall he live" (John 11:25-26). "I give unto them eternal life and they shall never perish and no one shall pluck them out of my hand" (John 10:29). "As we have borne the image of the earthly, so we must bear the image of the heavenly" (1 Cor. 15:49). It is as the poet says, "There is no death, what seems so is transition." The life which is thus declared to be permanent suffers no loss by the experience of death. It is "in the heavens." It dwells in "a building from God, a house not made with hands" (2 Cor. 5:1). This habitation is eternal. Those who die in the Lord are where Christ is. "This day shalt thou be with me in paradise" (Luke 23:43). The truth about them is that they are forever with the Lord.

The Bible speaks of the end of the present world order, of a final catastrophe which is to usher in a new heaven and a new earth wherein dwelleth righteousness. It speaks of a coming of Christ in glory, of a resurrection of the just and the unjust, of a final judgment, and of the ultimate assignment of every soul to his own place. Thus many Bible scholars speak of an intermediate state of the soul by which they refer to the condition of the soul between the period of death and the resurrection. And they mean to say further by the term, that while the condition of the soul after death is in the case of the Christian one of blessedness, the soul does not attain to its ultimate destiny until it is given a spiritual body at the resurrection. There has never been unanimous opinion about how all these events are related to one another. It is, perhaps, impossible for anyone ever to write the actual biography of the life of the soul after death. This is quite in keeping with the manifest divine intention that we shall walk by faith and not by sight and in no way compromises the comforting passages to which we have alluded in which the Bible sets forth the large blessedness which follows the death of a Christian. We are dealing with the sure Word of God and our inability to construct proper sequences and to relate properly the many mighty events predicted, does not detract from the truth of all that has been revealed.

God speaks in every verse and chapter of Scripture which deal with this great subject and we are warranted in deducting their full strength of consolation for the assuaging of sorrow. We are shut up to faith, but faith is a great light, which permits us to see that no damage results from death to those who die in the Lord, but rather infinite gain. Thus our last glimpse of them sees them "safe in the arms of Jesus" and we can leave them there in the confidence that God will perfect that which concerns them, if so be that the "building from God, a house not made with hands, eternal, in the heavens" is still less than the final best.

Simon Blocker

139 *A FAITH BY WHICH TO DIE*

In my Father's house are many mansions: if it were not so, I would have told you. I go to prepare a place for you. And if I go and prepare a place for you, I will come again, and receive you unto myself; that where I am, there ye may be also.   JOHN 14:2-3

For Christians this is meant to be a day of triumph, a day of triumph for our loved one who now has gone beyond the broken dreams of this earth and beyond the veil which hides the everlasting mysteries from us. This is what we have always said to ourselves in our hymns and in our prayers. It must not, therefore, be a day of rebellion, but of thanksgiving; not a day of bitterness, but of gentle remembrance; not a day of anger because God has taken someone whom we thought dear, but a day of gratitude because God has come to take one of His children to His heavenly home.

There are times when in the poverty of our faith and from the loneliness of our hearts we say that we have lost someone whom we have loved. But how can that be? How can we lose that which is held by the bonds of everlasting affection? The only time when we have lost anything is when we no longer know where to find it. *But we do know.* Our Lord Jesus said: "In my Father's house are many mansions: if it were not so, I would have told you. I go to prepare a place for you. And if I go and prepare a place for you, I will come again, and receive you unto myself; that where I am, there ye may be also." *We do know!* And speaking to those whose hearts were darkened by the shadow of death, He said, "Though he were dead, yet shall he live: and whosoever liveth and believeth in me shall never die" (John 11:25-26). Lost? No! *We do know.*

So this then is more than a day of sorrow. It may be a day of loneliness; our hearts were made that way. It may be a day of longing, for the mist of tears veils our eyes. But above all else let it be a day of faith. Are we afraid of death? Death is a throbbing moment; life is eternity. Death is a rippling eddy; life is the stream. Death is a cloud—and God's hand reaches through the cloud and touches us as He says: "It is time to come home." His voice pierces the cloud and whispering to our inmost heart says: "It is time to come home." Death—it is God coming to us, leading us on to another life, more knowing, more creative, rising beyond the hindrances that have slackened our steps on earth. And so we are not afraid and we are not rebellious. This is our faith. It is a wonderful faith. It is a faith by which we were reared; it is a faith by which we live; it is a faith by which we will want to die.

Arnold Hilmar Lowe

140   *THE WORLD BEYOND*

In my Father's house are many mansions: if it were not so, I would have told you. JOHN 14:2

Apart from the definite allusion to [the future life] which [Christ] made, the thought of it lies at the basis of all His teaching. It is part of its very warp and woof. We cannot subtract it from His teaching, any more than we can lift the background from a picture and expect what remains to have a true perspective. "In my Father's house are many mansions," He said; "if it were not so, I would have told you." In other words He assumed the fact of the other life. He took it for granted. It was the only thing that could give His teaching consistency, and satisfy the expectations which His whole influence had created in the minds of His disciples. He felt it to be so inevitable that He did not need to state it. This can be seen if we examine the effect of His message.

For one thing, He makes us feel the sacredness of personality. Every soul is precious to God. In every man there is something of infinite value, which God cannot bear should be lost. "What man of you, having an hundred sheep, if he lose one of them, doth not leave the ninety and nine in the wilderness, and go after that which is lost, until he find it?" (Luke 15:4). This idea has been the moving force of all human progress since Christ's day. It has broken the power of slavery, inspired factory reform, and sent men and women into the slums to rescue the victims of drink and vice. It has sent missionaries into distant lands, and made them feel it worth while if they could save one single life from the grip of heathendom. If a great building were on fire and part of it could be saved only at the cost of leaving someone in it to perish, men would pull that building to pieces if thereby they could rescue that single life. Jesus not only taught this sense of human value. His whole influence created it. Maeterlinck says, "When Jesus Christ met a Samaritan, met a few children, an adulterous woman, then did humanity rise three times to the level of God."

That was the motive power of Christ's own ministry of healing and preaching. But of what use is it if this life is all? He took Mary Magdalene from the life of shame she had been living; but for what, if her life was to end at the grave? Why save Zaccheus from dishonesty, if death was to make an end? The one ground on which it is consistent to believe that men are worth saving at the cost of any sacrifice is the fact of immortality.

Or again, think how He deepened personal affections. He strengthened and purified home love. He gave back to the widow of Nain her only son on the way to the grave. He loved little children and revealed them in a light of tender reverence that gave the world a new interest in all children. The whole field of human affections and friendships was enriched by His Spirit. He persuaded people to forgive their enemies. But if death is to end all, it seems sheer cruelty to kindle and deepen this love in our hearts. Why deepen it if it is only to end in unavailing sorrow? If there is nothing beyond, it would seem kinder to discourage these affections. Surely within this love there is the seed and promise of immortality. Love gives us, beyond anything else, the feeling that it is eternal. That is the conviction that rose in the heart of Charlotte Brontë when she was dying. "God will not separate us now; we have been so happy."

Or think of Christ's call to serve God's purpose. He took His disciples away from their fields and their fishing boats, and led them into the wider service of His Kingdom. It meant foregoing the gains they might have made. Was it all to be for nothing? Peter, indeed, put the question, and Christ answered, "Everyone that hath forsaken houses, or brethren . . . or lands, for my name's sake, shall receive an hundredfold, and shall inherit everlasting life" (Matt. 19:29). It is not an ignoble instinct that demands that we should see the fruit of our labor. Jesus assured His disciples that all their sacrifices and service would find their fulfilment in a Kingdom whose joy and victory they would share. The vision of the Kingdom of God has the power to awaken man's deepest energies of service. But why, if there be no abiding reality in it? Is it conceivable that Christ should kindle in men hopes that will not be realized? "Let not your heart be troubled. . . . if it were not so, I would have told you" (John 14:1-2).

But think also of His own love and the bond with Himself He creates in the hearts of men; for He kindles in the heart a love for Himself and a faith in Himself which is like no other bond. That was why the disciples broke down after Calvary. He had so loved them and taught them so to love Himself, that they had felt the friendship must be permanent. His death seemed to have shattered that dream. Their grief and dismay were the reflection of the death of this conviction. This assurance the resurrection restored and confirmed. They knew then that this love of Christ was a love from which nothing could separate them, because its springs were in the heart of God. For that love, our human springs have abiding value. This is the conviction that His message about the love of God, lit up as it was by His own Spirit, creates in the heart. This presumes immortality. It is the deepest basis of our assurance. If, as Jesus says, our human father-love can be trusted as a dim picture of God's love, there is assurance that He will not let us go. No father can bear the loss of one of his children or ever cease to love him. "For love," as Hocking says, "is the principle of individuation."

> God singles out unit by unit.
> Thou and God exist.

When a man has seen the love of God in Christ he knows that its beam is focused on himself. The surrender to that love brings us into a relationship with God from which nothing can separate us. That is the ultimate basis of our assurance of immortality. In his last letter to his wife, just before the end, Dr. Edward Wilson of the Antarctic wrote,

> Don't be unhappy. We are playing a good part in a great scheme arranged by God himself, and all is well. . . . We will all meet after death, and death has no terrors. . . . All is for the best to those that love God, and we have both loved him with all our lives. . . . Life itself is a small thing to me now. But my love for you is for ever, and a part of our love for God. All the things I had hoped to do with you after this expedition are as nothing now, but there are greater things for us to do in the world to come. All is well.[1]

James Reid

[1] From *Edward Wilson of the Antarctic* by George Seaver.

C. AND THIS IS LIFE ETERNAL

THE LIFE ETERNAL

And this is life eternal, that they might know thee the only true God, and Jesus Christ, whom thou hast sent. JOHN 17:3

We believe in the life eternal because the life eternal has been manifested to men. Jesus lived the life eternal.

And Jesus talked about life all the time. He at no time talked about death.

To be more accurate, Jesus did once speak of death. He said to His disciples, "Lazarus is dead." The report of Lazarus' sickness had come to Jesus. Then a little later Jesus said, "Our friend Lazarus sleepeth; but I go, that I may awake him out of sleep" (John 11:11). He had carefully avoided the word "death." Rather He used the word "asleep." It was only because the disciples did not understand, that Jesus said, "Lazarus is dead." Jesus preferred the word "asleep"; for sleep means rest and recuperation and a waking-up in the morning. When Jesus had come to the sorrowing sisters, He spoke out of the fullness of life that was His and said, "I am the resurrection, and the life: he that believeth on me, though he were dead, yet shall he live; and whosoever liveth and believeth in me shall never die" (John 11:25-26).

Jesus was as sure of immortality as he was of God. His fellowship with the Father was forever unbroken. His consciousness of God was a deep, underlying reality. And just so with His certainty touching the life eternal; it underlay all His teaching because it was with Him an abiding and all-controlling experience. The Eternal World was His native country.

We need not now recall the many things Jesus had to say about immortality. It will be enough to mention two memorable sayings. When the Sadducees who were skeptics concerning the doctrine of immortality came to Jesus with their stock-puzzle touching the much-married woman, as to whose wife she would be in the other world, Jesus answered, "Do ye not therefore err, because ye know not the scriptures, neither the power of God? . . . And as touching the dead,

that they rise: have ye not read in the book of Moses, how in the
bush God spake unto him, saying, I am the God of Abraham, and the
God of Isaac, and the God of Jacob? He is not the God of the dead,
but the God of the living: ye therefore do greatly err" (Mark 12:24,
26-27.) All this is to say that the personal relationship established between God and His children outlasts time and continues into eternity.
God's friends are His forever. Therefore, Abraham, Isaac, and Jacob
are not dead but alive.

The other reference is to the great words found in the fourteenth
chapter of the Gospel according to John, "the dearest words that ever
rang their sweet peal across the centuries"—"Let not your heart be
troubled: ye believe in God, believe also in me. In my Father's house
are many mansions: if it were not so, I would have told you. I go to
prepare a place for you. And if I go and prepare a place for you, I
will come again, and receive you unto myself; that where I am, there
ye may be also. And whither I go ye know, and the way ye know"
(John 14:1-4). There are not many words in this great saying. Details
are not entered into; nothing is said to satisfy the imagination. But
there is everything here to satisfy the heart. The saints' immortal hope
is not a fond fiction. Jesus would never have permitted His friends to
hug a delusion to their breasts. "If it were not so" He would have told
us. In the "Father's house" there is room, abundant room; there are
"many mansions." And whatever else may be there, Christ Himself
is there—"Where I am, there ye may be also." The fellowship begun
with Him on earth shall be continued forever. That hope fills the
heart with wistful longings, but for the time being we rest in this:

> My knowledge of that life is small;
> The eye of faith is dim.
> It is enough that Christ knows all;
> And I shall be with him.

Edwin D. Mouzon

142   ENDLESS LIVING

This is life eternal, that they might know Thee the only true God, and
Jesus Christ whom thou hast sent. JOHN 17:3

We are come together in this hour of sorrow to reaffirm our faith
in God and in His Son, Jesus Christ, whom to know aright is the life
eternal. We humble ourselves before God our Creator not because
we must but rather because we may. The Lord gives; the Lord
receives back unto Himself. Blessed be His holy name.

Eternal life is a free gift from God who is the Creator and Sustainer of all life. He offers, we receive; and together we live victoriously forever. This life was in our world before we appeared upon the scene; it will be here after we have gone away. During our sojourn here upon earth, we can, if we will, move into this divine life. It will bless and keep us here; it will bless and keep us there.

If we possess today the peace that passeth all understanding, it is because we have received it from God whom we have truly known in our daily living. To believe is not enough. It is easier to sit down and believe than it is to get up and live. To know God is to realize His presence, to become aware of His power in and around us. Our lives must receive the spirit of the living God and be healed and directed by it. So do we come to know Him in every pulse beat, and knowing Him and His Son Jesus Christ, we possess, and are possessed by, that quality of life which is endless. Eternal life is not a distant reward, it is an ever-present reality. It is potential and actual—here and now. This is the faith by which we live and this is the faith by which we are prepared to die, for whether we live or whether we die we are forever safe with the Lord who is Life Eternal. If we would die as those who are prepared to live, we must live as those who are prepared to die.

In the beginning God speaks our names and we awaken in our homes where loving care awaits us. The days come and go. Slowly and surely we learn the lesson of living. We come to know and respond to God's call through the redeeming spirit of His Son, Jesus Christ. Then one day when our learning is done, He speaks our names once again and we vanish from the faces of our friends and loved ones to be forevermore with Him, from whom we came, in whose will we live, and to whom we return.

To live with Him, to be assured of His loving care is the one goal of life. This is the only rational way of living, but it goes beyond our ability to understand. It is much deeper than our small human minds.

> I know not where His islands lift
> Their fronded palms in air;
> I only know I cannot drift
> Beyond His love and care.[1]

When we are comforted and reassured by our Christian faith, we are never without hope even though our sorrow and loss be tragically

[1] From "The Eternal Goodness" by John Greenleaf Whittier.

real. We can, if we will, hear the Master's voice saying, "In my Father's House there are many abiding places" (John 14:2).

And so, calmly and quietly, we note the home-going of the immortal spirit of one whom we have known and loved, and with courage and determination we move away from this hour, to accept once again the happy privileges and sacred responsibilities of those unlived days yet before us, with full assurance that all is well with us and our loved ones when our lives are under the guidance of God in whose likeness we have been fashioned.

> Candle-flame buffeted by darkness,
> The curve of purple iris petal,
> The rainbow arch against the waterfall,
> These I have seen . . .
> And these have passed away.
> Have passed whither?
> Into the great nothing? . . .
>
> Then fearless shall I face the baffling void
> For how can nothing take unto itself
> All lovely things,
> All fragile things that fade,
> And not itself become clothed
> With majesty and wonder?[1]
>
> *Lee C. Sheppard*

143   *CONFIDENT ASSURANCE*

If a man keep my saying, he shall never see death.   JOHN 8:51

Our Saviour Jesus Christ, who hath abolished death, and hath brought life and immortality to light through the gospel.   2 TIMOTHY 1:10

He will swallow up death in victory; and the Lord God will wipe away tears from off all faces.   ISAIAH 25:8

O death, where is thy sting? O grave, where is thy victory? . . . Thanks be to God, which giveth us the victory through our Lord Jesus Christ. 1 CORINTHIANS 15:55-57

Let not your heart be troubled.   JOHN 14:1

Do we really believe and accept these great assertions? Can we meet the threat and challenge of death in their confident assurance? Commonly we are apt to evade or postpone the encounter.

Let us make the encounter in the presence of Christ: how else

[1] From "Candle-flame" by Bonar Wilson.

should we? This faith which conquers death is rooted in Him; is begotten of our experience of God in Him. He is the Ever-living, who once was dead. It was He who said, "Because I live, ye shall live also" (John 14:19). It is He who has "brought life and immortality to light," revealing the real and enduring life to be a thing of the spirit. Eternal life is our inheritance and God, above time and mortal change, which He has redeemed for us, which is ours for the asking, by faith in Him, the Lord of life. "I *give* unto them eternal life; and they shall never perish, neither shall any man pluck them out of my hand" (John 10:28).

> There is not room for Death,
> Nor atom that his might could render void:
> Thou—*Thou* art Being and Breath,
> And what *Thou* art may never be destroyed.[1]

It is in this vision and faith and personal experience of eternal life that, if we are Christians, we have to find our focus of what, in the mere vision of time, appears such a sore and hurtful problem: the cutting off of an earthly term of life at an early age. In this connection, is there not significance in the fact that Christ died—by violence —at about thirty years of age? He is rightful Captain and Surety of all who unselfishly lay down their lives in youth; and time's years are not His measure.

Emerson wrote: "Let the measure of Time be spiritual, not mechanical. Life is unnecessarily long. Moments of insight, of fine personal relation, a smile, a glance—what ample borrowers of eternity they are."

But if there is any meaning in that, it requires the Christian faith of eternal life and its fulfilment beyond this mortal world.

But it is the separation, the sense of sundered love, of irreparable loss, which is hardest to accept, is it not? Here is the sting of death— for sin is sundered relationship—with God and with our human fellows. God is love—true and sustained relationship—and love is life eternal.

Well, why accept it? Christ is ours, livingly, the Reconciler, the At-one-ment. If we are, in Him, at one with God, we are at one with all His realm of life; we are admitted to the fellowship of all living. We do not submit to the victory of death; we enjoy the fruits of His victory. Let this work in your heart and mind.

[1] From "Last Lines" by Emily Brontë.

Somewhere thou livest and hast need of Him:
Somewhere thy soul sees higher heights to climb;
And somewhere still there may be valleys dim,
That thou must pass to reach the hills sublime.

Then all the more, because thou can'st not hear
Poor human words of blessing, will I pray,
O true, brave heart! God bless thee, wheresoe'er
In His great universe thou art today![1]

P. J. Fisher

144   *YEARNING FOR GOD*

As a hart panteth after the water brooks, so panteth my soul after
Thee, O God.   PSALM 42:1

While traveling in a horse-drawn cart in the heat of a blistering
June sun, our company, tired, thirsty, and hungry, stopped for lunch,
refreshment, and rest beside a large spring by the side of Mount
Ararat. A brook of clear cool water ran from that mountainside
spring. As we rested, we watched a deer go to the water. It was panting heavily as it plunged eagerly into the brook where it bathed
and cooled itself. When satisfied it moved slowly up the mountain.

That sight brought to our minds the words of the text. The
Psalmist, no doubt, had been inspired by an experience similar to ours.

The human soul travels through many mountain, valley, and desert
experiences in this life. When we are exhausted by our experiences
of need, sickness, disappointment, and death, our souls long and pant
for God. God's fountain of life is always full. The only way we can
quench our spiritual thirst is to plunge eagerly into the fountain and
drink to satisfaction.

In the Syriac Version of the Bible this text reads: "As a hart longeth
and craves for the water brooks, so my soul longeth and craves for
Thee, O Lord." In the presence of death, we long and crave for something better, something higher, than the failures and sadness of this
life. Nowhere can we find what our souls need but in God.

This quest for God and for eternal life cannot be given to us by
good legislators nor through the wisdom of beneficent men. It comes
freely and graciously from God, whenever we may open our hearts to
Him. No wealth, no position, no book can quench our thirst for God,
our desperate need of God; but a simple faith in God and in the
eternal life through the risen and ever-living Christ can satisfy our

[1] From "Somewhere" by Julia C. R. Dorr.

deepest longings, can answer our persistent questions, can quiet our most anguished fears.

Paul S. Newey

145 *THE PATHWAY OF LIGHT*

The pathway of the just is as a shining light, that shineth more and more unto the perfect day. PROVERBS 5:18

This is a tender hour, but in no wise an hour of tragedy. There is something utterly appropriate about the going of this one who has lived a long, happy, and useful life, who has put so much of goodness, kindness, love, and service for others and loyalty to God into her years. It is highly appropriate when such a person goes home, to the Home toward which she has journeyed for nearly *eighty* years.

This is not a time of darkness, but rather a time of light. It is not an hour in which to exaggerate grief, but rather an hour in which to comprehend more fully the measure of our gratitude to God for this life that was and *is.*

We shall not talk of death, but rather of life eternal. The harvest of the faith and life of your beloved beautifies the landscape for you and for all of us.

She was a consecrated Christian wife and mother. The tenderness of her love for her children, her interest in all they did, her training of them in the ways of God—all these concerns are a commentary upon her graciousness and goodness. She was always an inspiration to her pastor who found her confidence in God a benediction and a blessing.

Today we are on holy ground, for we pause near Heaven's gate through which your lovely mother and friend has just passed into the gardens of eternal life.

Particularly appropriate to this occasion are the words of Scripture, "But the pathway of the just is as a shining light, that shineth more and more unto the perfect day." This promise has back of it the authority of God, the affirmation of Christ Jesus whose whole life was a demonstration of its validity, and the witness of the saints of all generations. All Scripture and all Christian experience is saturated with this assurance.

He who faces the light walks in a lighted pathway. Only those who turn their backs to the source of light stumble amid their own shadows.

Long ago, in her early girlhood, our beloved friend turned her face, her heart, her whole life toward God the Father and set her feet upon "the pathway of the just." In the words of a slightly paraphrased verse:

> She gripped and held the hand of God,
>   The hand that led and blest,
> And let that peace whose storm is calm,
>   Hold kingship in her breast.

The longer she walked on this pathway the brighter the light became, for she was ever moving toward the source of light. The pathway was a shining light, shining more and more brightly. In her experience, as in the experience of every true disciple of Christ, evening was not a forerunner of darkness. Rather what some have mistaken for the colors of sunset were for her the beautiful anticipations of Eternal Dawn. She found another's experience to be her own: "At evening time it shall be light" (Zech. 14:7).

How truly was her faith revealed in the simple verse (which she dearly loved) by Bishop William Alfred Quayle:

> Tomorrow I shall die.
> I feel the coming of my grave.
> Hereafter I shall fly
> On wings of morning. Death's cold wave
>
> Affrights me not at all;
> I schooled me at the school of Christ.
> And when in death I fall,
> I answer to a holy tryst.

Such faith turns evening skies into the glow of morning's Eternal Day. She knew she was in God's keeping and that the end of her earthly life would only release her from all earthly limitations to the limitless life beyond.

> Think of stepping on shore and finding it Heaven!
> Of taking hold of a hand and finding it God's!
> Of breathing a new air and finding it celestial air!
> Of feeling invigorated and finding it immortality!
> Of passing from storm and stress to a perfect calm!
>   Of waking and finding it Home!

Such is your faith and in this is your comfort. Your heritage is a priceless one which all the uncertainties of life cannot possibly take from you. Yours is the memory of a mother whom you can always love and respect. Her felt presence will ever be an inspiration and a challenge. She waits beyond as she so often waited for you here. And the way to her has been illuminated by her faith and love, for "the pathway of the just is as a shining light, that shineth more and more unto the perfect day."

Louis H. Kaub

D. INTIMATIONS OF IMMORTALITY

This mortal must put on immortality.   1 CORINTHIANS 15:53

The question of immortality cannot be forgotten for long. We may become absorbed in present interests but through some tragic experience we suddenly realize the need of immortality. With the passing of each generation it continues to be a persistent question.

The fact that our friends and loved ones, as well as ourselves, face, as each man must, the experience of death, makes immortality a vital question, timely and timeless. Job asked, "If a man die shall he live again?" (Job 14:14). The same question arises in the minds of all who lose a loved one.

There are some things which indicate man's immortality. There is the indication of nature. We speak of one season as "dead of winter." Much of nature dies during that season but it lives again in the spring. Job reasoned from what he saw of a tree. "There is hope of a tree, if it be cut down, that it will sprout again . . . though the stock thereof die in the ground; yet through the scent of water it will bud, and bring forth boughs like a plant" (Job 14:7-9). Certainly if a tree lives again, man should. He later declared that he would see God even after the skin worms destroyed his flesh.

Immanuel Kant said that the eternal law of justice demanded a life beyond this one. He believed that sometime, somewhere, there would be a correction of wrong. He felt that a rational universe demanded immortality.

Some have pointed to the desire for immortality as an indication of its reality. There is food to satisfy hunger, water to quench thirst, and knowledge for the inquiring mind. Just as these fundamental desires have their fulfillment, so it is reasoned that immortality is necessary to satisfy the need and the desire for it.

There is also the intimation recognized as intuitive knowledge. This represents an unlearned human possession. It comes within the range of Plato's idea of *a priori* knowledge, knowledge included in man's original equipment as man. This sense of immortality has also been called the "surmise of the soul." We have a feeling, inward and yet assuring, of the truth of immortality.

Intimations of immortality, however, are not sufficient. We need a stronger word of assurance. That stronger word is found in the living Saviour. His resurrection demonstrated a life beyond the grave. He assured us by saying, "Because I live, ye shall live also" (John 14:19). Christ and the New Testament writers gave great assurance concerning the future life. Jesus spoke of the Father's house with many mansions. Paul mentioned the house not made with hands. John tells of all tears being wiped away, and of day which knows no night.

The Christian affirmation is that the soul is immortal and that the body will be resurrected. Life as we now know it in the flesh is not immortal. We now speak of mortal man. Nevertheless, this mortal shall put on immortality, and the corruptible will put on incorruption. Man's resurrected body, as well as his spirit, will be immortal. Paul adds, "Then shall be brought to pass the saying that is written, Death is swallowed up in victory." In the light of this he triumphantly asks: "O death, where is thy sting? O grave, where is thy victory?" Then he concludes the discussion with a note of victory, saying, "Thanks be to God, which giveth us the victory through our Lord Jesus Christ" (1 Cor. 15:54-55, 57).

A. Milton Smith

147   *BEYOND THE SHADOWS*

Whosover liveth and believeth on me shall never die.   JOHN 11:26

The time draws near for the ocean liner to start the voyage, and passengers stand at the rail. They look toward the land with interest and appreciation. The harbor is alive with light and color and activity. Gulls flash and wheel overhead and occasionally dart to the ocean for food; customs officers in the customs shed pore over their papers or examine passengers' baggage; seamen trundle cargo and baggage to the ship's deck; and, best of all, friends line the shore and wave their *bon voyage.*

Then, within a few minutes, the scene changes. A gray mist rolls in from the ocean, chilling cheeks and limiting vision. Ships that are near become blurred outlines in shadows that are barely pierced by the ship's lights. Soon the lights are hidden in shrouding fog. Occasionally the air is rent by the eerie sound of foghorns whose blast is muted by fog and distance.

Human life is like that. The world is a place of gaiety and interest. Here we find warm human friendship, colorful adventure, and vigorous activities. But these things come to an end. Gray shadows slowly sweep over the little landscape of our lives and we are left to our loneliness.

But although bereaved of our friends, we are not bereft of comfort. As the foghorn is a heartening reminder that the gray shadows are peopled by other ships, so do intimations of immortality give confidence about the well-being of those whom we have loved and lost awhile.

There is the hope of the heart. When death strikes a dear one, we cherish the confidence that he now dwells in the deathless land. He has passed beyond our sight, but not beyond our love. We had loved him with a deep affection that was independent of outer circumstance. Our affection was

> . . . an unchanging love
> Higher than the heights above,
> Deeper than the depths beneath,
> True and faithful, strong as death.

A love like that, we feel, ought not to be at the mercy of any physical change. So the heart insists that our dear one is gloriously alive.

At the same time, we uneasily wonder whether we are fooling ourselves by wishful thinking. Are there other grounds for believing in immortality in addition to the hope of the heart? What is the verdict of the mind? Man is the summit and crown of creation and the highest thing about man is his personality. Personality is strengthened and refined through struggle and discipline. Tennyson said:

> Life is not an idle ore,
>
> But iron dug from central gloom,
>   And heated hot with burning fears,
>   And dipt in baths of hissing tears,
> And battered with the shocks of doom,
>
> To shape and use.[1]

The process of producing fine personality is so tremendous that one's mind rebels against the idea that personality at last is snuffed out like a candle. It is more in accord with the fitness of things to

[1] From *In Memoriam*, St. CXVIII.

believe that this is a reasonable universe which provides for the survival of personality. So reason supports the hope of the heart. Belief in immortality reaches its fullness in the Christian Gospel. Here we find, not vague generalities but specific assurance. Intimations of immortality are merged into the larger concept of eternal life.

Jesus spoke of the hereafter not as something to be argued, but as a reality to be taken for granted. He declared that He Himself was the resurrection and the life and added, "He that believeth in me, though he were dead, yet shall he live" (John 11:25). In the sentence which follows, Jesus affirms that the eternal quality of life that He gives is not suspended at death, but goes on, unbroken, into the hereafter: "And whosoever liveth and believeth on me shall never die."

When Jesus drew within a few hours of Calvary, He spoke to His disciples those words which have comforted multitudes in the time of bereavement: "Let not your heart be troubled: ye believe in God, believe also in me. In my Father's house are many mansions. . . . I go to prepare a place for you . . . that where I am, there ye may be also" (John 14:1-3).

So we take courage. We believe in the Gospel of the living Christ. And when the sands of time run out, we will say with Anna Letitia Barbauld:

> Life! we've been long together,
> Through pleasant and through cloudy weather;
> 'Tis hard to part when friends are dear—
> Perhaps 'twill cost a sigh, a tear;
>   Then steal away, give little warning,
>   Choose thine own time;
> Say not Good Night,—but in some brighter clime
> Bid me Good Morning.[1]

Carl A. Glover

148   *LIFE AND IMMORTALITY*

If a man die, shall he live again? JOB 14:14

Our Saviour Jesus Christ, who hath abolished death, and hath brought life and immortality to light through the gospel.   2 TIMOTHY 1:10

Fully do we understand and pity the patriarch Job as he confronts the unknown with little to guide and help him in his quest after the haven of spent souls. 'Tis no equal case in our day after the fullest revelation of Jesus Christ. We have more than human aspiration,

[1] From "Life."

human experience, human speculation, human research to orient us in this search. We have a Saviour and Guide who has taken men to the portals of that other world, has returned from beyond the separating veil and spoken to them reassuringly, has stationed Himself at the door between two worlds, and has done everything but remove the thin curtain that divides us from His presence and glory.

Death is one of the primary realities of life. We are not like Prince Gautama who was carefully shielded from the knowledge that people die. All of us know that, from the tiny infant to the centenarian, our kind are being carried off to the silent city every day of the week. Every thoughtful person asks: "Is this the end of life?" And all our nature cries out for an answer. My friends, if Jesus had not furnished a clear answer to our heart-rending appeal, He could not have the right or title to Deity and He could not be considered the Son of God.

To us, death is of the night. Death strikes in the dark and retreats where none can follow. But our Saviour brought life and immortality out into the clearness of noonday with the light of Heaven shining plainly upon both.

He stirred up in men's hearts the burning passion to live forever when He showed what true life was. The strongest persuasion I know in favor of eternal life is based on our own inmost desire. When we are carried along by fullness of feeling and thinking, when all our nature is exhilarated, when we love truly, give freely, and spend bountifully, at such times we long to live on and on indefinitely. The complement of right, true, and full living is endless living. Jesus said live as I do and you will live forever! That is what I understand by His soothing assurance to Martha: "He that believeth in me, though he were dead, yet shall he live: and whosoever liveth and believeth in me shall never die" (John 11:25-26). The nearest approach we can make to believing in Jesus is to acknowledge Him as Saviour of sinners and to imitate, as children of God, the life of the Son of God.

He invested the work of man from the cradle to the grave with a dignity and splendor that carry it far beyond our brief day. Sinful, perverse, and fallen, man tries to kill time. He has many devices, but he never succeeds. Time eventually kills him. What success do you imagine a time-killer would have with eternity?

It is only after one has caught the glorious vision of days nobly spent that he can awaken, at morn, with Carlyle's salutation on his lips:

> So here hath been dawning
> Another blue Day;
> Think, wilt thou let it
> Slip useless away?
>
> Out of Eternity
> This new Day is born;
> Into Eternity
> At night, will return.[1]

For a Christian a day is not twenty-four hours of time, but twenty-four hours of eternity. Having entered upon eternal life with Jesus here, the grave only marks a change of environment not of occupation.

Jesus establishes communion with the Father in this life. It is beyond belief that such intimacy should end after threescore or more years. We, being evil, try to keep our friends forever; God who is infinite affection will surely make that friendship perpetual.

Through the good tidings concerning the Father and His children our Saviour has enhanced every human tie and provided that our work should be projected into the family and the Kingdom of God.

That is life in its noblest aspect. Have you ever read those memorable lines from "Rugby Chapel" which begin:

> But thou wouldst not *alone*
> Be saved, my father! *alone*.[2]

Run through that page once more to catch the radiance of a life that was lifted by the Saviour to the heights of brotherly service.

Finally, if our Saviour says to His disciples, "Be ye therefore perfect as your Father in Heaven is perfect," He arouses in each of us the expectation of a broader sphere and a fuller time for improvement. The ripest of saints does not find time in a short span of years to enter into all the perfections of the Father's character.

These are a few of the reasons why the apostle proudly claims that Christ has nullified death, has robbed the grave of its power over His followers.

There is no need that any of us die in the sense of being exterminated. Immortality is the continuation of that life which we are living here. But only as we think and act in accordance with the life of Jesus Christ are we living in a manner worth carrying on.

[1] From "To-day."
[2] From "Rugby Chapel" by Matthew Arnold.

Let me apply these teachings briefly with the prayer of George
Eliot:

> O, may I join the choir invisible
> Of those immortal dead who live again
> In minds made better by their presence: live
> In pulses stirred to generosity,
> In deeds of daring rectitude, in scorn
> For miserable aims that end with self,
> In thoughts sublime that pierce the night like stars,
> And with their mild persistence urge man's search
> To vaster issues.[1]

Know Jesus Christ as your Saviour and you will never live again the
paltry life of yesterday. If you long to join the choir invisible it may
lead you to join the choir visible. If you scorn miserable aims that
end with self, you will find yourself in blessed partnership with Him
who came not to be ministered unto but to minister. There are many
things you will not do when you realize that you will be called to go
on doing them forever. There are many other services you will render
when you realize that life is shared with God and Christ and needy
men.

James Dalton Morrison

149   *THE TRIUMPHANT CERTAINTY*

If a man die, shall he live again?   JOB 14:14

Because I live, ye shall live also.   JOHN 14:19

This is a question asked in the Old Testament and answered in the
New; asked in a good many cases, but nowhere perhaps so plainly
as in this chapter and book. But the question which is left a little
uncertain in the Old Testament, or to which an affirmative answer
is given with hesitating voice, becomes a triumphant certainty in
the New. Christianity came to tell us about the deathless, ageless life,
on the authority of Him through whom life and immortality have been
brought to light. His words ring in our ears in confirmation of this
text, which is our promise and our surety: "Because I live, ye shall
live also." "I am the resurrection, and the life: he that believeth in
me, though he were dead, yet shall he live: and whosoever liveth and
believeth in me shall never die" (John 11:25-26).

There is such an interest in the subject of personal immortality
that I question whether many others can compare with it in significance and importance. Men for the most part do want to live. Even

[1] From "O, May I Join the Choir Invisible."

some of those who say that they do not, if they could be assured that the best is true, and not the worst, would very soon change their outlook and their hopes, feelings, and desires.

> Whatever crazy sorrow saith,
> No life that breathes with human breath
> Has ever truly long'd for death.
>
> 'Tis life, whereof our nerves are scant,
> Oh life, not death, for which we pant;
> More life, and fuller, that I want.[1]

It is love that speaks with the loudest tongue here. There are some people to whom life has ceased to signify much since the dearest went away. Most of your interests now are upon the other side; you feel that the cruelest thing that ever came into your experience was death's invasion of your home, and if you could be assured that you will see your dead again, you would not trouble very much about your personal immortality—you would be glad to think that love can never lose its own.

It is for this reason that men are always asking, and will continue to ask, in the words of Job, "If a man die, shall he live again?" I have no hesitation about the answer. No, he will not; for the simple reason that he will never die. We have the highest authority for saying this. Deathless life is in Jesus Christ. The Master of the universe, who holds the keys of death and hell, is the One who came to save mankind.

The destiny of humanity is bound up with the life of Jesus Christ. To Him do you belong, not to yourself; not your own are you, but bought with a price. Jesus Christ has rights over your souls, and it is in Him that all your hope is centered, not only for yourself, but for your dear ones. If Christ were wrong in the authority He claimed and the assurance with which He spoke, it is a dismal fact for humanity today; but if He were right, all the best we hope for and expect is bound up in our kinship with Jesus Christ. "Because I live, ye shall live also."

You remember the story of the old Scottish woman, who was asked by her minister to test her—so great was her love for the Master, so sure was she of His goodness—"But, Jenny, woman, suppose at the last, after all, your Lord should let you down to hell?" "Ah, weel," she said, "be it as it pleases Him: He will lose mair than me." Goodness has a claim upon God. Goodness is an apologetic for immortality.

[1] From "The Two Voices" by Alfred Tennyson.

Produce a saint, and you produce something far more worthy to live than this world of bricks and mortar, stones and lime, sea and air. Nay, you have produced a faith that it cannot be otherwise, and that it shall live. To have lived with God is the promise that you will live for aye. "Because I live, ye shall live also."

Life, on the authority of Jesus, is one; death is an episode, an event in continuous life. Jesus, the Soul of the universe, has charge of yours. When death comes, he is but a messenger to call personality to its own. "Beloved, now are we the sons of God, and it doth not yet appear what we shall be: but we know that, when he "—or it—" shall appear, we shall be like him; for we shall see him as he is" (1 John 3:2).

The persistence of personality means the persistence of all the relations that make life glad and good—the persistence of memory, thought, feeling, desire, affection. Morality is pivoted upon personality. Make a noble man, and you take with him to the eternal world the relations that have helped to make him noble. Can the dead, then, forget? No; they wait for the great reunion; "they without us should not be made perfect" (Heb. 11:40). "Shall we see our dead again?" say some. Yes, you will; they are safe in the arms of Jesus; in the unseen you will meet them all. And I sometimes long to think the black sheep will be there with the rest. Moreover, I feel that the cruelest stroke of fate which has ever come to any man in this life, in the removal of one who taught him to be noble, might be God's call to a higher citizenship here in preparation for the citizenship beyond.

There may be some man or woman who feels bitter because death has robbed him or her of all that gave meaning to life. Do not feel like that any more; set your affections on things above. If you only knew, you would make Christ your Trustee, and never question Him again. You little know what your dead have been saved from and saved to. Your little child who has gone to Heaven is wiser than you, and he will be your teacher bye and bye.

Jesus, the Conqueror and King, is the pledge and the guarantee of all spiritual reunions above. Oh, it is worth our while to trust Him, to leave all to Him, to live as in His presence, to make Him the sacrament that puts us in touch with eternity. He is the golden bridge over the gulf of death.

> Think, when our one soul understands,
>   The great Word which makes all things new,
> When earth breaks up and heaven expands,
>   How will the change strike me and you
> In the house not made with hands?

Oh, I must feel your brain prompt mine,
Your heart anticipate my heart;
You must be just before, in fine,
See and make me see, for your part,
New depths of the Divine.

A little girl had been accustomed always to bid her father good-night in the same words. She was an only child, and loved as only children are. She used to say, "Goodnight, I shall see you again in the morning." The time came when death's bright angel—bright to those who go, dark to those who stay—summoned her to heaven. In her last moments, she called her father to her side, and putting up her little arms, she clasped them around his neck, whispering with her rapidly dying strength, "Goodnight, dear father, I shall see you again in the morning." She was right, as the child always is right about the highest things. "Sorrow endureth for a night; joy cometh in the morning" (Ps. 30:5).

R. J. Campbell

150   *LIFE AFTER DEATH*

If a man die, shall he live again? JOB 14:14

Thirteen hundred years ago, Christian missionaries went to the court of King Edwin of Northumbria. After listening to them, a bearded earl inquired, "Can this new religion tell us what happens after death?" In more recent times, Robert G. Ingersoll, the agnostic, asked the same poignant question, "Is there beyond the silent night an endless day?"

It is an undeniable fact that in man's deepest instincts is what might be both a suspicion and a hope that this present life is not the whole story of our existence. The earthly life, incomplete and unjust as it is, demands a denouement.

If it be objected that what the Bible teaches about life after death has not been proved by experience, we reply that at any rate it has not been disproved, that it does not contradict any known fact, that it satisfies our deepest longings, fulfills our ideas of what ought to be, and, what is more important still, it has been ratified by that indisputable fact, the resurrection of our Lord Jesus Christ.

You can take heart, sorrowing one, for Christ has burst the bars of death. He has proved His power over the last enemy. Those dear ones, who have passed on humbly believing in Him, are safe in His keeping. Because He lives, they shall live also.

Not that the Bible gives a complete picture of the life to come. That would be impossible, as impossible as it would be for a chicken to comprehend the reality of the world outside its shell before the shell is broken. With our finite minds, we cannot grasp infinity. So, on many respects of the life to come, the Bible is of necessity obscure. It does assure us though that for all who sincerely trust in Christ on this earth, the future will mean something richer, fuller, and more satisfying than they have known. "When he shall appear, we shall be like him; for we shall see him as he is" (1 John 3:2). The apostles on the Mount of Transfiguration recognized Moses as he talked with Christ. It is true to say

> We shall know each other better,
> When the mists are rolled away.

That dear one who has just passed on you will meet again. You will take up the threads of fellowship with *him* just where you have now laid them down.

Could anything be more reassuring than Christ's own words, clear and emphatic as they are: "I am the resurrection, and the life: he that believeth in me, though he were dead, yet shall he live" (John 11:25). And again, "I go to prepare a place for you . . . that where I am, there ye may be also" (John 14:2-3).

If these words do not answer all your questions, they do at least give you a sure foundation upon which you may build your hopes, a vantage ground from which you can see above the gray mists to the towers of the celestial city.

Your sadness will turn into gladness if you will realize that in the streets of that city you will meet your loved one once again, will meet *him* to part no more.

J. Calvert Cariss

151 *WE ARE NOT DEFEATED*

Because I live, ye shall live also. JOHN 14:19

We came into this world without our consent. We are going out, perhaps, against our will. We are travelers and we pass this way but once. It is evidenced on every side that this is not our home and that we did not come here to stay. We are in a vacillating and changing world. The mountains, the forests, the landscapes, everything around us changes. Even we are not the same as we were yesterday. "We all do fade as a leaf" (Isaiah 64:6). We "are like the grass which groweth up" and "is cut down, and withereth" (Ps. 90:5-6).

When we realistically consider these facts we are likely to acknowledge defeat. We are brought face to face with the proof of these realities. There is no denying, and it is foolish to close our eyes to them. When we lift up our eyes we behold and when we listen we hear from Him who is the "same yesterday, and today, and forever" (Heb. 13:8), the One who changeth not. It is He that giveth to us the victory through our Lord Jesus Christ. Therefore, even though we are "sown in weakness" we are "raised in power" (1 Cor. 15:43). We turn our eyes to Him who came among us, challenged all that is mortal, and conquered all things. The last enemy that He conquered was death. We see Him standing at the brink of the grave saying: "O death, where is thy sting? O grave, where is thy victory?" (1 Cor. 15:55). He then turns to us and says without apology, "Because I live, ye shall live also."

It is a glorious feeling to remember that we are the children of God. If then we are children, we are also heirs of God. If we are heirs we are not only heirs of this world, but the universe belongs to us. If this is not our home, *and it isn't,* God does not permit us to be homeless. He has prepared a place for us. He has not left us in doubt as to this fact, neither has He left us in darkness. Jesus said: "I am the way" and "Whither I go ye know, and the way ye know" (John 14:4). To defeat us while in this Way the enemy would first have to defeat God, but if we walk in this Way then our victory is assured.

Death comes stealthily into our gardens and steals away our flowers, *but* it cannot take away the power and presence that grew them. So they grow again. It comes into our homes and takes away our loved one, *but* it can only take away that which is mortal. It must keep its hands forever from all that which is eternal. So, faith brings to us the message of victory and by faith in the Eternal Father we triumph. "Because I live, ye shall live also." This truth is described for us in the poem "There Is No Death" by John L. McCreery:

> There is no death! The stars go down
> To rise upon some other shore,
> And bright in heaven's jeweled crown
> They shine for evermore.
>
> There is no death! The forest leaves
> Convert to life the viewless air;

The rocks disorganize to feed
The hungry moss they bear.

There is no death! The dust we tread
Shall change beneath the summer showers
To golden grain, or mellow fruit,
Or rainbow-tinted flowers.

And ever near us, though unseen,
The dear immortal spirits tread;
For all the boundless universe
Is life—there are no dead![1]

Adolphus Gilliam

152   *CHRIST'S BELIEF IN IMMORTALITY*

Because I live, ye shall live also.   JOHN 14:19

It was more than ordinary grief or sympathy that was the fountain
of the tears of Jesus. He was in sympathy with the mourners, and felt
for them, but there was that in the whole scene with which He had no
sympathy; there was none of that feeling He required His disciples to
show at His own death, no rejoicing that one more had gone to the
Father. There was a forgetfulness of the most essential facts of death,
an unbelief which seemed entirely to separate this crowd of wailing
people from the light and life of God's presence. "It was the darkness
between God and His creatures that gave room for, and was filled with,
their weeping and wailing over their dead." It was the deeper anguish
into which mourners are plunged by looking upon death as extinction, and by supposing that death separates from God and from life,
instead of giving closer access to God and more abundant life—it was
this which caused Jesus to groan. He could not bear this evidence that
even the best of God's children do not believe in God as greater than
death and in death as ruled by God.

This gives us the key to Christ's belief in immortality. It was Christ's
sense of God, His uninterrupted consciousness of God, His distinct
knowledge that God the loving Father is *the* existence in whom all
live—it was this which made it impossible for Christ to think of death
as extinction or separation from God. For one who consciously lived
in God to be separated from God was impossible. For one who was
bound to God by love to drop out of that love into nothingness or
desolation was inconceivable. His constant and absolute sense of God
gave Him an unquestioning sense of immortality. If we ask why it was

[1] Quoted in part.

impossible He should have any shadow of doubt of a life beyond
death, we see that it was because it was impossible for Him to doubt of
the existence of God, the ever-living, ever-loving God.

Marcus Dods

153   *THE GROUND OF IMMORTALITY*[1]

Art Thou not from everlasting, O Lord my God, mine Holy One? we
shall not die.   HABAKKUK 1:12

Presumptuous words these surely from the creature to the Creator:
"Thou art from everlasting [therefore] *I* shall not die." What right
have we to measure our lives with *Him*? He is from everlasting; we are
of yesterday. He has the dew of His youth; our days decline as doth a
shadow. He is the same yesterday, today, and forever; our lives are
changed as a vesture every hour. Would it not be more becoming for
us to say, "Thou art from everlasting, therefore *we* must die."

Nay, my soul, thou hast not rightly read the ground of thine own
hope. The prophet is not seeking to have his own life made equal to
God's; he is seeking to have God's own life in *him*. Bethink thee what
mean such words as these, "Because I live, ye shall live also" (John
14:19), "I live; yet not I, but Christ liveth in me" (Gal. 2:20), "Christ
in you, the hope of glory" (Col. 1:27). They mean that thy immortality is God's immortality. Thy hope of vanquishing death is thy possession in thyself of the deathless One. It is because the Everlasting is
thy God that His everlastingness is anything to thee. Were he merely
outside of thee it would be indeed presumption in thee to measure
thy years with Him. But He is not outside of thee. He has breathed
into thy nostrils the breath of His own life, and it is by that breath
that even now thou livest. It is by that breath that even now thou art
victor over death from moment to moment, from hour to hour, from
day to day. It is by that breath that, when flesh and heart faint and
fail, thou shalt be victor over death still, shalt find the strength of thy
heart and thy portion forever.

George Matheson

154   *THE CROWN OF LIFE*

Be thou faithful unto death, and I will give thee a crown of life.
REVELATION 2:10

In these words we have the Divine assurance that life may have
beauty, strength, and completeness. Our experiences in the process of

[1] Slightly adapted.

living are often fragmentary and seem to lack unity and wholeness. There are so many disappointments and losses that we often find it difficult to maintain a sustaining faith in the meaning and ultimate worth-whileness of life. We, therefore, need such comfort and guidance as the words of the text bring to us. These words challenge and direct us in the process of living. These words assure us when we stand at the portals of death. It is a great joy to know that there is a way which leads to the crowning of life.

In all ages men have longed for such assurance. Life here and now is never wholly satisfying. Men have always longed for a more enriching experience and a more perfect expression of life. With deep longing they have hoped that sometime, somewhere, and somehow life would be perfected. They have built their hopes into picturesque and often fanciful utopias. In fellowship with their god and gods they have hoped to find fullness of life.

This hope has spurred men on, but it often has left them without a satisfying assurance. In the revelation of God in Christ we have a sure ground for hope. This assurance is grounded in the fact that God seeks to give life. He shares His life with man that man may enter into life. Jesus, whom God sent for our salvation, said concerning His mission, "I am come that they might have life, and that they might have it more abundantly" (John 10:10). In the text He says, "I will give thee a crown of life."

There are several things in this text's assurance of the crown of life which should be carefully noted.

First, the crowning of life is an act of God. This is in full accord with the total revelation of life in the Holy Scriptures and in the Living Word. Life is a mystery. Many attempts have been made through scientific studies to discover the source of life. These have revealed many interesting and worth-while facts about life, but they have not solved the mystery of life. Based upon the truth of Divine revelation we accept God as the Source and Giver of life. He is the life. He alone can give life. The crowning of life is, therefore, an act of God. It is only in and through God that man can come to such a crowning experience.

How God gives life is also a mystery. How He caused nature to be impregnated with the dynamic of life, how through Him man became a living soul, and how through faith in Jesus Christ man may have eternal life are facts shrouded in mystery too great for our understanding. There is, however, an approach in the Holy Scriptures which satisfies the mind and strengthens the faith. All life is given through the self-giving of God. In creation, in the preservation of the created order, and in redemption God has given and continues to give life through His own self-giving. In the process of living man not only becomes aware of the expression of God's power but of God in His loving self-giving for the enrichment of man. Here we have the deepest meaning of life. Life is the gift of God in which He gives Himself. The fullness and meaning of life are found in the fellowship of life and in service with God.

This is further expressed in the words of the text in the affirmation that, second, the crowning of life is conditioned upon the faithfulness of man. God gives, but the entrance into life is determined by man's relationship to God. Faithfulness means, first of all, a response of man in terms of faith. To neglect or reject God always means the loss of life. This is true individually and corporately. We have such a low tide of noble and enriched and enriching life in this world because there are so many people who seek to live without the acknowledgment of God. Only as men accept in faith the grace of redemption in Christ Jesus do they find life. Jesus bore our sins to the cross, made an all-sufficient atonement for sin, entered the realm of death and destroyed its power, arose from the dead, and lives forevermore as Saviour and Lord. In Him there is life. But unless men believe and accept the offered grace they do not enter life. In faith we lay hold upon this offered life.

Faithfulness also means unwavering adherence to the truth of our redemption through Christ. We are not saved through our skills nor through our wealth, but through Christ. It is Christ crucified which is the ground of our hope. There is always a danger that men may forget what God has done to bring them into life and the fullness of life. We need in faithfulness to hold fast to the Gospel of our salvation.

Faithfulness also means that we continue in our comradeship with God in the effort to bring to all men the knowledge of the truth of our redemption. Jesus said to His disciples before He left them, "Ye shall be witnesses unto me" (Acts 1:8). This is what He says to all of His children. Unless we are faithful in our witness we will not come to the crowning experience.

These words are, therefore, also a challenge to rethink the meaning of our relationship in and through Christ. They point to the fact that, third, the crowning of life means the achievement of the Divine purpose and entrance into fullness of life. God is, therefore, interested in this experience. We, too, should be profoundly interested.

We cannot fully understand all that this will mean, but we are assured it means deliverance from all sin and all the effects of sin. It means being ushered into the presence of God, where there is fullness of joy and where there are pleasures forevermore. And it means our eternal at-homeness with God. In this confidence we can live in assurance of the worth of life. In this hope we can die in peace. In this intimate fellowship with God life will come to its crowning experience. Let us then hold fast our profession. Let us yield fully to God. Let us give ourselves with all diligence to faithfulness—unto death. Then we shall receive the crown of life.

John S. Stamm

155   *THE WITNESS OF NATURE*

The Creator has not left us in doubt on the subject of immortality. He has given to every created thing a tongue that proclaims a life beyond the grave.

If the Father deigns to touch with divine power the cold and pulseless heart of the buried acorn and to make it burst forth from its prison walls, will He leave neglected in the earth the soul of man, made in the image of his creator? If He stoops to give to the rosebush, whose withered blossoms float upon the autumn breeze, the sweet assurance of another springtime, will He refuse the words of hope to the sons of men when the frosts of winter come? If matter, mute and inanimate, though changed by the forces of nature into a multitude of forms, can never die, will the imperial spirit of man suffer annihilation when it has paid a brief visit like a royal guest to this tenement of clay? No, He who, notwithstanding His apparent prodigality, created nothing without a purpose, and wasted not a single atom in all His creation, has made provision for a future life in which man's universal longing for immortality will find its realization. I am as sure that we shall live again as I am sure that we live today.

In Cairo, I secured a few grains of wheat that had slumbered for more than thirty centuries in an Egyptian tomb. As I looked at them this thought came into my mind: If one of those grains had been planted on the banks of the Nile the year after it grew, and all its lineal descendants had been planted and replanted from that time until now, its progeny would today be sufficiently numerous to feed the teeming millions of the world. An unbroken chain of life connects the earliest grains of wheat with the grains that we sow and reap. There is in the grain of wheat an invisible something which has power to discard the body that we see, and from earth and air fashion a new body so much like the old one that we cannot tell the one from the other. If this invisible germ of life in the grain of wheat can thus pass unimpaired through three thousand resurrections, I shall not doubt that my soul has power to clothe itself with a body suited to its new existence, when this earthly frame has crumbled into dust.

William Jennings Bryan

E. THE PATH OF LIFE

156   *THE GLORY OF THE UNSATISFIED*

See, I have set before thee this day life and good, and death and evil
. . . therefore choose life, that both thou and thy seed may live.   DEUTER-
ONOMY 30:15, 19

In the book of Deuteronomy are written words as true today as
they were almost twenty-five hundred years ago: "I have set before
thee life and death . . . therefore choose life." Each generation between that time and our own has faced that fateful decision—life or
death. Almost as a corollary of the above passage are these words from
the book of the Revelation: "I will give unto him that is athirst of
the fountain of the water of life freely" (Rev. 21:6). These words
describe that bent of soul which is the secret behind the attainment
of life. He who is athirst, unsatisfied, finds life.

Many books have been written suggesting when life begins—at
forty, sixty, even at eighty. Each stresses the fact that the future belongs to those who are mentally and spiritually unsatisfied. Plato did
not lay down his pen until he was eighty. Michelangelo expressed his
genius in marble until he was almost ninety. Gladstone was prime
minister of Great Britain when he was eighty-five. All of these suggest that fullness of life belongs to those who are eternally unsatisfied.
Furthermore, all progress lies this way. When as a very young man
Abraham Lincoln traveled down the Mississippi River to New Orleans
and saw slaves shackled together on the river boats, he wrote in a
letter to a friend, "That sight was a continued torment to me." That
spirit of torment is the spur at the heart of all reform and all progress. John Greenleaf Whittier wrote:

> And step by step since time began
> I see the steady gain of man.

But that gain has not been as steady and easy as he makes it sound.
Often man has taken two painful steps forward and slipped three back.
But wherever gain has been registered, it has been due to the great
army of the unsatisfied. The true pioneers in any field are the unsatisfied.

This is all related, of course, to the far reaches of faith, the lure of aspiration, the pull of glorious adventure. It opens vistas that extend through all eternity. If the best in life belongs to the unsatisfied, to those who never cease the quest here, why shall it not be true of the hereafter? This instinct for eternal life, found in people of all generations, must have a counterpart in reality. The tendency of man to be unsatisfied with the best this life has to offer must indicate that the ultimate satisfaction lies beyond this "bourne of Time and Place." The very word "unsatisfied" throws a light upon the true nature of immortality itself. It can scarcely mean a static existence in some realm however beautiful, but is rather an active, vital experience of growth and accomplishment and an altogether glorious adventure.

Our former physician passed away recently. He had been a wonderful man, a skilled physician and an earnest Christian, untiring in his ministry to the needful. As the disease that took him got ever and ever firmer hold upon him, and he knew that the end was near, he said to his wife: "It's going to be a great adventure." That's it; not dissatisfied and discontented because of disappointed hopes, but unsatisfied, ever athirst, eternally unsatisfied.

Henry Irving Rasmus, Jr.

157   *LIFE'S AFTERGLOW*

Now abideth faith, hope, love.   1 CORINTHIANS 13:13

The most beautiful part of the day comes in the cool of the evening. After a hot summer's day, with the freshness of the gathering shadows, a silence comes across the face of the earth as if all nature were waiting for the pageantry of the night.

Then, for a magnificent moment, there is the startling beauty of the day's afterglow. While we know that the indescribable colors are created by the sun's rays striking back upon the rarefied matter suspended in the upper air, still to many it is God's sign of beauty that the darkness of the coming night will soon give way again to the splendor of the dawn.

So in death we think of life's afterglow. Every life leaves after life's day is over some inspiration of goodness, beauty, and truth that remains to comfort and sustain a sorrowing heart. The Apostle Paul, as he brought to a close the immortal thirteenth chapter of First Corinthians, wrote that faith, hope, and love have the power to endure and abide.

The first Easter came as an afterglow experience. Christ's day of life seemed over. Death's cruel dealing on a cross seemed to write the final words on a high note of faith: "Father, into thy hands I commend my spirit" (Luke 23:46).

Then the night of death was lightened by the colors of life. Two weary disciples making their way from Jerusalem to Emmaus found their hearts warmed within as the living presence of Christ, in an afterglow experience, was made real to them. With startling rapidity the night of death in the thought of the disciples was changed to the vivid colors of faith, hope, and love as they realized that death had but brought Christ closer to their own lives and that He was alive forevermore.

So for us in life's afterglow we recognize that this, too, is a service of faith. We do not understand the mystery of death, but it is in the heritage of a great faith that we lay our blessed dead away. In this we find our comfort and our strength.

Each night throughout life we have drifted off to sleep in the certainty that there will be an awakening in the morning. Yet sleep must be very similar to the experience of death. In fact, Jesus spoke of death as a quiet sleep with the awakening in the House of Many Mansions. So in life as we live with faith why should there be any fear in our thought of death, for a dear one awakens in God's world of eternal life?

It is from our faith in God that we receive our comfort and our strength. We know that we need not face death alone. Neither do we need to face life alone, for always there is the presence of God. How often as we wonder if we really can live on in the face of some difficulty and hardship we find that God opens an unexpected door and a new way is before us? Again and again, when all doors ahead seem closed, God's love and care makes it possible to go on by another way. Yes, here is our comfort and our strength.

This faith has been tested many times, yet it has always brought strength and peace. It is the faith revealed in the words of Moses who when facing death said, "The eternal God is thy refuge, and underneath are the everlasting arms" (Deut. 33:27). It is the faith of the 23rd Psalm, "Yea, though I walk through the valley and shadow of death, I shall fear no evil: for thou art with me." It is the assurance of the 121st Psalm, "The Lord shall preserve thy going out and thy coming in from this time forth, and even for evermore." Its final assurance comes from the lips of Christ, "Because I live, ye shall live also" (John 14:19).

In this service of faith we lay our blessed dead away in the assurance of the faith that our God who has prepared this world for life will keep the sacred soul for which the ages have been preparing. The God who orders the planets in their courses, who brings the stars nightly to the sky, and who controls the tides and the endless spaces of the universe, is a God whom we can trust in death to bring our beloved to the life that is eternal.

This is also a service of hope and not of despair or defeat. It was in the power of the afterglow experience that the disciples went forth to proclaim the message of the Risen Christ. The early disciples met death with the thought of victory. Instead of laying their dead away with wails of despair, they sang songs of hope. So we, in this memorial service, have the background of great music. Here is the assurance of the hymns of the church. We want the old hymns of tender association, such as "Abide with Me" and "Still, Still with Thee." And we think of the final refrain in the Lord's Prayer, "For thine is the kingdom and the power and the glory forever."

As a symbol of our hopes we surround our loved one with living beauty. We try to make the place where our memorial service is held as much like a garden as possible. Flowers are a symbol of our living hope. Out of the seed, through the strength of the sod, the call of the sun, and the awakening knock of the rain, God brings forth the beauty of a living flower. So, for us, too, flowers express the thought that our God is not the God of the dead but of the living.

In our hope we find a power that is greater than grief. Grief in death is always poignantly real. Yet in our hope we find a comfort stronger than the deepest grief. Psychologically we know the laws of handling grief. We should not bury our sadness in our subconscious life but we should express it at the time of death that we may go on to think of our loved one in thoughts of joyous life. We should remember our dear one in the vitality of life so that the halls of memory bring back to us the happy moments of bygone days. We should talk about our beloved naturally with someone else who appreciated the beauty and fineness of his life. And, lastly, we should look ahead, knowing that we must pick up life, fill moments that we have spent in joyous, loving fellowship with our dear one with other tasks and work that must be done. The joy of life is always on ahead. And it is our hope in the certainty of our Christian belief that God will not deny our living hope but bring it to fruition in a reunion with the family of God in some new dawn.

Robert Millikan, looking back across a life's study of the secret of

God's scientific law, said, "The Divine Architect of the Universe has not built a stairway that leads to nowhere." If this is the faith of a scientist, how much more it can be our hope for we know that God has not given us our longing for life eternal without the certainty that our dream will come true.

The Old Book also tells us that there is the lasting afterglow of love. This is also a service of abiding love. William Penn said that they who love beyond this world can never be separated by anything that happens here. Thus we have the comfort of an abiding love.

Certainly we can find comfort in the knowledge that our dear ones will live eternally within our love. As long as love endures, the one who has meant so much will live in that love. Many ministers no longer use the phrase in the wedding service, "until death do us part," but have changed it to, "love throughout all eternity," for we know the one whose memory we revere shall always live in our love. We also realize that he will live in the eternal love of God. Our loved one will be wherever God is and God is love and His love is everywhere.

As we take the body to its final resting place, and then return to our homes, we should not think that we are leaving our departed there. His love will go with us to the final resting place, return with us, and be a part of our lives forever.

During the last war I preached a sermon titled "The Triangle of God's Love." I said that we should think of ourself as one part of the triangle, someone whom we love as the other part of the triangle, and in our love and prayer reaching up to God our life would be joined in the apex of His love.

A young pilot who heard that sermon soon left to fly over Germany. He was shot down and taken prisoner. When he returned he said that the last sermon he heard had been a source of real comfort to him. Many a night when he could not sleep he would go out and look up at the stars and think of his love reaching up through prayer. Longing for his wife who was at home in the assurance that her prayer and longing was also reaching up and out to him and in the triangle of that love he found his strength renewed.

So our love and prayer will ever reach out and up to God and we believe our loved one in the eternal life of God will also be reaching out to us and in the triangle of God's love there is no death, but life, eternal life forevermore.

Yes, the darkness of death is dispelled by the light of the afterglow of faith, hope, and love, and across the years we hear Christ say, "My peace I give unto you: not as the world giveth, give I unto you. Let not your heart be troubled, neither let it be afraid" (John 14:27), and with the assurance of our faith, hope, and love we may face the future with confidence and courage and the assurance that God will supply our every need.

Frank A. Court

158   *THE DEVOUT LIFE HERE AND HEREAFTER*

I have set the Lord always before me: because he is at my right hand, I shall not be moved. . . . In thy presence is fulness of joy; at thy right hand there are pleasures for evermore.   PSALM 16:8, 11

I have put these two verses together because they present striking parallels in expression, and a close connection of thought. As to the parallel expressions, notice "before me" in the one verse, and "in Thy presence" in the other. The two phrases, though not identical, are synonymous. There follow another pair of parallels, "my right hand" in the former clause answering to "thy right hand" in the latter. Then as to the connection of thought, the former verse describes the devout life as it is lived here on earth, the latter is most naturally and adequately understood as pointing to the devout life as it is perfected in Heaven.

It is, perhaps, the clearest expression of confidence in immortality to be found in the Old Testament, and it is instructive to notice the way by which the Psalmist comes to that confidence. My two texts are linked together by two intervening verses, which begin with a "therefore." "I shall not be moved; therefore"—because of my present experience of the Divine presence, and the stability which it brings— "therefore my heart is glad, and . . . my flesh also shall rest in hope. For thou wilt not leave my soul in hell; neither will thou suffer thine Holy One to see corruption" (Ps. 16:9-10). That is to say, the Christian experience of communion on earth necessarily leads on to the expectation of its own persistence, and makes it ridiculous to suppose that such a purely physical thing as death should have any power over such a bond. You might as well suppose that a sword could wound a soul.

But that is not all that the connection of these two verses suggests. It implies the correspondence of these two phases of the devout life. Not only is the one the ground for believing in the other, but the one is the germ of the other.

For the Christian life on earth and in Heaven is continuous, and that which is but tendency and thwarted aim and unreached direction here will become fact hereafter. "To morrow shall be as this day, and much more abundant" (Is. 56:12). Continuity and increase lie at the basis of the Christian hope. And if ever we are to have present confidence of immortality, or ever to possess the reality of it in a future life, it must be because we here have set the Lord always before us. If we are ever to be set at His right hand in the heavenly place, it will be as the natural culmination and termination of our having set Him at our right hands amidst the struggles and strifes of earth.

Alexander Maclaren

159   *THE PATH OF LIFE*

Thou wilt shew me the path of life.   PSALM 16:11

The word which brings us together at this hour is life not death, for Jesus said, "I am the resurrection, and the life: he that believeth in me, though he were dead, yet shall he live." So we who have known and loved God, the God and Father of our Lord Jesus Christ, do not fasten our thought on death but on the life He gives.

Long ago the Psalmist affirmed the truth which Jesus taught when He said, "Thou wilt shew me the path of life." Four words in this text are fraught with meaning.

Consider first the word "Thou." The Psalmist points us to the one and only source of life, God. How many are the agencies upon which we rely in our pursuit of life. In our quest for pleasure and happiness little time is given to the all-important matter of religion. Popular opinion teaches that sincerity in any faith is all that is required. What an appeal this makes to the average person. Of old the prophet Isaiah cried: "To the law and to the testimony" (Is. 8:20). In his time he found men who were seeking other deities, but the teaching of prophet and priest, past and present, points unerringly to the One who said, "I am the way, the truth, and the life" (John 14:6).

Consider, second, the word "me." The personal pronoun emphasizes our personal relationship to God. May we never forget that before our lives can be made a blessing to others, we must make our peace with God. In the busy round of duties and in our sincere desire to help others in need there is a tendency to neglect or postpone this very important matter which each must settle sooner or later. The urge to hasten to the help of someone else may be charitable and the proof of selflessness, but in reality the greater need may lie deep in the heart of the helper. Well has the hymn writer penned these inspired words:

> I need Thee, oh, I need Thee
> Every hour I need Thee
> Oh bless me now, my Saviour,
> I come to Thee.[1]

Let us not overlook the word "path." The way to eternal life is nowhere in the Scriptures spoken of as a road or a broad way. In the Sermon on the Mount Jesus taught that "strait is the gate, and narrow is the way, which leadeth unto life" (Matt. 7:14). We are so accustomed to paved four-lane arteries of transportation that it is difficult for us to comprehend that the Way of Life is a mere path. Yet the Psalmist says, "Thou wilt shew me the path," and a path it is. And being only a path there is reason to believe that those who travel it are not as numerous as those who favor the broad way. Among believers there is a common saying that there is, however, room for two, your Saviour and you, side by side.

Finally, consider the word "life." What a myriad study it is. Scientists labor faithfully to reveal its secrets and every clue is exploited to prolong life and to make it more enjoyable. And yet at the same time more and more institutions for the care of the sick and diseased are being erected! Life offers many such dilemmas, but we may confidently look beyond our finite minds for explanations. And even as the apostle Peter did when he said, "Lord, to whom shall we go? thou hast the words of eternal life" (John 6:68). And the Saviour speaks to us as he spoke to those who loved Him long ago: "I am come that they might have life, and that they might have it more abundantly" (John 10:10).

There is physical life and we know that God is the giver of this, for our origins are in Him. And there is eternal life, which begins in the heart of the believer when he accepts the Lord Jesus Christ as his Saviour. Paul wrote, "Therefore if any man be in Christ, he is a new creature" (2 Corinthians 5:17). And there is the *more abundant life* which our Saviour has promised. When more abundant life is given to and accepted by the believer, that believer is then beyond the sting of death. He walks in the path to life everlasting, a path through Him who said, "I am the resurrection and the life: he that believeth in me, though he were dead, yet shall he live."

Wallace S. Bragg

[1] From "I Need Thee Every Hour" by Annie S. Hawks.

160   *LIFE'S DIMENSIONS*

In the time of sorrow consider. ECCLESIASTES 7:14

There are many things which we may well consider at this time of sorrow. First, we need to realize that *life is a mystery*. The Creator of life needed no patent, for no one else has been able to create life. Man with all his varied abilities to discover and to invent has not been able to make even a small seed that could produce an ear of corn. No man has ever been able fully to comprehend life and its physical, mental, and spiritual development. No man has ever been able to guarantee the continuance of life. Andrew Carnegie once offered one million dollars to any physician who could prolong by ten years his life, but no one could make such a guarantee.

Life may well be a mystery, but let us remember that *life is a gift from God*. Says Genesis 1:27: "So God created man in His own image." Says Psalm 8:4-5: "What is man that Thou art mindful of him? . . . For Thou hast made him a little lower than the angels, and hast crowned him with glory and honor."

Never must we cease to thank God for His gift of life and especially for our precious loved ones whom He has given to us. This is particularly true of the gift of a mother, for, as a poet has written:

> Sometimes I think God grew tired of making
> Thunder and mountains and dawn redly breaking;
> Weary of fashioning gorges and seas,
> Sometimes I think God grew tired of heating
> The earth with the sun, and of fully completing
> The whole of the world! God grew tired, and so
> He took just a bit of the soft afterglow,
> He took just a petal or two from a flower,
> And took a songbird from a sweet scented bower.
> The dewdrops He took from the heart of a rose,
> And added the freshness of each breeze that blows
> Across long green meadows. He took all the love
> Left over from His heaven above.
> His kind fingers mixed them—God's hand and no other—
> And made, for the first time, the soul of a mother.[1]

Furthermore, *life is an opportunity*. Each day of life brings new experiences and special opportunities wherein we may help others and thereby make our own lives a blessing. Few have a greater privilege

[1] "The Soul of a Mother" by Margaret E. Sangster.

than a mother. She can take the various experiences of life, the joy and the sorrows, and, mixing them with her own faith and love, can cause them to work together for good in the lives of her children. T. W. Fessenden acknowledges this in his tribute:

> You painted no Madonnas
>   On chapel walls in Rome,
> But with a touch diviner
>   You lived them in your home.
>
> You wrote no lofty poems
>   That critics counted art,
> But with a nobler vision
>   You lived them in your heart.
>
> You carved no shapeless marble
>   To some high souled design,
> But with a finer sculpture
>   You shaped this soul of mine.
>
> You built no great cathedrals
>   That centuries applaud,
> But with a grace exquisite
>   Your life cathedraled God.[1]

The person who discovers the opportunities of life usually realizes, too, that *life in an influence*. The most significant fact accompanying life is influence. We are continually lifting people up or dragging them down by our influence. The influence of a mother in our lives is greater than that of anyone else. In Ezekiel 16:44 are found these words: "As is the mother, so is her daughter." In 1 Kings 22:52 are found these words: "Ahaziah . . . walked . . . in the way of his mother." In 2 Chronicles 22:3 are found these words: "His mother was his counsellor." Those of us who have been privileged by having Christian mothers know that even now she "being dead yet speaketh" (Heb. 11:4).

> She always leaned to watch for us,
>   Anxious if we were late,
> In winter by the window,
>   In summer by the gate;
>
> And though we mocked her tenderly,
>   Who had such foolish care,
> The long way home would seem more safe
>   Because she waited there.

[1] From "To Mother."

> Her thoughts were all so full of us,
> She never could forget!
> And so I think that where she is
> She must be watching yet,
>
> Waiting till we come home to her,
> Anxious if we are late—
> Watching from Heaven's window,
> Leaning from Heaven's gate.[1]

In this time of our sorrow, let us, finally, consider that *life is an eternal reality*. Death and the grave are not the end. While the body of the loved one is placed in the grave and eventually returns unto the dust from which it came, there is the spirit which goes on into eternity. Christ revealed unto us both by His teaching and by His own resurrection that death is not the end. He tells us plainly that there are really two eternities: one is called hell, a place of suffering, sorrow and remorse; and one is Heaven, a place of great beauty, blessed fellowship, and wonderful service. He came into the world and He died on the cross that it might not be necessary for us who have sinned to spend eternity in hell. By His marvelous grace and our faith in Him we enter into the heavenly home to abide forever.

In the hour of sorrow may we remember that the lessons are unto the living. May we properly consider that life is a gift from God and that by His redemptive grace we can make the most of our days here and be ready when He calls us to come up higher. Then may He say unto us: "Well done, thou good and faithful servant: thou hast been faithful over a few things, I will make thee ruler over many things: enter thou into the joy of thy Lord" (Matt. 25:21).

Vance H. Webster

161   *THE LIFE CHRIST GIVES*

When Christ came into the world, He found death the king of terrors; He left it only the king of mysteries. He found the grave a black point which vanished into nothingness; He left it a golden cloud behind which God and the soul meet in an eternal friendship. He found death set forth by the skull and the cross-bones, the skeleton and the scythe; He left it an event so victorious that earth's most beautiful flowers are not sweet enough to garland the glorious event called dying. He found it with one song; it was a dirge, and He turned it into

---

[1] "The Watcher" by Margaret Widdemer.

a symphony; with one record, a slab with an epitaph upon it; He left instead a gate of pearl; with one color, black, He turned it to gold; and for the skeleton he substituted an angel, who whispered, "He is not here: for he is risen" (Matt. 28:6).

Newell Dwight Hillis

F. DEATH THE GATE OF LIFE

Except a corn of wheat fall into the ground and die, it abideth alone.
JOHN 12:24

The universal and inexorable doom of all life is here pronounced by Him who abolished death. Jesus Christ abolished death in the only way in which a stubborn fact can be abolished—by showing that it is not what it appears to be.

Death appears to be the seal of failure, it is the condition of success; it appears to be an end, it is also a beginning; it appears to be a humiliation and a curse, but its cleansing waters purge the soul of her travel-stains, and land her refreshed upon the farther shore.

Death, says the book of Genesis, is a punishment. Death, says science, is no punishment, but a law of nature. Death, says Jesus Christ, is nothing save the gate through which one passes into immortal life. Death is a punishment if we will have it so. If we turn into ends what were meant to be instruments; if we use that wonderful idealizing power which belongs to us to give a false and spurious substance to fleeting shadows whose nature it is to come and go, and to desire which, so idealized and intensified, can never be satisfied, then death, which dissolves these cloud-palaces into thin air, will be to us a punishment—a punishment for mistaking shadow for substance, and attempting to slake the divine thirst of the soul in the waters of a mirage.

Death is a law, if we will have it so. The rhythm of reproduction and dissolution, of growth and decay, may seem to swing evenly backwards and forwards. The study of nature may, and probably will, lead us only to the manly resignation of Marcus Aurelius, and to the Stoic's resolve to steel the heart against emotions which tend to discontent or rebellion against nature's laws. "Depart, then, satisfied, since He Who releases thee is satisfied." Very many have tried to be content with this courageous submission, and to "cut down long hopes with a narrow compass."

And yet, if we will have it so, death is the gate of life. What was the secret, the hidden source, of St. Paul's joyous attitude towards the thought of death? Why did he look forward to "finish his course with joy," instead of only to "depart satisfied"? What made him so sure that "to die is gain"? His belief in the resurrection, of course, but this belief rested not only on what he saw in the clouds on the road to Damascus, not only on the reports of the Twelve and the survivors of the "five hundred brethren" who had seen the risen Christ, but on the overpowering conviction, to which the resurrection of Christ opened his eyes, that death has no sting to those who know the hidden laws of life. The passage from death unto life is no unique portent; it is the open secret of the universe, which Jesus Christ brought to light. In the world without it is exemplified in every harvest-field. "That which thou sowest is not quickened except it die." The seed "dies," it does not perish entirely, else the analogy would fail; but it dies as a seed, and takes new life as a blade. In the world within St. Paul knew what it was to die to the old man, to die and be buried with Christ, and to rise again into newness of life.

W. R. Inge

163 *THE VICTORY*

If a man keep my saying, he shall never see death. JOHN 8:51

He that believeth in me, though he were dead, yet shall he live; and he that liveth and believeth in me shall never die. JOHN 11:25-26

What mean such words as these, for something they must mean? Do such words mean only that we shall rise again in the resurrection at the last day? Surely not. Our Lord spoke them in answer to that very notion.

"Martha said to Him, I know that my brother shall rise again, in the resurrection at the last day. Jesus said unto her, I *am* the resurrection and the life"; and then showed what He meant by bringing back Lazarus to life, unchanged, and as he had been before he died.

Surely, if that miracle meant anything, if these words meant anything, it meant this: that those who died in the fear of God, and in the faith of Christ, do not really taste death; that to them there is no death, but only a change of place, a change of state; that they pass at once, and instantly, into some new life, with all their powers, all their feelings, unchanged—purified doubtless from earthly stains, but still the same living, thinking, active beings which they were here on earth. I say, active. The Bible says nothing about their sleeping till the Day of Judgement, as some have fancied. Rest they may;

rest they will, if they need rest. But what is the true rest? Not idle-ness, but peace of mind. To rest from sin, from sorrow, from fear, from doubt, from care—this is the true rest. Above all, to rest from the worst weariness of all-knowing one's duty, and yet not being able to do it. That is true rest; the rest of God.

Death is not death if it kills no part of us, save that which hindered us from perfect life.

Death is not death, if it raises us in a moment from darkness into light, from weakness into strength, from sinfulness into holiness.

Death is not death, if it brings us nearer to Christ, who is the fount of life.

Death is not death, if it perfects our faith by sight, and lets us be-hold Him in whom we have believed.

Death is not death, if it gives us to those whom we have loved and lost, for whom we have lived, for whom we long to live again.

Death is not death, if it joins the child to the mother who is gone before.

Death is not death, if it takes away from that mother for ever all a mother's anxieties, a mother's fears, and lets her see, in the gracious countenance of her Saviour, a sure and certain pledge that those whom she has left behind are safe, safe with Christ and in Christ, through all the chances and dangers of this mortal life.

Death is not death, if it rids us of doubt and fear, of chance and change, of space and time, and all which space and time bring forth, and then destroy.

Death is not death; for Christ has conquered death, for Himself, and for those who trust in Him.

Charles Kingsley

164   *VICTORY OVER DEATH*

This is the victory that overcometh the world, even our faith.   1 JOHN 5:4

The Christian thought of death is a thought of victory. First, the power of memory and influence is victorious over death. We say that Beethoven is dead, but Beethoven will never die. In notes upon a million pages, in harmonious vibrations from a million violins, cellos, and oboes, Beethoven will go on blessing the world. Something from his mind and heart will always be very much alive.

More than one of us could tell that some dear one, a parent, a wife, husband, or friend, though dead for years or decades, is more real as far as concerns those forces that affect life than the person sitting in the next chair. Daily our thoughts, ideals, and conduct are determined by the influence of that person.

In the second place, we Christians are sure that, in addition to the "earthly immortality" of which we have been speaking, God's faithful children enter a heavenly immortality. When life is finished here it moves on through the gateway of death into endless life, life eternal. Stripped of the limitations of the flesh, the real self, the individual personality, persists.

I shall mention three things that undergird our faith in immortality. Not least of the facts which make eternal life credible and necessary is what we have already mentioned, these dear ones whom we have known and loved. An eternal quality of life in them we have seen and approved. The goodness, truth, and love which were a part of them cannot be sealed in a tomb. Living close to such values we awaken to the conviction that such personalities cannot end in death. As the universe so carefully conserves its material energy, it must also conserve the highest value we have known—human personalities.

Faith in a personal God calls for the immortality of human beings that love and serve Him. Having once yielded to the conviction that behind our universe is a personal God, that in His faith and experience Jesus was right that God is a Heavenly Father, then the next inevitable step is to believe that God's human children will be cared for eternally.

For Christian people, of course, Easter itself offers the crowning assurance that the faithful child of God is victorious over death. We are sure that "it was not possible that he should be holden" (Acts 2:24) of death, that Christ rose from the grave.

This is victory over death and our common attitude of morbid sorrow is all wrong. I am not suggesting that it is possible not to have a heartbreaking sense of personal loss and grief when a cherished friend slips away. I am saying that above and beneath that sense of personal loss and grief there should be a sense of joy as one whom we have loved has triumphed over death and enters as a victor into the presence of God.

A friend tells of a man who, disliking the traditional funeral service, planned his own. He asked that his friends, gathered for his funeral, should, first of all, join in singing "Praise God from Whom All Blessings Flow."

This recalls the word of Sir Edward Burne-Jones. He attended the funeral service of Robert Browning in Westminster Abbey. He did not like it. Knowing Browning, he was sure that his funeral service should have sounded the note of victory. He said: "I would have given something for a banner or two, and much I would have given if a chorister had come out of the triforium and rent the air with a trumpet."

Robert Louis Stevenson tells of a lad who was shipwrecked on a tiny isle just off the coast of Scotland. Within sight lay the quiet farmhouses of the mainland, but he was isolated by the angry sea that closed him in. Despair and fear possessed him, until at last he discovered that at low tide the water which separated him from life and hope was shallow enough to be waded. "The terror was only make believe." This is the Christian's conviction about death: the terror is only make believe. "This is the victory that overcometh the world"— and the fear and pain of death—"even our faith." Our faith brings victory.

Frank B. Fagerburg

165   *PRECIOUS DEATH*

Precious in the sight of the Lord is the death of his saints.   PSALM 116:15

There are some things in the Word of God which if viewed in a cursory manner seem completely contrary to human thinking. One of them is the Scriptural concept of death. To us, to men everywhere, death brings sorrow and tears. It is something that we instinctively avoid when it is at all possible, for within every man lurks the fear of death and dying. God, however, takes a decidedly different view of death. God says that death can be precious.

"Well," someone will say, "I can understand that death might be desirable under certain circumstances. If a man has suffered intense agony over an extended period of time, he might desire death and even welcome it as a release from his suffering. His family, too, might welcome death for him, rather than to watch him continue to writhe in agony."

True, but what of the little child who is suddenly called from the home of young parents? What of the young mother who is called from the home in which her husband and children need her so deeply? Can death be desirable in cases like these? The answer of the Word of God is that death can be precious even in cases like these.

There are inevitable questions which people will ask concerning the Scriptural assertion that death can be a precious thing. To whom is death a precious, desirable experience? The text answers that death can be a precious thing to God. It does not suggest that death can be a desirable experience to the physician. For him, death is defeat. It means that medical science with all of its advancements has failed to stem the tide of death. Nor does the text suggest that death is always a precious experience to the one who is taken. Many who know God well and who rest calmly in the promises of God abhor, nonetheless, the thought of death. It means separation from those whom they love and care for. Nor does the text suggest that death is necessarily a desirable thing to members of the family who must be left behind. However deep and abiding their faith, however certain may be their knowledge that their beloved one has gone to be with God in Christ, their loss in separation is great and soul-searching. No, the text does not suggest that death is precious to the doctor, to the one who experiences it, or to the family that remains behind, but death can be precious to God.

Why is this true? Because it marks the completion of a project God set out long ago to accomplish. When God sends a life into this world, He does so with the purpose of molding that life until he is fitted for eternal life with God. Then one day God sends the messenger of death into that life. It may be after a year, or ten years, or eighty years. Whenever the time comes, the process of molding and remaking has been completed. It means that that life has now become acceptable to God in Christ. It means that God now considers the life fitted for eternity. When that time arrives, when the divine molding process has been completed, God sends the angel of death to call the soul home unto himself. It is a precious moment to God, for it means that his work in that life has been completed.

One further question awaits an answer. The question is this: is death always precious to God? Whenever a man dies, whenever a woman is called from this life, is that a precious experience to God? Not so! Death is precious to God only in the lives of a certain people. The full text reads: "Precious in the sight of the Lord is the death of his saints." A more lucid translation of the original reads: "Precious in the eyes of the Eternal is the death of his devoted" (Moffatt).

It is apparent that not every life represents a successful molding and remaking process. The flame of the Spirit does not remove the dross from every life. So death can be a precious experience or a terrifying experience. It is a precious experience for those who have successfully walked the rocky road to Calvary, for those who have been graduated into a larger, better world with God. It is a terrifying experience for those who have failed to see the beacon light of the cross, for those for whom there is no God, no Christ, no Saviour. What will death mean *to God* in your case? What will it mean *to you*?

Gordon H. Girod

166   *WHY DID THIS HAPPEN?*

Jesus answered and said unto him, What I do thou knowest not now; but thou shalt know hereafter.   JOHN 13:7

There are many things that happen to us in this life for which we can find no answer. Experiences which we cannot understand baffle us. There seems sometimes to be no reason or purpose in what has taken place. In the dark hour of a great loss, sick with loneliness and anguish, our hearts cry out for an explanation. In such times we may find strength and guidance in the words of Jesus spoken on the eve of the crucifixion to the perplexed disciples in the upper room. These words speak to us as we confront life's heaviest losses. They apply to us as we stand bereaved and mystified in the presence of events for which we can find no answer.

When the minister stands, as he often does, with a heartbroken family after the sudden death of a young person, he knows that there is one reminder that may prove helpful to those who grieve. It is this: beyond the tragic event, an event that defies man's explanations, there is a purpose which faith alone can see amid the shadows and which patience will in time reveal.

We live out our lives in the presence of mystery. There are so many experiences we cannot understand. We cry out for light:

> Behold, we know not anything;
> I can but trust that good shall fall
> At last—far off—at last, to all,
> And every winter change to spring.
>
> So runs my dream: but what am I?
> An infant crying in the night:
> An infant crying for the light:
> And with no language but a cry.[1]

If we could only be certain that this crushing blow is not from the hand of blind fate, but is permitted by a Heavenly Father who is "afflicted in all our afflictions"! We are not alone in our desire for

[1] From *In Memoriam* (St. LIV) by Alfred Tennyson.

assurance as we pass through the dark night of our soul: many of the
choice people in each age have grappled with this matter. Out of this
same state of mind and heart, however, have come some of the most
beautiful and tender words of hope and guidance that have ever fallen
upon the weary of heart as they groped in the shadows. John Henry
Newman in 1833, perplexed in mind and sick in body, wrote a hymn
that was to become the prayer for millions of people in each generation:

> Lead, kindly Light! amid the encircling gloom;
>   Lead thou me on!
> The night is dark, and I am far from home;
>   Lead thou me on!
> Keep thou my feet: I do not ask to see
> The distant scene; one step enough for me.
>
> So long thy power hath blessed me, sure it still
>   Will lead me on,
> O'er moor and fen, o'er crag and torrent, till
>   The night is gone;
> And with the morn, those angel faces smile
> Which I have loved long since, and lost a while.[1]

In the hours of great anguish there is a question that comes back
again and again to our minds. The query is summed up in the word
"Why." How often do we hear persons say: *Why* did this happen?
Why was this useful person taken? *Why* was this young person, so full
of promise, cut off before the chance to make a contribution to life
was granted?

Jesus, who was Son of Man as well as Son of God, knew well this
word. It was his word amid the darkness and anguish of Calvary. Out
of the depths of an indescribable loneliness and desolation come the
words, "My God, my God, *why* hast thou forsaken me?" In all of the
Holy Scriptures there is no verse more difficult to explain. Surely
the Master was never closer to the suffering heart of humanity than
when he uttered this cry. "And all the millions of whys which have
arisen from agonized souls, jealous for the honor of God but perplexed
by His providence, were concentrated in the *why* of Christ."

The final word from the cross may be, by the grace of God, our
word. And for us also light may come out of darkness, trust out of
uncertainty, and peace out of anguish. "Father, into thy hands I
commend my spirit" (Luke 23:46).

[1] From "The Pillar of the Cloud" by John Henry Newman.

Yea, once Immanuel's orphaned cry his universe hath shaken—
It went up single, echoless, "My God I am forsaken!"
It went up from the Holy's lips amid his lost creation,
That, of the lost, no son should use those words of desolation![1].

"For my thoughts are not your thoughts, neither are your ways my ways, saith the Lord" (Is. 55:8).

While life often confronts us with that which we can neither understand nor explain, yet life is not all mystery. If the unexplainable experiences of life are a terrific storm that blasts upon the citadel of faith, let us remember that that stronghold can be so constructed that it will not fall. Our great defense is trust in the goodness and wisdom of God.

For the Lord will not cast off for ever: For though he cause grief, yet will he have compassion according to the multitude of his mercies. For he doth not afflict willingly nor grieve the children of men. (LAM. 3:31-33)

It was this confidence that grew in the heart of the Apostle Paul, nourished on the presence and promises of Christ, that enabled him to say: "Our citizenship is in heaven whence also we wait for a Saviour, the Lord Jesus Christ; who shall fashion anew the body of our humiliations that it may be conformed to the body of his glory" (Phil. 3:20 R.V.).

"What I do thou knowest not now; but thou shalt understand hereafter" (John 13:7).

Sometime, when all life's lessons have been learned,
    And suns and stars forevermore have set,
The things which our weak judgments here have spurned,
    The things o'er which we grieved with lashes wet,
Will flash before us out of life's dark night,
    As stars shine most in deeper tints of blue;
And we shall see how all God's plans were right,
    And what most seemed reproof was love most true.[2]
                                        Clyde V. Hickerson

167   *CONFIDENT DYING*

Father, into thy hands I commend my spirit.   LUKE 23:46

Let no one talk lightly about death. It is a terrible reality. Sometimes death means release from the limitations of the body as well as the end of physical suffering and pain. At times death becomes a

[1] From "Cowper's Grave" by Elizabeth Barrett Browning.
[2] From "Sometime" by May Riley Smith.

revealer of those things that are most worth-while, clearly showing us that some of the things to which we give our attentions are not worthy of our devotion. But then again death comes as a terrible destroyer of hopes, a blaster of real happiness, and a challenge to faith.

No matter when or where death reaches us it never should find us unprepared, for we know it is appointed for man to die. It is here in the presence of death that our Christian faith gives us, not only light concerning the mystery of death, but provides strength for the mastery of life. Jesus taught us not only how to live, but He showed us how to die in confidence. That is what He meant when He said, "Father, into thy hands I commend my spirit."

Death to the Christian, as it was to the Lord Himself, is a home-going of the soul. As a seed that is put into the ground dies into life, so death becomes an open door through which we enter into the full life for which Christ redeemed us.

Jesus came from the Father, lived with the Father, and returned to the Father. So it may be for us. The reason for our confidence is not our goodness nor our achievement, not even our religion, but Jesus Christ the Lord. We are not saved by character but by Calvary. Therefore, even this temporal life takes on eternal significance and we live for the things that cannot perish, since we trust in Him who said, "Because I live, ye shall live also" (John 14:19).

David I. Berger

168   *PREPARING FOR DEATH*

Take ye heed, watch and pray: for ye know not when the time is. MARK 13:33

Men do not love to think of death, because they are not on good terms with him. They resort to forgetfulness. They occupy themselves, often, intensely. They rush into pleasures. They count him to be no kind companion, and no pleasant friend, that will insist upon reminding them of dying and death. It is a gloomy thing. All the offices of death are gloomy; and they are made more so by the heathen practices of Christian communities.

Now, death is not in itself anything terrible, as a mere physical event. Most persons die with as little pain as a child goes to sleep; and all the suffering which precedes death is so little in the majority of instances that if it were all summed up and put upon a man who is alive and well, he would be ashamed to shed a tear, or to shrink from the bearing of it. Death in and of itself is merciful. It was not meant that men should be crowded out of life as through a door. When men are prepared to die, nature is as gracious to them in dying as to an apple, when it is ripe and ready to fall from the bough. The stem itself prepares, as a part of its ripeness, to let go; so that when the least breath of wind, after the moistening by the dew in the night, shakes the apple, it falls easily to the ground.

We do not cling to the bough of life very tenaciously. We do not need to be torn from it by rude handling. Dying is not a thing specially to be dreaded. No man ever has the toothache in good earnest, no man ever has the rheumatism or neuralgia, that he does not suffer every hour more pain than dying inflicts upon men ordinarily. There are exceptional cases, but this is the general rule. Death is a thing, therefore, not to be dreaded as a physical experience.

In regard to death as the interruption of our plans and affections, it is a thing, certainly, more painful, and to be apprehended with less composure; because death does overhang men in the midst of their love, and in the midst of their schemes; and they have seen among their neighbors what disasters have followed it. One prophesies, and asks: "What will become of my children? What will become of my estate? What will become of these mighty interests which have devolved upon me, and which my hands have controlled and guided?" So that there is a reason more worthy than the fear of pain, why men do not like to think of death.

And yet, even this, philosophy, without any consideration of religion, might very much ameliorate. For, since the world began, has it ever been found that a man died whose place could not be supplied? Has the world mourned because a family mourned? Have children that have lost the guiding parent not been able to find their way into life and through life? Nature is made so large and so bountiful, and the economy of God's providence is such, that, after all, those who think that they are so important to their estate, to their business, to their families, overestimate. To be sure, if they should die, the household would not be carried on as they are carrying it on; but it would not be destroyed.

Besides, we are not as necessary as we think. The sun will come up tomorrow if you do die. The stars will shine if you are not here to see them. Summer will come if your plough is still. The world is not made to turn on you as a pivot. You occupy a very small place. Your little will, and your little purposes, scarcely crease the great orb of affairs. And no man is so necessary that of the stones God cannot raise up one to take his place. The work that you have in undivided hands, God scatters and divides up among a hundred.

So men overestimate their importance, and think that death is a terrible thing because they are conceited in regard to their relations here in this world.

But the true significance of death lies in the fact that it brings men into final moral relations with God; that it brings moral character and conduct to a final test; that it brings men into judgment for all the deeds done in the body—for every word; for every thought; for every habit; for every element of character. At death men enter into the presence of God. There is a settling of their estate; and their estate follows their nature and character. They that have done good rise to honor and glory and immortality; and those that have done evil sink to shame and woe. That is a reason why men dread death; and it is a good reason for dreading it. But it is not a good reason for not thinking about it. It is not only a good reason why men should not love to cherish in their bosom the thought of death, which is so full of fear, but it is a good reason why they should take away fear from the thought of death. For, death may come to us either dark, revengeful, prophesying mischief, or it may come as the coming of the Son of Man, full of hope and promise and cheer.

A wise foresight of death also gives unity, consistence, and steady purpose to the whole of our life, now scattered into details, or gathered together like a sand-heap in which the particles are in juxtaposition, but not in union. He who thinks from day to day that death is but a hand-breadth; that death comes to terminate this life, and then begins the other, the eternal, and the real life, cannot but find, not only that it will minister to wisdom and prudence, but that it will soften many hard places, and relieve many sharp sufferings.

If one thinks wisely of death, not only will it not be a fear and a terror, but it will be a guardian angel. There is no thought sweeter to those that believe in Christ, than the thought that He will bring them from the dead, even as He was raised from the dead. There is no thought in which, with more joy, men bathe their fevered brow, than the thought, "Ere long I shall die; I shall go forth from this struggle—from this strife of tongues; from this bitterness; from this injustice; from this partial life; from this unmanliness. It will be but a little while before I shall go forth and be at rest."

Henry Ward Beecher

FOR A YOUTH

169   *THE DESTINY OF MEN*

And as it is appointed unto men once to die, but after this the judgment: so Christ was once offered to bear the sins of many; and unto them
that look for him shall he appear and the second time without sin unto
salvation. HEBREWS 9:27-28

Many treat the spiritual world as if it were entirely lawless. They
think of it only with sentiment and as governed by chance. Resting
in a false view of the fact that God is love and that they are "pretty
good," they feel assured that all will go well. They know that there
is law in nature, which must be respected; but they have a gambling
spirit concerning eternal things.

God, however, reveals the spiritual world as both love and law.
Love and law are in all departments of it. There is no holy love without law. Love without law is lust and brings ruin. Spiritual blessings
are conditioned by law. "God is law and love is the way He rules us;
God is love and law is the way He loves us." We reap as we sow in
the spiritual world just as in the physical world.

Our young friend, who has been taken from us, believed in God
and in His love; so *he* accepted the expression of this love in Jesus
Christ who bore his sin on the cross. He believed in God's law, so *he*
obeyed Him. There was marked earnestness and sincerity in *his*
spiritual life in the Church, in prayer, in Bible study, in offerings to
the cause of Christ. Christ loved the Church and gave Himself up for
it; so did our friend.

Death is not annihilation, but the separation of the spirit from the
body. It faces everyone, and everyone should face it. Man's body is
mortal and subject to death. "Death passed upon all men, for that all
have sinned" (Rom. 5:12). Death has been left in the world that man
might not be immortal in his sinful condition. It is also a constant
reminder of his frailty and of the certainty of his passing into the
presence of God. For the Christian, death becomes the gateway into
the presence of the Lord. Because of the uncertainty of death's coming, it behooves one to "boast not thyself of tomorrow" (Prov. 27:1).
Death came unexpectedly to our young brother, but he was ready
for it.

Spiritual as well as physical judgments are inevitable in a universe
of righteous law. There are two phases of judgment after death.
One is the judging of the work of God's people, the judgment of

awards. The Lord comes to "take account of his servants" (Matt. 18:23). Then shall be revealed whether the Christian life has built the imperishable—"gold, silver, precious stones"—or the perishable—"wood, hay, stubble." Paul declares that some "shall be saved; yet so as by fire" (1 Cor. 3:15), like people escaping from a burning building with all their accumulations burned up. Our friend's work will come into judgment. As we have all known, he was a faithful, loyal, earnest servant of the Lord Jesus Christ. His work will stand.

There will also be the execution of the judgment which is already determined upon earth. "He that believeth not is condemned already, because he hath not believed in the name of the only begotten Son of God" (John 4:18). One does not have to wait until after death to know whether the word will be "Come, ye blessed of my Father" (Matt. 25:34) or "Depart."

He who once was offered to bear the sins of many, shall appear again with salvation for those who wait for Him.

The coming again of the Lord was a truth dear unto our *brother,* and *he* sought to live the kind of life of which *he* would not be ashamed if the Lord came in *his* day. The Lord has, however, sent for *him.* And while we feel sorely bereaved to lose *him* from our midst and *his* going is a great bereavement for this home, yet *his* life has been a blessing which shall continue with us.

Earle V. Pierce

G. HIS RESURRECTION AND OURS

CHRIST OUR HOPE

Because I live, ye shall live also.   JOHN 14:19

Man needs a hope, resting on something which is beyond the sphere of sense and time. And God has given him one in the resurrection of Jesus Christ from the dead. Our Lord, indeed, taught in the plainest language the reality of a future life:

> In my Father's house are many mansions . . . I go to prepare a place for you. (John 14:2)
>
> Lay up for yourselves treasures in heaven, where neither moth nor rust doth corrupt. (Matt. 6:20)
>
> These shall go away into everlasting punishment: but the righteous into life eternal. (Matt. 25:46)
>
> He is not a God of the dead, but of the living: for all live unto him. (Luke 20:38)

Passages of this kind from among the very words of Christ might be multiplied. But, in teaching that man would thus live after death, our Lord was teaching what, with various degrees of distinctness, pagans and Jews had taught before Him. He contributed to the establishment of this truth in the deepest conviction of man. Not merely lessons taught in words, but a fact palpable to the senses. When He rose, after saying that He would rise from the grave, He broke up the spell of the law of death. He made it plain within the precincts of this visible world that a world unseen and eternal, but most real, awaits us hereafter. He converted hopes, surmises, speculations, trains of inference, into the strongest certainties.

"Because I live, ye shall live also." This was the motto which henceforth faith, under the guidance of reason, described as the legend which was traced over the doorway of Christ's empty sepulchre. For that He had risen was not a secret whispered to the few; it was a fact verified by the senses of more than five hundred witnesses. It was established in the face of a jealous, implacable criticism, which endeavoured to silence by violence its eloquent protestation that there is indeed a world beyond the grave.

H. P. Liddon

171 *THE ASSURANCE CHRIST GIVES*

Why should it be thought a thing incredible with you, that God should raise the dead? ACTS 26:8

It is the glory of the Christian creed that in tones of ringing conviction it announces the certainty of life beyond the grave. The power of the apostles' preaching lay in their assertion that they had positive knowledge of facts which give assurance of our common hope of immortality. We who are here today have accepted their message. We believe in life eternal. We are sure that at death the soul is not unclothed, but clothed upon its immortal spiritual body. We believe that life here is a preparation for life unending. We believe because of apostolic witness. We believe on the authority of Jesus Christ.

Jesus, in His teaching, said very little about the future life; He simply took it for granted. That is the way He dealt once with a question about the resurrection life. Had not the questioners heard about the resurrection life? Had not the questioners heard how God declared Himself to be the God of Abraham and the God of Isaac and the God of Jacob? He is not the God of the dead, but of the living; therefore, these patriarchs live in the world beyond. When questions were asked as to relationships hereafter for those whose bonds here were as close as in marriage, He simply answered that in many such matters we must be content to remain ignorant; there are no terms in our vocabulary by which they can be explained. Such earthly relations will be lifted into something more beautiful, more satisfying, not less personal or individual, but more expansive. "Eye hath not seen, nor ear heard, neither have entered into the heart of man, the things which God hath prepared for them that love him"(1 Cor. 2:9).

So then, Jesus never attempted to explain difficulties—how can they be explained when there is no language of human experience in which to phrase the explanation? He did not give any descriptions of the other life—when all is said, details are of little value by comparison with the great fact itself; details which are not yet understandable would but blur the picture. Jesus simply took for granted that death is only a turn in the road to life eternal. God being what he is, and man being God's child, it could not be otherwise. "In my

Father's house are many mansions:" He says, and then adds quietly, "if it were not so, I would have told you" (John 14:2). In other words, Jesus fills men's hearts with trust in a heavenly Father; He makes them understand the real value of human life; having done this, it is unnecessary to argue as to what such a Father will do with so precious a gift as that of life. Jesus makes belief in immortality rest back upon God's moral character. Once we see God as Jesus tells us of Him, we are not afraid to make the leap of faith which accepts all the rest without question.

In Christ we have more than intuition; we have positive assurance. People talk glibly, in these days, about the fatherhood of God, but in plain fact apart from this Christian faith the idea of God as a loving Father is but a dream, a vision of what God must be to meet our needs. With Christianity it is not a dream; it is solid reality; we *know* that God is love, because He has written the fact on the pages of history in the earthly life of His Son. It would be almost impossible to believe it, apart from this record, so terrible is the burden of the world's pain, "distributed to good and bad alike, without regard to our moral desert."

A God, therefore, who created men for such a life as ours, and then cut off that life as soon as its earthly span of years was over, would not be a righteous God. Let me repeat, then, that faith in immortality grows out of the teaching of Christ as to God's character.

I think it is with some such feeling as this—though not with our full acceptance of the revelation through Christ—that Hugh Walpole tells of his faith in immortality, a faith which he announces as intuitional, something which he feels has so clearly been "given" him that he would not think for a moment of arguing about it, explaining it, defending it. He says: "I have become aware, not by my own wish, almost against my will, of an existence in another life of far, far greater importance and beauty than this physical existence, beautiful and important though that is. I know that the knowledge of this other life leads to increasing happiness and interest; that it brings me, however slowly and with however many personal stupidities, ignorances, and clumsy faults, to a new tolerance, a new sympathy, a new understanding of the life we now live." Of this we have assurance in the teaching of Jesus.

Charles Fiske

172   *SURE OF GOD'S LOVE*

I am the resurrection, and the life: he that believeth in me, though he were dead, yet shall he live: and whosoever liveth and believeth in me shall never die.   JOHN 11:25-26

These thrilling words come singing their way across the centuries to sustain and strengthen us today, as they have comforted millions since Jesus spoke them. Because we can be sure of God's love for us, when we eagerly give ourselves to Him, we begin to understand what Robert Browning had in mind when he exclaimed:

> So, the All-Great were the All-Loving too—
> So, through the thunder comes a human voice
> Saying, "O heart I made, a heart beats here!
> Face, my hands fashioned, see it in myself!
> Thou hast no power nor mayst conceive of mine,
> But love I gave thee, with myself to love."[1]

This is the truth upon which we depend in life's last crisis. If there is a God such as Browning describes, we can meet any emergency with fearless confidence.

Maude Royden tells of hearing in Hyde Park one Sunday afternoon a speaker who was attacking the providence of God on the grounds that the war showed Him to be cruel or heedless. She writes that the crowd listened to the speaker with interest, doubtless thinking, "Well, God must be horribly cruel to allow such things to happen." Then the man turned from the main theme of his discourse and began to attack Jesus Christ. Suddenly an auditor who was not a Christian, who did not in any way believe that Jesus was God, was filled with the fury of indignation. He exclaimed: "Say what you like about God. There's nothing bad enough you can say about Him, if He really made the world like this. But let Jesus Christ alone!" The crowd who had been with the speaker while he arraigned the justice of God, cheered and applauded, saying: "Yes, let Jesus Christ alone!"

We feel our hearts throb in unison with the protest of the man who spontaneously shouted his disapproval at the condemnation of Christ. But this is the vital and all-important point: if one accepts and approves of Christ's character, as did this man, he must have the same

[1] From "An Epistle Containing the Strange Medical Experience of Karshish, the Arab Physician," by Robert Browning.

confidence in the friendly character of the universe as Jesus Himself had. The universe cannot produce something greater or finer than it is.

Jesus says quite plainly that He represents in character and in nature the spirit of the universe. He insists that when one has *Him,* he knows the nature of the power of the world. It is not blind force; it is not chance; it is not fate; it is not harsh, cold, impersonal law. It can be none of these. It is friendliness and goodness and truth. It is righteousness that cares. It is all these together—in One Person. Jesus trusted God, and God did not betray His confidence. This is the glorious truth which sustains and strengthens us today. The Spirit of the universe did not betray His confidence! Understanding this, we know that neither chance nor fate rules the world, but the wise love of God which has been seen in Jesus Christ.

This truth makes all the difference in the world at a time like this. We cannot explain *what* has happened, nor can we fully understand *why* it has happened, but we can place our confidence in Christ. It is not *what* we believe, but *whom.* "He that hath seen me hath seen the Father" (John 14:9).

There is no need of closing our eyes or minds to unanswered questions. They are too numerous: they keep forever besieging us. But there are some things of which we can be sure.

> I know not where I'm going, but I do know my Guide,
> And with childlike faith I give my hand to the Friend that's
>   by my side;
> The only thing I ask of him, as he takes it is, "Hold it fast;
> Suffer me not to lose my way, but bring me home at last."

So, again we hear words of Divine comfort: "God shall wipe away all tears from their eyes; and there shall be no more death, neither sorrow, nor crying, neither shall there be any more pain: for the former things are passed away" (Rev. 21:4). In spite of our lack of detailed information concerning the future, we have enough knowledge to assure us. We may not know the geography of tomorrow's world, but we know Him who will lead us into tomorrow—and beyond!

With all the confidence which has come to us from Christ, tens of thousands of men and women have refused even to permit their trust to be called faith; they insist it is personal experience. So, happily they join another in saying:

When I go down to the sea by ship,
And Death unfurls her sail,
Weep not for me, for there will be
A living host on another coast
To beckon and cry, "All hail!"[1]

G. Ray Jordan

173   *YE SHALL LIVE ALSO*

Because I live, ye shall live also.   JOHN 14:19

The resurrection of Jesus Christ was an experienced fact for the first disciples. Calvary had been to them a bitter disappointment, shattering their fondest hopes and their most cherished dreams. There came with Easter the restoration of these hopes and dreams and the rising of their souls to the full glory of life triumphant. The certainty of their faith in the risen Lord transformed their lives and made possible the subsequent achievements of the Christian tradition. New and victorious meaning had been imparted to life. "Because I live, ye shall live also."

Death has no power over Christ nor over those who find life's meaning in Him. From time to time during this earthly pilgrimage, the individual experiences intimations of a life after death, but for the one whose life is linked with Christ, personal immortality becomes an absolute certainty. No longer is it a vague possibility, but it becomes such a reality that death loses its sting and the grave relinquishes its victory.

Man's deepest longing is not to die but to live. Immortality is often difficult to explain, because we do not literally see it. But we do not see, in any literal sense, any of the great powers of the universe. No one ever saw an idea or a purpose, but these are great forces in life. No one ever saw a Christian virtue, yet this can be the most precious adornment of humankind. No one ever saw love, but love is the greatest power in the world. Only an individual's outer shell is visible. The real self, its ideas and purposes, memories and hopes, virtues and love, is invisible. It is this real self which enters eternal life, wherein all values are preserved, freed from the changes and chances of mortal life.

Death becomes a graduation from this imperfect primary department into a higher and more perfect rank of learning and living. The

[1] From "Beyond the Horizon" by Robert Freeman.

individual, clothed with a new form suitable to his celestial environment, is more splendidly equipped for a larger life of divine service.

The human heart, of course, is saddened when a loved one passes through the valley of the shadow of death. Anguish is felt when the soul longs

> for the touch of a vanish'd hand,
> And the sound of a voice that is still![1]

The Christian, however, draws his consolation from a faith that undergirds him with the knowledge that at last there will come the happy and permanent reunion.

The poet Whittier pictures with these words what the Christian knows within his soul:

> Yet Love will dream, and Faith will trust,
> (Since He who knows our need is just,)
> That somehow, somewhere, meet we must.
> Alas, for him who never sees
> The stars shine through his cypress-trees!
> Who, hopeless, lays his dead away,
> Nor looks to see the breaking day
> Across the mournful marbles play!
> Who hath not learned, in hours of faith,
>   The truth to flesh and sense unknown,
> That Life is ever lord of Death,
>   And Love can never lose its own![2]

Christ gives to human life a meaning and a value that are eternal, and there is no danger of their ever being lost. The disciples who followed Jesus along the shores of a Syrian sea found their faith vindicated and triumphant in the risen Lord of Easter morning. "Because I live, ye shall live also."

The tomb, as Victor Hugo once reminded us, is not a blind alley, but a thoroughfare. It closes on the twilight; it opens on the dawn. The life with which we are entrusted is imparted with permanent meaning and eternal value by the victorious Christ. Our work does not end with the grave. It begins again the next morning. Through the power of Christ, we can walk and live in this faith, that as soon as we are absent from the body we shall be at home with the Lord.

Paul Lambourne Higgins

---

[1] From "Break, Break, Break" by Alfred Tennyson.
[2] From *Snow-Bound* by John Greenleaf Whittier.

174   *HIS RESURRECTION AND OURS*

If a man die, shall he live again?   JOB 14:14

Who has not asked this question, in suspense, in hope, or in fear? We know that we must all die: we know that those who are dearest to us must die: can our eyes penetrate beyond the veil which death lets fall? Is there any answer in the nature or heart of humanity to the question of Job, "If a man die shall he live again?"

I

The great passages in the Old Testament, in which the hope emerges, come upon us suddenly. This passage in Job is one. The tried man is in the very extremity of his distress. He feels—for so he interprets his distress—that God for some reason is angry with him, and that His anger will endure till he dies. His disease is mortal, and will carry him to his grave. But is that all? Job finds his faith in God come to his relief. For God is righteous, the vindicator of righteousness, and it is not possible for Him to abandon a righteous man as Job would be abandoned, if his death ended all.

The idea comes to Job through his faith in God, that Sheol may not be the final outlook, and he puts it into the pathetic prayer: "O that thou wouldest hide me in Sheol, that thou wouldest keep me secret, until thy wrath is past, that thou wouldest appoint me a set time, and remember me!" (Job 14:13). How patient such a prospect would make the suffering man. How uncomplainingly he would face the dreary underworld if he knew that it was only a temporary interruption to his communion with God. "All the days of my warfare would I wait till my release should come. Thou shouldest call, and I would answer Thee: Thou wouldest have a desire to the work of Thine hands" (Job 14:14-15).

This is only the yearning soul, its faint anticipation, born of faith, of what might be; but in a later passage we see it flame up triumphantly, though it is but for a moment. "I know that my redeemer liveth, and that he shall stand up at the last upon the earth, and after my skin hath been thus destroyed, yet from my flesh shall I see God, whom I shall see for myself, and mine eyes shall behold and not another; though my reins are consumed within me" (Job 19:25-27)— that is, I faint with longing for that great vindication.

Both in Egypt and in Greece faith in immortality, such as it was, rested simply on conceptions of man's nature; here, as everywhere in revealed religion, it rests on the character of God. He is the Eternal Righteousness, and His faith is pledged to man whom He calls to live in fellowship with Himself. All things may seem to be against a man; his friends may desert him, circumstances may accuse him; but if he is righteous, God cannot desert him, and if he must die under a cloud, even death will not prevent his vindication. His Redeemer lives, and one day he shall again see God. And to see God is to have life, in the only sense which is adequate to the Bible use of the word.

II

Christians believe in their own resurrection to eternal life, because they believe in the resurrection of Christ. But faith does not depend upon—it does not originate in nor is it maintained by—the resurrection of Christ, simply as a historical fact. The resurrection of Jesus is not simply a fact outside of us, guaranteeing in some mysterious way our resurrection in some remote future. It is a present power in the believer. He can say with St. Paul—Christ liveth in me—the risen Christ—the Conqueror of death—and a part, therefore, is ensured to me in His life and immortality.

This is *the* great idea of the New Testament whenever the future life is in view. It is indeed very variously expressed. Sometimes it is *Christ in us,* the hope of glory. Sometimes it is specially connected with the possession, or rather the indwelling, of the Holy Spirit. "If the Spirit of him that raised up Jesus from the dead dwell in you, he that raised up Christ from the dead shall also quicken your mortal bodies by his Spirit that dwelleth in you" (Rom. 8:11). It is easy to see that the religious attitude here is, precisely what it was in the Old Testament, though as the revelation is fuller, the faith which apprehends it, and the hope which grows out of it, are richer.

Just as union with God guarantees to the Psalmist a life that would never end, so union with the risen Saviour guaranteed to the Apostles, and guarantees to us, the resurrection triumph over death. Here is a faith in immortality which is moral and spiritual through and through —which rests upon a supreme revelation of what God has done for man—which involves a present life in fellowship with the risen Saviour—which is neither worldly nor other worldly, but eternal— which has propagated itself through all ages and in all nations— which in Jesus Christ invites all men to become sharers in it—which is the present, living, governing faith of believing men and women

in proportion as they realize their union with the Saviour: a faith
infinite in its power to console and inspire: a faith not always easy
to hold, but demanding for its retention that effort and strain in
which St. Paul strove to know Him, and the power of His resurrection, and the fellowship of His sufferings, becoming conformed to His
death, if by any means he might attain to the resurrection of the dead.
And all this, which fills the epistles of the New Testament, goes back
to the words of Jesus Himself: "Abide in me, and I in you" (John
15:4); and, "Because I live, ye shall live also" (John 14:19).

III

"If a man die," asked Job, "shall he live again?" Let us put it
directly, if *I* die, shall I live again? It is not worth while putting it as
a speculative question: the speculators have not been unanimous nor
hearty in their answer. Faith in immortality has in point of fact
entered the world and affected human life along the line of faith in
God and in Jesus Christ His Son. Only *one* life has ever won the
victory over death: only one kind of life ever can win it—that kind
which was in Him, which *is* in Him, which He shares with all whom
faith makes one with him. That is our hope, to be really members of
Christ, living with a life which comes from God and has already
vanquished death. God has given to us eternal life, and this life is in
His Son. Can death touch that life? Never. The confidence of Christ
Himself ought to be ours. If we live by Him we have nothing to fear.
"He that eateth my flesh, and drinketh my blood, hath eternal life;
and I will raise him up at the last day" (John 6:54). "Verily, verily, I
say unto you, If a man keep my saying, he shall never see death"
(John 8:51). "I am the resurrection, and the life: he that believeth in
me, though he were dead, yet shall he live: and he that liveth and
believeth in me, shall never die" (John 11:25-26).

James Denney

175   *LIFE AND HOPE FROM ABOVE*

I am he that liveth, and was dead; and, behold, I am alive for evermore.
REVELATION 1:18

All our highest knowledge and experience, every fact of nature and
of human life, points to the probability of life continued beyond the
grave. Men have always felt within themselves the longing for immortality. We see the evidence of this in the pyramids of Egypt, in the

legends of Greece, in the history and customs of every race. And the higher men have risen, the deeper this longing has become; the greater and nobler the soul, the more impossible for it to believe in its own extinction.

We cannot believe that the purpose of our creation is fulfilled by our brief existence on this earth. God has woven the hope of immortality into the very texture of our being. And yet, confronted with the great fact of death, this hope of the future life is inadequate and uncertain.

As we meet the deep sorrows of life, as we stand beside the new made grave, we need something more than the speculations of philosophy or the guesses of human reason. The help that we need is given to us in Christ, the Son of God.

It is Christ who has changed hope into assurance, a speculation into faith, longing into certainty.

In the risen Christ we have God's own answer to the longing which He has implanted in our souls.

The message of Christianity to the world is not a vague philosophy of the immortality of the soul.

There would have been no Gospel from above in that, nothing that could have produced those results which the gospel has brought to pass in the lives of men.

It is the actual resurrection of Jesus Christ from the grave, the fact that He rose on the third day from the dead, which has brought life and hope from above, and has met the need and longing of the world.

And if this is true of Jesus Christ can we doubt as to who He is, and what our faith in Him ought to be?

It is this stupendous fact of Christ's resurrection which changed the course of history, which inspired the apostles with a faith that nothing could resist, which for 2,000 years has given faith to the dying and comfort to the mourners, which has been the divinest force for good this world has known and is today a mightier influence than ever before.

And so, with the Christian Church throughout the world, we lift up our prayers and hymns and thanksgivings to Him who says to us, "I am he that liveth, and was dead; and, behold, I am alive for evermore," and whom we shall soon meet face to face in the life beyond.

William T. Manning

176   *IF CHRIST BE NOT RISEN!*

If Christ be not raised, your faith is vain; ye are yet in your sins. Then they also which are fallen asleep in Christ are perished. . . . But now is Christ risen from the dead. 1 CORINTHIANS 15:17-18, 20

"If Christ be not risen, *then they also which are fallen asleep in Christ are perished.*" Those whom we are accustomed to call "the blessed departed"—obliterated, annihilated. Blown out of existence, as you would blow a candle out. "Cast," said Tennyson, "as rubbish to the void." Never to be met again. Perished.

Now why? Why is that involved in it? You can see why. You scarce need to ask. For if Jesus never rose, how should they? If the one finally perfect life that has ever appeared on earth did not get through this thing called Death—how should any one else? They are perished.

Well, does it matter? Ah, don't say that! Don't mock us. Does anything else matter? As long as love is love, as long as one human heart cleaves and clings to another, it matters all the world!

You can't live without it. There was an old Welsh saint of a former generation, a great soldier of Christ—Christmas Evans they called him—and when the day came for him to die, he bade his friends at the bedside farewell, and turned his face to the wall; and in a little while, suddenly they saw him wave his hand triumphantly: "Drive on! Drive on!" he cried, as if he were seeing Christ's chariots come to take him, "Drive on!" And so he died. What if that were just delusion, and there were no chariots there? "The angels!" cried a young boyish Covenanter on the scaffold in the Grassmarket, just before the axe of death descended, "the angels! They've come to carry me to Jesus' bosom!" And so he passed out. But what if that last cry were mistaken? What if Macbeth were right?

> Tomorrow, and tomorrow, and tomorrow,
> Creeps in this petty pace from day to day,
> To the last syllable of recorded time;
> And all our yesterdays have lighted fools
> The way to dusty death. Out, out, brief candle![1]

What if the Venerable Bede's image of our human life were all that could be said about it—a bird flying out of the dark into a brilliantly lighted banqueting-hall, flying across that brilliance for a moment, then out at the other window, out into the night again? Then we can

[1] From *Macbeth*, Act V, Scene 5.

only tell God that it is cruel of Him to put such love in our hearts, and snap it in the end! There is a picture by a great artist which shows God in the act of making His world. And as the vision of human life, with all its tragedy and loss, begins to shape itself out of chaos, a figure is seen starting up and crying to the Creator, "God, if it is a world like that you are going to make, stay your hand! Don't make it at all!" That is how we should feel if death finishes love and destroys forever. And if Christ is not raised, it does.

But if Christ be risen from the dead—then they that have fallen asleep in Christ are alive, are ours, are here! "Is there no one," said Cromwell, as he lay dying and looked round on the faces of his weeping friends, "is there no one here who will *praise the Lord?*" That is the new note. Grim, portentous, solemn Death—you thought you would rob me, did you? You were wrong.

> O thou soul of my soul! I shall clasp thee again,
> And with God be the rest![1]

So Paul here has looked the grim thought—Christ not risen—in the face, and challengingly has drawn three inevitable conclusions—faith gone, forgiveness gone, immortality gone. But then, while the shudder of it is passing over his readers' souls, comes his sudden burst of triumph. "But now," he cries, and every word of it is a trumpet-note, a shout, a battle cry—"but now is Christ risen from the dead"—and with that he sweeps the horror from his soul. "Now is Christ risen!"

And if you ask him, "How do you know it, Paul?" he has two answers. "Know it? Why, I have spoken with men who have seen Him! Peter, Andrew, and John, and a hundred others, men who have had their whole life changed from top to bottom by the experience of seeing Him!" Can you say that? Have you ever spoken to a man who has seen the risen Christ? Some one surer of that than of anything else in life? That is one glorious line of evidence.

But Paul had another, an even greater. "Christ risen—how do I know it? I have seen Him myself, seen Him with these very eyes, seen Him with this very heart!" And if any one had dared to suggest to Paul that Christ was not really alive—"Not alive, man?" he would have answered, "Why, He arrested me riding to Damascus, and He has been power to my life ever since! I have seen Him, felt Him—and I *know*." Can you say that? Say it in all sincerity, and with no exaggeration at all—"It is not I who live, but Christ who lives in me: and I

---

[1] From "Prospice" by Robert Browning.

have actually felt His presence and His power"? Then you have the evidence in yourself. You *know*. And you can say, with Savonarola, "They may kill me if they please; but they will never, never, never tear the living Christ from my heart!"

James S. Stewart

177   *THREE GLORIOUS REALITIES*

Because I live, ye shall live also.   JOHN 14:19

As we stand today in the presence of this dead body—this house of clay—from which the soul has departed, we acknowledge

I. The Reality of Death.

Death's only flowers are faded garlands on coffin lids.

Death's only music is the sob of broken hearts.

Death's only pleasure fountains are the falling tears of the world.

Death's only palace is a huge sepulchre.

Death's only gold are bones scattered at the grave's mouth.

Death's only light is the darkness of the tomb.

Death is a king of terror with no rival.

Death oft mocks our hopes like a coarse comedian.

Death is an inexorable jailor who imprisons many in heavy slumber.

Death—once in the centuries long gone—closed the eyes, stilled the heart, folded the hands, and stopped the feet of Jesus. For all who loved Him, dark and bleak and comfortless was the night—after Jesus died.

But we think, too, of

II. The Reality of Christ's Resurrection.

"But now is Christ risen from the dead" (1 Cor. 15:20).

So it is a living Christ we have today. A Christ alive!

A Christ alive—no mere shadow Christ of legend and myth.

A Christ alive—no hypothetical Christ of sentimental conjuring.

A Christ alive—no immanent Christ of nature.

A Christ alive—no pale Christ of historical imagination.

A Christ alive—no mere dream Christ of culture and romance.

A Christ alive—no mere heroic Christ of the poet's imagination.

A Christ alive—no mere artistic Christ of the painter's dreamy conception.

A Christ alive—no cold marble Christ of the sculptor's chisel.

A Christ alive—no mere ivory Christ on a crucifix.

A Christ alive—no dead-figure Christ protected by a creedal sarcophagus.

A Christ alive—no mere eulogized Christ of the orator's post-mortem rhetoric.

A Christ alive—today's Christ, no radiant apparition Christ of yesterday.

A Christ alive—no coffined Christ of the embalmer's art.

Alive is our great Christ—linking the exploits of the fathers to the achievements of the children, acknowledging no mastery in hostile circumstances, offering the inexhaustible fountains of his strength, rejuvenating and transforming human lives, vitalizing the hidden mysteries of our own being, lightening our loads and brightening our roads.

We must think, moreover, of

III. The Reality of Our Own Resurrection.

Jesus said: "Because I live, ye shall live also."

Paul, the Apostle, said: "For as in Adam all die, even so in Christ shall all be made alive" (1 Cor. 15:22).

The pulse of immortality will give forth vibrations in the grave. The sheeted dead shall come forth—the dead in Christ first. God will drag the deep for his beloved. God will ransack the tomb and torture the mountains for his own; but He will find us and bring us up to the glorious victory. And we shall come up with perfect eyes, with perfect hands, with perfect feet, with perfect body—all our weakness left behind. The resurrection of our bodies is embraced in the work of redemption. And as Jesus' resurrection was necessary to complete the work of redemption He came to perform, so by a parity of reason our resurrection is necessary to complete the work with reference to us. And He will complete it, never you fear!

As believers we are not in our sins. We are emancipated children of grace. They who have fallen asleep in Christ have not perished. They opened their eyes in the Saviour's presence, and in the presence of his loveliness their Heaven was begun. Our horizon shines with the light of eternal hope! The glory of the resurrection is ours!

Ours is the inheritance incorruptible and undefiled. Listen to the heartbeat of the Apostle Peter across the centuries and may we join with him in saying, "Blessed be the God and Father of our Lord Jesus Christ, which according to his abundant mercy hath begotten us again unto a lively hope by the resurrection of Jesus Christ from the dead, to an inheritance incorruptible, and undefiled, and that fadeth not away, reserved in heaven for you, who are kept by the power of God through faith unto salvation ready to be revealed in the last time" (1 Pet. 1:3-5).

Robert G. Lee

178   *THE OTHER SIDE OF DEATH*

That disciple whom Jesus loved saith unto Peter, It is the Lord.   JOHN 21:7

In Jesus' reappearance after the resurrection, nothing is more evident than that the passage through death had wrought no essential change upon His humanity. He showed the same care-taking toward the disciples, the same authority over their life and work, the same spirit of close and holy companionship, as before. "Go tell my brethren that they depart into Galilee, and there shall they see me" (Matt. 28:10). "Come and break your fast." He had laid down His life, and had taken it again.

Shall we not learn from Him who thus became the first-fruits of those that slept, the truth of the identity of personal being, and the persistence of love, here and on the other side of death? Said Bernard of Clairvaux, in the funeral sermon for his brother Gerard: "Thou hast discarded thine infirmities but not thine affection. 'Love never faileth'; thou wilt not forget me at the last."

What is it that makes one's friend dear, or one's own life precious? Not circumstances, not place and time, not the tie of outward association, not the flesh: these are but the treasure-box in which lies the untold wealth. It is the real human self that gives the transcendent worth to life and love. And over his personal self death has no power. Out of the divinely appointed sleep it will awake the same. Death is not the loss of personality. There are those whom I long with inexpressible longing to see again. The time that has intervened, with its long dreamy succession of days and nights, since they went away, has not dimmed the image of them I hold in my heart. Often has my spirit been prone to cry out with tears, that even for one short hour I might see their faces, and talk with them about many things, as in the days of long-ago. How welcome would they be this moment at my side!

> Whatever change the years have wrought,
> I find not yet one lonely thought
> That cries against my wish for them.

My Father and my God, Thou hast awakened this love and longing,
unsubdued by time or death. Thou hast given me these brothers and
sisters of the soul. Are they not in Thy keeping there, in the world
of spiritual realities, as I in this fleeting world of flesh and time? Let
me meet not another, but themselves again.

John A. Kern

179   THE REALITY OF THE UNSEEN WORLD

I ascend unto my Father, and your Father; and to my God, and your
God.   JOHN 20:17

I often think that there is some faint echo of the power of Jesus'
resurrection when for the first time the death of a dear friend comes
into a man's life and makes it thenceforth different, never again what
it has been before. I do not mean the mere soberness and solemnity
which the whole thought of living from that hour assumes; I do not
allude to the mere sadness of bereavement, but I speak of that new
sense of reality in the world beyond the grave which comes to all of
us when for the first time we can think of one who has been intimate
in our interests as having gone there and sat down in the intimacy of
its interests, which have heretofore been so foreign to us and so far
away. Heaven has at once an association with us. We have a relation
there. One name is known in its mysterious streets, and so its streets
become less mysterious and remote to us.

It is somewhat as when a mother in some little country village sends
her boy to the great city, and at once feels familiar with the great city
because somewhere, lost in among its hurrying thousands, her boy is
there. His familiar life, transported to it, seems to make it familiar.
She feels as if she knew all about it. She talks of it with a kind of affection, as if it were almost her home, because it is the home of one
she loves. She catches every mention of it as if it were a message meant
for her. To go there is the constant dream of her life, and she feels
as if when she came there she would know at once the streets in which
her heart has had its home so long. So when a dear friend dies and
goes to heaven, heaven at once catches and naturalizes into itself all
our love for him. We read about it as if we knew it, and when we
think of going there ourselves we think of it as going home, because
our heart has had its home there so long .

It is not evident, then, from this what it was that Jesus did for all
the world, and what it was His desire to do for all of us, by His resur-

rection? First, by His life and death He had made the closest appeal that ever has been made to the human heart. He had taught man to love Him. He had called out the deepest and tenderest affection. With all this He passed down into the grave. We saw Him go in at the black door. We watched and waited after He had disappeared, till at last from a region that before had been to us like a land of ghosts, the region beyond the grave, the land of those who live again, we saw Him come out, still clothed with our affection, still bearing our hearts with Him.

At once that strange land lost its ghostliness. He was there, not changed, but still such a one as we could love. His life there made it all real to us. We understood Him when He said, "I ascend unto my Father, and your Father; and to my God, and your God." They were ours as well as His. We knew them as ours by knowing them as His. Already, just as the mother in her village lives yet in the great city, and her life is different because her child is there; as the friend lives in heaven while he is still on the earth, and his life is altered and is happier and higher because his friend has gone to bliss, so the true Christian lives in the spiritual world in which Christ is, even while he lives still in the body. His life is different this side the veil because his heart has passed through with his risen Saviour to that now familiar realm of life that lies beyond. In Paul's wonderful words, he is "risen with Christ." In the words of our collect for Ascension Day, which have the whole truth in them, "Like as he does believe our Lord Jesus Christ to have ascended into the heavens, so he also in heart and mind thither ascends and with Him continually dwells."

Phillips Brooks

H. THE GOD OF ALL COMFORT

Blessed be God . . . the God of all comfort; who comforteth us in all our tribulation. 2 CORINTHIANS 1:3-4

The God of Jesus and of Paul is a God of comfort. Paul, in writing to the Corinthians, said, "Blessed be God . . . the God of all comfort; who comforteth us in all our tribulation."

The problem of suffering is a universal problem. No one can escape it. "Man is born to trouble, as the sparks fly upward (Job 5:7). It is an ancient problem. Job faced it in the long ago. Job was one of earth's saints who lived in the early twilight of God's revelation to man. He was sore troubled. He was wealthy, but he lost his wealth. He had a family of beautiful children, but he lost them one and all. He was strong and robust, but he lost his health. He had a wife and friends, but he lost their sympathy. His heart was broken.

Where could he go? To whom could he flee for comfort? Who could heal his broken heart? Who could satisfy his soul and bring peace to his troubled breast? There was only One, and that One was God. Hence, turning away from human sympathy and help, he raised the cry that through all centuries has come from the heart of man: "Oh that I knew where I might find him!" (Job 23:3).

Today we are confronted with the same problem that Job faced centuries and centuries ago. Why, if God be Father, is the world full of pain? Why, if God be love, do the innocent suffer? Why is it that in this world we have tribulation? Why are our loved ones taken from us, sometimes so suddenly that they have scarcely time to say goodbye? Why are these pathetic lines of Longfellow so sadly true?

> There is no flock, however watched and tended,
> But one dead lamb is there!
> There is no fireside, howso'er defended,
> But has one vacant chair.[1]

These are vital questions which touch every human heart, and we can but say there is One and, only one, who can help us solve the prob-

[1] From "Resignation" by Henry Wadsworth Longfellow.

lem of human suffering. There is only one who can bring light out of darkness; there is only one who can heal the heart that is broken by grief or who can bring peace to the troubled soul. And that one is God, the God of whom Paul spoke when he said, "Blessed be God . . . the God of all comfort."

I commend you to this God of all comfort. He is a God who never fails. He did not fail Christ. He did not fail Paul. He did not fail our fathers and mothers, and He will not fail you.

When Moses was about to bid a final farewell to the Israelites, he said to them, "The eternal God is thy refuge, and underneath are the everlasting arms" (Deut. 33:27). These words form one of the finest expressions of faith to be found anywhere in the language or literature of men. They were true when they were first uttered. They are true today. They will be true always. "The eternal God is thy refuge." Have faith in Him. Jesus, speaking to His disciples on that sad and tragic night in which He was betrayed, said, "Ye believe in God, believe also in me" (John 14:1). That is what we need today—faith in the God revealed by Christ, faith to believe that He remembereth his children, and that "all things work together for good to them that love God" (Rom. 8:28).

> Not now but in the coming years,
> It may be in the better land,
> We'll read the meaning of our tears
> And there, sometime, we'll understand.

Somebody has well said, "I feel that if I can believe in God, I shall have all I need." How true this is! To believe in God is the sublimest and most comforting fact in all the world.

James L. Gardiner

181   *EYES TOWARD THE ETERNAL*

So I never lose heart . . . because I keep my eyes not on what is seen but what is unseen. For what is seen is transitory, but what is unseen is eternal.   2 CORINTHIANS 4:16, 18 (GOODSPEED)

Nowhere do we need to be reminded of this truth more than in the presence of death. Even those who watch and wait are never fully prepared for its coming.

In its more obvious consequences, death is complete and final. A familiar form passes from sight, a handclasp ceases, a voice becomes silent. Those who remain must face far-reaching changes and readjustments. A friend, speaking an honest mind from the depths of a paralyzing bereavement, exclaimed: "O the terrible finality of it all!"

Death seemingly is cruel, complete, final. Yet we are loath to close the book of life at this point. In our grief we must never overlook the affirmation of faith that death, for the one passing through the valley of the shadows, is but an incident, an event in an ever-ongoing personal experience with Christ.

For those who love God, death is but a step in an unending adventure. It finds expression in a wonderful poem:

> Build thee more stately mansions, O my soul,
>   As the swift seasons roll!
>   Leave thy low-vaulted past!
> Let each new temple, nobler than the last,
> Shut thee from heaven with a dome more vast,
>   Till thou at length are free,
> Leaving thine outgrown shell by life's unresting sea![1]

And death brings, for those of us who remain, the distinctive service of helpfulness. The old Greeks, in whose language much of our New Testament was written, discovered that if a person really cared about the circumstances of his fellows, he might enter vicariously into that person's experience. They called this *syn-pathos*, meaning "with suffering." From it comes our great word "sympathy." By means of sympathy we may enter into the minds and hearts of those who suffer and share their experience.

The old Latins, in whose language much of the history of the early church was written, discovered one thing more. When sympathy was unfeigned and sincere, a miracle in response from the bereaved was wrought. This they called *con-fortis*, meaning "together strong." From it comes our great word "comfort."

As we close ranks about the sorrowing, they lift their faces, smile through their tears, take a fresh hold on life, and together we carry on. Just as the locks of a canal lift a boat to the higher levels of sailing, so it is here. Thus may we think of death! Thus may we seek to serve!

> By faith sometime this bit of service small
> We shall discover helped to build
> The greater structure God hath willed.[2]
>   *Thomas Alfred Williams*

[1] From "The Chambered Nautalis" by Oliver Wendell Holmes.
[2] From "The Mystery" by Edgar A. Guest.

182   *DEATH BECOMES LIFE*

Seek him that maketh the seven stars and Orion, and turneth the shadow of death into the morning. . . . The Lord is his name. AMOS 5:8

Blessed be God, even the Father of our Lord Jesus Christ, the Father of mercies, and the God of all comfort; who comforteth us in all our tribulation, that we may be able to comfort them which are in any trouble, by the comfort wherewith we ourselves are comforted of God. 2 CORINTHIANS 1:3-4

How blessed we are that we have a God of comfort to whom we can turn in hours such as this. How grateful we are that in His provision for us He has given unto us loved ones and friends. Certainly their companionship, their sympathy, and their many deeds of kindness mean much when we are called to walk through the valley of sorrow.

The God of comfort has also given unto us the gift of memory. That is a precious gift, for through it we remember and relive the pleasant experiences of the past. Through it we find comfort and help in the hours of sorrow and loneliness.

Our greatest source of comfort is in God Himself: His presence, His peace, His promises, His power. He has said: "The Lord is nigh unto them that are of a broken heart" (Ps. 34:18). With what assurance and hope He speaks through His Word:

The Lord is my light and my salvation; whom shall I fear? the Lord is the strength of my life; of whom shall I be afraid? . . . I had fainted, unless I had believed to see the goodness of the Lord in the land of the living. Wait on the Lord: be of good courage, and he shall strengthen thine heart: wait, I say, on the Lord. (Ps. 27:1, 13-14)

God is our refuge and strength, a very present help in trouble. (Ps. 46:1)

He that dwelleth in the secret place of the most High shall abide under the shadow of the Almighty. I will say of the Lord, He is my refuge and my fortress: my God; in him will I trust. (Ps. 91:1-2)

I will lift up mine eyes unto the hills, from whence cometh my help. My help cometh from the Lord, which made heaven and earth. (Ps. 121:1-2)

Let not your heart be troubled: ye believe in God, believe also in me. In my Father's house are many mansions: if it were not so, I would have told you. I go to prepare a place for you. And if I go and prepare a place for you, I will come again, and receive you unto myself; that where I am there ye may be also. And whither I go ye know, and the way ye know. Thomas saith unto him, Lord, we know not whither thou goest; and how can we know the way? Jesus saith unto him, I am the way, the truth, and the life: no man cometh unto the Father, but by me. (John 14:1-6)

David said, "When my heart is overwhelmed: lead me to the rock that is higher than I" (Ps. 61:2). There is no time in life when we recognize our helplessness more than in the hour of death. There are so many things we would like to do and so little we can do. In our insufficiency we are glad to have a God, who is higher than we are, to whom we can turn for His sufficiency. He who had the power to make the seven stars and Orion is the only one who has the power to help us in a time like this. He alone can turn the shadow of death into the morning of life.

God turneth the shadow of death into the morning of rest. After one has gone through the weariness of the flesh and the sufferings of a lingering illness, how wonderful it is that "he giveth his beloved sleep" (Ps. 127:2). How we would like to have our loved ones remain with us, and yet we would not bring them back, even if we could, if coming again to us they would have to continue to suffer. God has said, "There remaineth therefore a rest to the people of God" (Heb. 4:9). God has said, "Blessed are the dead which die in the Lord from henceforth: Yea, saith the Spirit, that they may rest from their labors" (Rev. 14:13).

We are grateful to a God who can give rest and peace in the place of the weariness and the sufferings of this life. The Scriptures teach that at death the spirit of the Christian goes to be with the Lord. Paul wrote, "To be absent from the body, and to be present with the Lord" (2 Cor. 5:8).

> Oh, say, "He has arrived!"
> And not that "He has gone."
> May every thought of him
> Be in that Land of Morn.
>
> Arrived! To hear His voice
> And see His welcoming smile;
> And then to greet again
> Those he has lost a while.
>
> Arrived! To tread no more
> The weary path of pain,
> Nor feel the waning strength
> The body feels, again.
>
> To be forever free
> From all that limits love,
> In joyful service thus
> He now may tireless move.

Then say not, "He has gone,"
Nor think of him as dead;
But say, "In the Father's House
He has arrived"—instead.

God turneth the shadow of death into the morning of the resurrection. In Old Testament times man hoped that there was life after death and groped after it. But he never was certain. "Jesus Christ, who hath abolished death, and hath brought life and immortality to light through the gospel" (2 Tim. 1:10). Christ said: "I am the resurrection, and the life: he that believeth in me, though he were dead, yet shall he live" (John 11:25). In the Christian there is a glorious resurrection. In ancient times the mourners buried their loved ones facing the west, toward the sunset, darkness, and night; but after Christ arose from the dead Christians buried thier loved ones facing the east, toward the sunrise, light, and the dawn of a new day.

God turneth the shadow of death into the morning of rewards. "Precious in the sight of the Lord is the death of His saints" (Ps. 116: 15), exclaimed the Psalmist. Death, for God's saints, is a homecoming, wherein He reveals those things which He "hath prepared for them who love Him" (1 Cor. 2:9).

The Lord hath graciously drawn aside the curtain of Heaven that we may know that it is a place of great beauty and of a blessed fellowship. Many are the rewards which God shall give unto His faithful children. In 1 Corinthians 3:14 we read: "If any man's work shall abide . . . he shall receive a reward." In Hebrews 6:10 we read: "For God is not unrighteous to forget your work and labor of love." In Revelation 14:13 we read: "Blessed are the dead who die in the Lord . . . their works do follow them."

Amos tells us that the One who can turn the shadow of death into the morning of rest, resurrection, and heavenly rewards is the Lord: "The Lord . . . is his name" (Amos 4:13). Therefore, he says, "Seek Him." During our lives here we should seek Him, His forgiveness, His grace, and His help, so that when we pass through the shadow of death we may enter into "sunrise with Jesus for eternity."

Vance H. Webster

183 *THE SOUL'S ASSURANCE*

Jesus saith unto her, Mary. JOHN 20:16

Here is a word to a woman by a Man who knew what life and death are all about. Anyone looking for ·comfort and consolation in any dark hour, may well look for them in such a person.

It teaches two things. First, God is nearest in time of sorrow and trial. When Moses was about to pass from the sight of his people, he said to them: "This commandment . . . is not hidden from thee this day, neither is it far off. It is not in heaven, that thou shouldst say, Who shall go up for us to heaven and bring it unto us. . . . Neither is it beyond the sea, that thou shouldst say, Who shall go over the sea for us, and bring it unto us, that we may hear it, and do it? But the word is very nigh unto thee, in thy mouth, and in thy heart, that thou mayest do it." God does not leave you in your sorrow. You do not need to implore His help. Just look into your heart, and hold out your hand, and you will find Him there.

A little picture called *The Presence* hangs on the wall in my home. It shows a beautiful cathedral with its high altar, its long nave, and row upon row of empty chairs. Like all cathedrals, the door is open to anyone who may wish to enter and pray. A burdened soul has wandered in, and is kneeling quietly and penitently at the back of the last row of chairs. But scarcely has the worshiper knelt in prayer when a second figure emerges through the doorway and stands directly behind the kneeling penitent. It is Jesus come to give comfort and encouragement in the hour of the penitent's distress and to assure the soul of his Divine presence. Anyone can discern quickly enough that Jesus does not move up to the altar or to the pulpit where the priest and prophet of God ministers, for there is no ministering servant there, but He stands beside the worshiper and moves with him in the hurly-burly of life. Was Mary's soul still troubled? She knew she was not deserted when she experienced her Lord's presence.

Then, too, it says that death is not the end. Walking in fellowship with God in this life is good, but there is a fellowship to be revealed greater than anything one can experience here. Mary would not need the physical face of Jesus to prove His immortality. She would know that a personality so vibrant, so vital, so Divine, as that of Jesus, could not be conquered by death. She would know

> Though dead, not dead;
> Not gone, though fled;
> Not lost, though vanished.
> In the great gospel and the tree creed,
> He is yet risen indeed;
> Christ is yet risen.[1]

[1] From "Easter Day (Naples 1849)" by Arthur Hugh Clough.

What a contrast between the restless, perplexed, and ever-inquiring spirits of those today who go seeking evidence at the hands of clair-voyants and spiritualists, and those whose spirits are merged with the quiet assurance of Jesus who said, "Let not your heart be troubled: ye believed in God, believe also in me" (John 14:1). These latter, even in the face of the greatest disasters, the loss of loved ones and the grief that comes with disappointed hopes, never sit quietly in any garden without meeting their Master.

> I see His blood upon the rose
> And in the stars the glory of His eyes,
> His body gleams amid eternal snows,
> His tears fall from the skies.
>
> I see His face in every flower;
> The thunder and the singing of the birds
> Are but His voice—and carven by His power
> Rocks are His written words.
>
> All pathways by His feet are worn,
> His strong heart stirs the ever-beating sea,
> His crown of thorns is twined with every thorn,
> His cross is every tree.[1]

Frederick Keller Stamm

184   *COME UNTO ME*

Come unto me.   MATTHEW 11:28

Again we have met to pay our tribute of love to one who has shared life with us, and who now has laid *his* burdens down. Reverently do we come, and in silence, as we face the great mystery. Deep within our hearts is the desire to share in sympathy with the ones who most in-timately are bereft, and to renew again the hope we share as Chris-tians. To love is to enter through a door that leads to life's meaning. To lose a loved one is to throw us back upon the deepest faith we possess. How much we are, in times like this, like little children lost in a dark wood. It is then that we long to hear a well-loved voice call-ing us back to the light.

For many generations the Bible has been such a voice. When our fathers were grieved, they turned to the Word of God for strength, and so may we. The Psalmists and the Prophets, Paul and Jesus, speak words of comfort out of the deep to the deeps. So may we listen to Him who knew life as none other ever knew it, and who spoke words

[1] "I See His Blood upon the Rose" by Joseph Mary Plunkett.

of hope we all may hear and believe. "Come unto me," He said, "and I will give you rest." And rest is good.

Whatever the mystery of this hour may be, rest is at the heart of it. Here is a boon that comes at last to every pilgrim of time. How rest renews a child after a busy day at his games. How rest refreshes a man after the strain of a day of work. But complete rest seldom is found, however much it be prayed for. There always is a residue of weariness. Then comes the end of days, the laying down of the burdens of time, and the blessedness of eternity, with rest as God's good gift.

And Jesus promises His gift of peace. How often the heart is disquieted with questions that are not answered. The strain of effort and the unfulfillment of hope are common experiences. To fret at times is a burden we all bear. The spirit becomes a troubled sea and we yearn for a quiet harbor behind some sheltering headland. If the peace of time be partial, the peace of eternity is complete, like the peace of an ineffable sunset when all the west is hammered gold, and a voice whispers to our spirits, and we are freed for the hour from the strains. "My peace I give unto you" (John 14:27), says Jesus, and we may trust Him to the end.

The homing instinct is in all living things. "I want to go home," cries the child when night comes. "Take me home," calls the old man when away from well-loved scenes. Among all the words of the language "home" is one of the dearest. But home is something more than a roof or walls, or carpets on the floor, or the sound of dear voices. Home is a sense of security. It is being safe behind eternal battlements that keep pain away. It is a faith that love will heal the final hurt and speak the last word.

So beneath the loneliness of the hour may there be an abiding gratitude: gratitude to God for the one we remember today and the gratitude for the hope in immortality which faith in our Lord renews within us. So may we go our ways, knowing that our friend is with God, where rest and peace and home are His good gifts.

John Greenleaf Whittier, the Quaker poet, gives expression to the mood of us all as we remember the past and think of God:

> I cannot think that thou are far,
> Since near at need the angels are,
> And when the sunset gates unbar
> Shall I not see thee, waiting, stand,
> And white against the evening star
> The welcome of thy beckoning hand.

Walter Amos Morgan

185   *TO HEAL THE BROKENHEARTED*

He hath sent me to heal the brokenhearted. LUKE 4:18

When Jesus was asked to read the Scripture lesson in his home synagogue in Nazareth, he turned to the passage in Isaiah which, better than any other, described the basis of his ministry. One of the reasons He had come was "to heal the brokenhearted." He was an ambassador of God's comfort.

Healing was always an important part of His task. Take away the healing miracles from the Gospel record and a large and essential element is lost. In all His healing work, it was evident that He went beyond the body to the spirit. That what He wanted most to touch and to help was man's soul. Jesus was concerned with the whole man, and into the deep and mysterious areas of the emotional life He was especially eager to bring the strength and love of God.

One marvels at the way our Lord understood people. He realized the burdens they were carrying, as though every one of them had rested directly upon Him. No more understanding a summons has ever been given to the overborne than His, "Come unto me, all ye that labor and are heavy laden, and I will give you rest" (Matt. 11:28). And as His own life developed He became ever more able to help others. The ostracism from His church and tradition, the hatred of the religious leaders, the closing in of a work which He had hoped would expand and flourish—all this deepened and saddened the Master's spirit and helped Him understand the sharpest wounds of the human heart. He could be of such help to others because He understood them, because, whatever their need, He had that need too.

One of the ways in which He "healed the brokenhearted" was to help men keep sorrow in its proper place. He never lets us lose our perspective, no matter how "overmastering" some of our experiences may seem. Sorrow can seem to blot out all the rest of reality, and nothing is real save this bitter pain, this awful loss. It is then that Christ reminds us of what else is true in life. In our loss, we are to remember the good gifts which God has provided. In our separation, we are to recall the days of blessed fellowship. In our awareness of mortality, we are to think also of eternal life. Grief must not be allowed to obscure all else; it must see itself as under the wide arch of Heaven and know itself to be a part of the vast range of human experience. This is simply to say that Jesus bade men put their sorrows in the setting of their faith in God. "In my Father's house are many mansions. . . .

I go to prepare a place for you" (John 14:2), and death becomes only
part of a great journey, always under the eyes and in the love of the
Father toward whose home one moves. Our spirits are quieted when
we think of the way the sorrows of life form part of the whole of life,
in which the love of God is ever present and ever strong.

Moreover, He "heals the brokenhearted" by persuading men that
they are not alone, that they have not been isolated from the rest of
mankind by what they have gone through. This is the greatest burden
which comes with grief—the burden of loneliness. "I, I only am left,"
is the natural feeling. There may be many people near by, but they
do not seem real. They have not felt what I am feeling; therefore they
do not count, they cannot help. A great wall seems to rise between the
afflicted heart and the rest of humankind.

The path back to the human is by way of the divine. It is Christ
who takes our hand and puts it again into the hand of our brother. In
a simple and beautiful act from the cross He revealed this truth. Two
figures bowed with grief are at the foot of the cross. They are among
the small circle of the brokenhearted who kept watch on Calvary. One
is a woman, the mother of Jesus; the other is John, the disciple whom
Jesus loved. Each is alone, isolated in grief, cut off from all others.
Jesus turns to Mary, and says, "Woman, behold thy son!" He turns to
John, and says, "Behold thy mother!" And it is recorded that the
disciple "took her unto his own home" (John 19:27). Alone in their
grief, they had found one another and their fellowmen, *through Him.*
Thus, in our time, by keeping us aware of one another, Christ heals
the brokenhearted.

Phillips P. Elliott

FOR A SERVICE MAN

186   *GOD SHARES OUR SORROW*

He that spared not his own Son, but delivered him up for us all.
ROMANS 8:32

Our reaction to death is conditioned by the way in which death
comes into our homes and lives.

If death comes at the end of a long and useful life, it comes as a
welcome guest. I have known older folk who longed for death, who
prayed for it. Their bodies were old and weak with age. They felt
helpless and inactive. Their choicest friends had gone and they were

lonely here. They looked forward to the coming of death as one might anticipate the dawn of a new day.

If death comes at the end of a long illness, during which suffering has become increasingly severe, it comes as a welcome guest. Sometimes the clearest evidence we have of the mercy of God is when He lays upon a body racked with pain the soothing hand of death.

The coming of death, however, is not nearly so welcome when it comes into our midst suddenly and with startling alarm. We are left stunned. When death takes from us young life with potentialities unrealized and years of life unfulfilled, we are left bewildered. Our hearts cry out, why? why? why? And our faith is tested to the breaking point.

We shall keep steady in an hour such as this if we seek some message from God. What does He say to our anguished hearts in this trying moment?

I think that He would remind us that length of years does not always mean completeness of life. Some lives are fulfilled in a much shorter time than others. Some of the finest things of earth do not last long. The most beautiful flowers last but a season. Man seems to place more inportance on length of days than does God. He seems to be more concerned with life's quality than with its durability. He called unto Himself His only begotten Son after He had journeyed the paths of this world for less than half of the years allotted by the Psalmist of old.

And I think God would remind us that one of the best evidences we have of quality in life is the willingness to lose life in fulfilling some worthy purpose. When a person plunges into a great cause, and believes so deeply that he is willing to lose his life for it, he has achieved a nobility of life, a heroism, which is not limited by the barriers of time. That sort of life is timeless. It is immortal.

Then I think God would remind us that such a sorrow as we face is not experienced by ourselves alone. Our grief is shared by many. Some of us in this very room know what it means to lose a son. The hearts of this entire community are suffering with you today. Homes in every land are pierced by the sorrow and pain we feel. And more especially, too, does God share our sorrow.

Sir Harry Lauder lost a son in the first World War. One evening, we are told, he was walking down the street with a small lad at his side. They passed a home where a service flag, bearing a gold star, hung in the window. The boy inquired what that meant. Sir Harry told him that the parents in that home had lost a son at the front. They walked on for some time in silence and finally they saw the evening star just appearing on the distant horizon. "Look," the boy said, "God is hanging out his service flag. The star is gold. He, too, must have lost a son at the front."

God did have a Son who died for humanity in the service of a great ideal. And even as the New Testament tells us, "He spared not his own Son, but delivered him up for us all." That is why God so intimately shares your grief and mine.

Francis W. Trimmer

187   *OUR HOPE IN GOD*

Philip saith unto him, Lord shew us the Father, and it sufficeth us. Jesus saith unto him, Have I been so long time with you, and yet hast thou not known me, Philip? he that hath seen me hath seen the Father; and how sayest thou then, Shew us the Father? JOHN 14:8-9

Every right-thinking man wants to come to the end of his days with a record that will win the commendations, not only of his fellows, but primarily of God. In the presence of death, as in the presence of birth, we probably have an awareness of God such as we have not at any other time. Then it is that we realize our ultimate hope rests not in our own good works, but in the character of the God in whose keeping we are.

We are not left without knowledge of the character of God. Our Bible is a book of discovery, a book of the discovery and of the revealing of the character of God. Abraham, in the door of his tent in the desert, pleading with God to save the city of Sodom, asked a question revealing an insight into the character of God. This insight many of us today have not come fully yet to possess: "Peradventure there be fifty righteous within the city: wilt thou also destroy and not spare the place for the fifty righteous that are therein? That be far from thee to do after this manner, to slay the righteous with the wicked: and that the righteous should be as the wicked, that be far from thee: Shall not the Judge of all the earth do right?" (Gen. 18:24-25). Abraham saw God as the Judge within whose providence naught but that which is right was possible.

Amos discovered God as a god of justice; Hosea discovered God as a God of love. But the greatest discovery and the greatest revelation of the character of God came in Jesus Christ. Jesus discovered God as

His Father and as our Father. In Jesus Christ God is revealed as a Christlike God, a God of sympathy and understanding and love. So in the words of our text, "Jesus saith unto him, Have I been so long time with you, and yet hast thou not known me, Philip? he that hath seen me hath seen the Father." Canon B. H. Streeter said that the question deep down in his heart was whether God could be as good as Jesus Christ, and then declared that out of his heart of hearts came the answer, that God must be as good as Jesus Christ, for the furnace cannot be weaker or feebler than its spark. Our hope is in God, the God of our Lord and Saviour.

The God in whose keeping we are, here and yonder, now and then, is a Father who is ever seeking His own. Surely that is the meaning of the parables of the lost coin, the lost sheep, and the prodigal son. The parable of the prodigal son should not be thought of as the parable of the prodigal son; no, rather, as the parable of the Seeking Father.

To make possible our finding, God as our Father has placed within each one of us "the Father's drawings." And we are persuaded that "the Father's drawings," if not resisted, in the hour of departure from this life will draw us into the Father's House.

Here as we commit to our Father the spirit of *him* whom we have loved long since and lost awhile, may we rest in the assurance that the God and Father of our Lord Jesus Christ does not merely accept from us the one we love; no, rather, God has sought and found *him* and has taken *him* unto His house of many mansions.

Edmund Heinsohn

188   *THE VALLEY OF SHADOW*

Yea, though I walk through the valley of the shadow of death, I will fear no evil: for thou art with me. PSALM 23:4

"The valley of the shadow"—this figure gives us some comforting thoughts about death. It is not a state, an enduring condition, or an abiding-place. It is a passage, a transition, a valley through which we walk. The valley may be darksome and lonely, and infested with evil things; but we do not pitch our tent there; we pass through it to our rest.

In death the spirit leaves the body, and passes out: just as an artizan will leave the workshop at the evening hour, shutting blinds and doors as he passes out to his home, and leaves it deserted and still;

but his voice is to be heard in his home-circle, as he makes glad the wistful hearts that had waited for him; and whose joy had been incomplete till he came.

In Damascus there is a long, dark, narrow lane, ending in a tunnel. It has been there for ages. The traveler descends, and passes through; but on the other side he emerges into the court yard of an oriental palace, flashing with color and sunlight. This is a figure of a believer's death. Christ is called the first born from the dead. Dying is being born, out of the confinement and darkness of earth into the glorious light and liberty of the heavenly life. It is a physical act, which affects the body, but does not touch the faculties or acquirements of the individual soul. "Absent from the body, and present with the Lord" (2 Cor. 5:8). No staying in a state of unconsciousness; but an exodus, a passage, a walking through a brief valley, sunshine on this side, sunshine on that, and just a moment, a parenthesis, a hand-breadth of gloom.

Death is the gate to life. Our beloved are not dead; they are the living, who have passed through death into the presence of the King. And whenever we stand beside our dear ones, called to this exodus, we may address them with words of comfort and of hope: "Go forth, O Christian soul, from this world, in the name of God Almighty, who created thee; in the name of Jesus Christ, the Son of the Living God, who suffered for thee; in the name of the Holy Ghost, who was poured out for thee!"

F. B. Meyer

189   *GOD MAKES A DIFFERENCE*

Whither shall I go from thy spirit? or whither shall I flee from thy presence? PSALM 139:7

Surely goodness and mercy shall follow me *all* the days of my life. PSALM 23:6

A father, writing to a son serving in the overseas armed forces, closed his letter with these words: "Remember, my son, no one is ever far from God."

It appears that this faith must have been in the mind of the Psalmist when he put down these words: "Whither shall I go from thy spirit? or whither shall I flee from thy presence?" For these verses are not saying that God is a superpoliceman who keeps us under His eye. Rather they tell us that man cannot go where God is not. We can never remove ourselves from His love and care. As Whittier says in "The Eternal Goodness":

> I know not where His islands lift
> Their fronded palms in air;
> I only know I cannot drift
> Beyond His love and care.

Thus these words of our Scripture should be of great comfort and assurance in times of deep sorrow. And while in this kind of a world we may not be able to escape sorrow and suffering, yet we are confident that we need not face these experiences alone. God is standing by!

Try to picture Jesus going into the garden of Gethsemane and finding there only a vast indifference. Christian faith says that God is here and His eternal purpose comprehends all life.

One day I stood where I should have been able to see the Mount of the Holy Cross in western Colorado, but clouds and mist shut out my view. Yet I was reminded of these words from one I know who loved the mountains: "You always know the mountains are there, even behind the clouds, and that makes a difference."

Today when clouds of sorrow seem to hide the face of God, we know such is not the case, for we cannot be where God is not, and that makes the difference between hope and despair.

Let that faith be the sustaining factor in this experience, assuring us that as God has been with us in all our yesterdays, He will be with us in our unknown tomorrows. As an old saint of God put it: "O Lord, help me to understand that you won't let anything come my way that you and I can't handle together."

The man of faith finds strength and courage even in life's darkest hours because God is with him. "Surely goodness and mercy shall follow me *all* the days of my life. . . ." Because this is our faith today we can say:

> I will not doubt, though all my ships at sea
> Come drifting home with broken masts and sails;
> I shall believe the Hand which never fails,
> For seeming evil worketh good for me;
> And, though I weep because these sails are battered,
> Still will I cry, while my best hopes lie shattered,
> "I trust in Thee!"[1]

Warren S. Bainbridge

[1] From "Faith" by Ella Wheeler Wilcox.

190   *THE GIFT, THE GRIEF, THE GLORY*

The Lord gave, and the Lord hath taken away; blessed be the name of the Lord.   JOB 1:21

We are gathered to pay tribute to a departed loved one and neighboring friend. In the perplexity of this occasion we can find our answers, comforts, and instruction only in the Word of God. Cold and meaningless are the philosophies of men today. Made weak by the breaking burden of grief, we need the strength of eternal wisdom.

In such a dilemma, ah, even worse, Job said, "The Lord gave, and the Lord hath taken away; blessed be the name of the Lord." It is easy to go part way with Job in this statement, but if in his deep and multiplied sorrow he could bless God, we do well to examine what he had that we today so sorely need.

"The Lord gave." We are thinking of life today and so we are quick to agree that all life is a gift of God. All the facts of life and the reality of living is a reminder of the gracious gift of our loving God. We are not the evolvement of matter nor the accident of nature. We are created beings of God. What is Job saying, God has given? This physical life we so enjoy and yearn to hold is a gift of God.

God's second gift is the gift of happiness. We recall many hours of happiness with our departed loved one and friend. The ability to do the things that make for happiness and the capacity to enjoy it is a function of the inner man, which means that this, too, is a gift of God. Happiness adds a quality to life. Happiness helps to make others better. Happy people are the best loved and most sought. God gave us happiness that we might be better people.

The third gift of God we think about in this memorial service is God's gift of salvation. "Thanks be unto God for His unspeakable gift" (2 Cor. 9:15). Of what value is life if there is no salvation? Could there possibly be happiness without salvation? We know that God's gift of salvation through His Son as the Saviour of the world is what makes life worth-while and that which gives us such joy. Salvation is God's gift to dry our tears, to lift the burden of death from our hearts, and to comfort all who mourn. Fret not, there is hope.

"The Lord taketh away." Hardly have we, like Job, listed the gifts of God than we remember that all these things seem vain today. God

has taken away. There have been many other losses and deep sorrows in life, but now has come the greatest loss and the bitterest grief. The Lord has taken a loved one and a home has been broken.

God has taken a life! We believe that He created life and we must confess that He has a right to do with life as is well pleasing to Him. That which He let loose for awhile to function and be called life He has called home for another and more glorious purpose.

It, therefore, naturally follows that God has taken back the second of His gifts, happiness. We feel with Robert Burns,

> But pleasures are like poppies spread:
> You seize the flow'r, it's bloom is shed;
> Or like the snow falls, in the river,
> A moment white then melts for ever.[1]

For there is no happiness in death. There are only tears and troubled hearts and puzzled thoughts. We wonder if God has forgotten and forsaken us. Like babes we cry and ask God if He does not know how dearly we love the flesh and all the things attached to it.

Then we recall His third gift which He has never removed and which none can take from us. As we remember the gift of salvation, hope shines through the gloom in the valley of the shadow of death. God has taken a life. God has given tears, but God has not forgotten us. In Christ Jesus we have a salvation sure and steadfast, eternal and blessed.

Therefore, we join Job and say, *"Blessed be the name of the Lord."* If physical life is taken, eternal life is just beginning. If joy gives way to grief in this life, we know there are no tears, no grief, no weeping, no heartaches in Heaven.

Since all life is in the hand of God, eternal life must be so much better. Real happiness is not of the earth, but of Heaven. Our tears wash away the veil of grief and doubt, and, by faith, we see a better life, a certain way, a sure hope.

Faith will overcome grief. True resignation to God will bring assurance and peace. God with His supreme will determined our coming into this world and our leaving. We had nothing to do with the choice of coming, but we may exit from either side the stage of life. Life was not ours to choose. Eternal life is ours to have or not to have.

[1] From "Tom o' Shanter."

Because we are of the flesh we naturally grieve and sorrow this day. Let us now show the confidence of our faith by our sincere testimony, as we say,

> Blessed be the hand that gives,
> Still blessed when it takes.

Arthur House Stainback

FOR A CHILD

191 *A FATHER'S GRIEF*

I shall go to him, but he shall not return to me. 2 SAMUEL 12:23

If there is any one universally accepted fact, it is the innocence of little children. As we look into the face of a newborn child or watch a youngster at play, we realize that here is life in all its potential sweetness for the babe does not know what evil is, and is incapable of saying, thinking, or doing anything that is wrong. Surely those who have felt the tug of tiny arms and have listened to the early prattle of lisping lips know how precious these younger days are.

In the second book of Samuel there is the unforgettable story of David, King of Israel, overwhelmed with grief when his firstborn babe by Bathsheba is sick unto death. David fasts and prays for seven days and seven nights. He grovels in the dirt; he humiliates the flesh as with all his soul he entreats God to spare the child's life. Those of the royal household fear lest by his deep grief he should unsettle his mind. Then comes the seventh day, and child dies.

"What shall we do?" they asked themselves.

And David seeing them talk, knew that the child was dead. "Is the child dead?" he asked.

"He is dead," they told him.

He then called for water, bathed himself, went to the house of the Lord for prayer, and returned to the palace where he called for food. All was done just as he required, but it was evident that an explanation was expected. Why should David grieve so deeply while the child lived, and then when death came, dress himself, wipe away his tears, and return to the everyday routines of living just as if nothing had happened?

"While the child was yet alive," David explained, "I fasted and wept: for I said, Who can tell whether God will be gracious to me, that the child may live? But now he is dead, wherefore should I fast?

can I bring him back again? I shall go to him, but he shall not return to me."

Few parents indeed are able to look upon the loss of a little one in the way that David did. Many are anxious at the time of critical sickness and then become inconsolable at the time of death. They grieve like "Rachel weeping for her children, and would not be comforted, because they are not" (Matt. 2:18). Some carry for years the very bitterest scars within their hearts for they blame God saying: "He has done a shameful thing to take my babe from me." Yet fortunately, there are others who are able to see that the loss of a tiny life comes as a source of grief to the Almighty Himself, for surely God would have all these precious little ones grow into the fullness both of their physical being and of their character as God-fearing men and women.

In this hour of sadness, may those whose hearts are broken, find comfort in knowing that the little soul in all its innocence and purity has but returned to Him who gave it, and that even now while we mourn he is at peace in his Heavenly Home.

Will A. Sessions, Jr.

192   *WITH THESE WORDS*

But I would not have you to be ignorant, brethren, concerning them which are asleep, that ye sorrow not, even as others which have no hope. For if we believe that Jesus died and rose again, even so them also which sleep in Jesus will God bring with him. For this we say unto you by the word of the Lord, that we which are alive and remain unto the coming of the Lord shall not prevent them which are asleep. For the Lord himself shall descend from heaven with a shout, with the voice of the archangel, and with the trump of God: and the dead in Christ shall rise first: Then we which are alive and remain shall be caught up together with them in the clouds, to meet the Lord in the air: and so shall we ever be with the Lord. Wherefore comfort one another with these words. 1 THESSALONIANS 4:13-18

A mother who lived with a son in another city went to be with the Lord. She was the widow of a Baptist preacher. Her son had shared family devotions, Bible study, and church attendance. But when his father died he drifted away from the things of God. When his mother died, he collapsed.

I sent him a telegram in which I said: "LOVE, PRAYERS AND SYMPATHY. READ FIRST THESSALONIANS FOUR THIRTEEN EIGHTEEN."

·He read the telegram perfunctorily and laid it aside. When the funeral was over and everybody had gone he settled down in the quiet of his home to nurse the greatest sorrow he had ever known. He was going casually through the messages of condolence from friends. When he came to the one which I had sent him he noted the Bible reference, 1 Thessalonians 4:13-18. He turned to the reference in his mother's Bible. On the margin of the Bible beside this reference were these words in his mother's own handwriting: "Our hope of Heaven."

He read and reread this Scripture. He could hear his mother's voice as she had read the Scriptures to him when he was a little boy. Better still he heard the voice of God.

Faith returned. Hope revived. He read many other portions of Scripture, including Psalm 23 and John 14. He wanted to go to the house of God, so long now neglected.

Some months afterwards, while filling preaching engagements in that city, I called this young man and asked if he would come to the hotel and take me to the cemetery to visit his mother's grave. At her tomb in the mausoleum I read this inscription on the door of her room:

I THESSALONIANS 4:13-18.
OUR HOPE OF HEAVEN.

Her son said to me: "That message changed my life. It turned me around. It saved me." And I could see what it had done to him and for him. He was no longer cold and hard, critical and cynical. He was warmhearted, gentle, and kind. His wife had a new husband. His daughter had a new father. His church had a new, faithful, and loyal member.

Since then I have sent the same message and Bible reference to hundreds of others.

I commend all sorrowing saints to the Word of God and "to the word of his grace, which is able to build you up" (Acts 20:32).

"Wherefore comfort one another with these words." Among "these words," in 1 Thessalonians 4:13-18, is the word "sleep." This word comes from the same Greek source as our word "cemetery." When I made this discovery I resolved to stop calling the place where we take our dead, the "cemetery" or the "burying ground" or the "grave yard," but to call it "the sleeping room of the saints."

I find that it is a great comfort to sorrowing loved ones and friends to say that we are taking the body out to the "sleeping room of the saints" to await that glad, glorious morning when Jesus, "the first-fruits of them that slept" (1 Cor. 15:20), comes to awaken them.

I have seen burials in all parts of the world. I have seen Chinese bodies thrown out in the fields for the hogs and the dogs to destroy. I have seen the Hindus in India take their dead to the burning ghats. I have seen the Parsees take the bodies of their dead to the roof of their temple where the vultures swooped down upon them. I have seen an African throw the body of his wife or child into a river.

And all of them did so without any hope of ever seeing their loved ones again. They sang no hymn of hope, but chanted only dirges of despair.

We Christians mourn but not as those who have no hope. Our dead are only asleep and we shall see them again.

> There is no death;
> Our loved ones fall
> And pass away.
> They only await
> The Savior's call;
> To reign in His
> Eternal Day.
>
> *M. E. Dodd*

FOR THOSE WHO SUFFER TRAGIC DEATH

193   *YOU ARE NOT ALONE[1]*

I am not alone, because the Father is with me.   JOHN 16:32

Dear friends, we are assembled in respectful memory of a mother and a son whom we have known and loved and whom we will ever cherish in tender memory. In God's own good time we will know and understand what now is a vast tangle of mystery and loneliness. Both of these came to an untimely death in what will always be a mystery to us. Jesus our Saviour said, "Judge not, that ye be not judged. For with what judgment ye judge, ye shall be judged: and with what measure ye mete, it shall be measured to you again" (Matt. 7:1-2).

One thing we know: had this mother, because of an overload of

---

[1] This message was given at a double funeral service for a mother, who, after a complete nervous and emotional collapse, took the lives first of her twelve-year-old son and then of herself. She was one of the loveliest and most respected members of her church and community. Attending the service were relatives and friends and a large number of children from the Sunday School, the public school, and the scout troop. The pastor considered especially these children who greatly needed guidance in a tender and difficult hour.

cares and responsibilities, come to complete physical exhaustion and
illness, during which she was not like herself, we would have surrounded her with a double measure of love and understanding. There
would have been no condemnation. For similar reasons, human beings
often come to deep mental illness and to complete mental collapse,
which, utterly unpredictable, is often devastating to the person and
disastrous to others.

This, too, we know: for many months she spent long hours, prac-
tically every afternoon, by the bedside of a beloved relative, a victim
of a relentless disease for which our medical science knows no cure.
She suffered, as only love can suffer, with and for her close relative
and the members of the household. Several times she said to me that
she wished she could take the whole burden of pain and anguish
upon herself. Deep was her suffering because her love and sympathy
were genuine. These days of anxiety took a terrific toll of her energies,
more, perhaps, than any of us can measure. During recent months she
has known fears and apprehensions, however baseless, that she herself
was a victim of the same disease and would bring upon her family
a long vigil in terrible suffering through sympathy.

In a moment of deep despondency, when her reason was held
prisoner by paralyzing fear, life ebbed out for mother and son. Only
Eternal God can know the sickness and suffering which had gripped
her mind and spirit. But God *does* know. As for me, I shall always
remember the goodness, the kindness, and the patience which characterized her life. The rest I can safely leave to the Father's love and
mercy.

Let us turn to God the Father and to Christ Jesus our Saviour for
comfort and assurance. When Jesus faced what He knew would be
certain death, He said, "Behold, the hour cometh, yea, is now come,
that ye shall be scattered, every man to his own, and shall leave me
alone: and yet I am not alone, because the Father is with me." We
believe that Jesus is saying now to those whose shock has turned to
bewilderment and grief, "Ye are not alone for the Father is with
you." What a difference this assurance made to Jesus in the dark
gloom of Gethsemane and when He gave His life upon the cross.
What a difference this assurance can make to each of you today. Hear
the Saviour's voice, "Let not your heart be troubled . . . *believe in
God*" (John 14:1). Let not your hearts be troubled today, baffled, distressed beyond comfort, the prisoner of unrelenting grief. Believe
in God the Father, for you are not alone. This is God's sorrow even

more than it is your sorrow. We need not fear if we trust God completely, for death cannot end life. God is the God of life.

A little child in the confusion and perils of traffic in a great city is not afraid as long as he knows his father holds his hand and guides him. So let us, the children of God, grip more firmly the hand of our Heavenly Father, for He will lead us safely through the sorrows which beset us. He is not far from any one of us. This God and Father is with you now and forever. Your loved ones are in His care and keeping, and God is loving, merciful, and just. His judgments are just and they are kind, for they spring from Fatherly understanding. They are not based on partial knowledge and prejudice, the ghost writers of human indictments and verdicts. Lay hold of the promises of your Father and Saviour. Hear God's voice: "Fear thou not; for I am with thee: be not dismayed; for I am thy God: I will strengthen thee; . . . yea, I will uphold thee. . . . When thou passest through the waters, I will be with thee; and through the rivers, they shall not overflow thee . . . for I am the Lord thy God, the Holy One of Israel, thy Saviour . . . I am with thee" (Is. 41:10; 43:2-3, 5).

Bishop Quayle wrote this witness:

> If Thou wilt stay beside me
> When life's mercies turn to dust,
> Then joy and peace abide me,
> And I dwell in perfect trust.

Thomas Moore wrote these precious words:

> Come, ye disconsolate, wher'er you languish,
> Come, at God's altar fervently kneel;
> Here bring your wounded hearts, here tell your anguish—
> Earth has no sorrow that Heaven cannot heal.

> Joy of the desolate, Light of the straying,
> Hope, when all others die, fadeless and pure,
> Here speaks the Comforter, in God's name saying—
> "Earth has no sorrow that Heaven cannot heal."

In the moments of your greatest loneliness remember the words of Jesus, "I am not alone, for the Father is with me." In this great truth He found comfort. In this is your comfort adequate and sure.

Louis H. Kaub

194   *INTO THY HAND*

Into thine hand I commit my spirit. PSALM 31:5

Father, into thy hands I commend my spirit. LUKE 23:46

Since another one among us has laid aside the garment of flesh, we who remain seek fittingly to recognize the completion of a life upon earth. We gather here to reaffirm our faith in God, to bring our tribute of grateful thoughts for the one whom we hold in remembrance, and to dedicate ourselves anew to the ends which make life good.

In this presence we acknowledge the Lordship of God. He alone is "from everlasting to everlasting" (Ps. 90:2). From Him our life comes, by Him it is upheld, and into His keeping we commit the spirits of those who have passed beyond our mortal vision.

This occasion reminds us that this earth is not our lasting dwelling-place. Our bodies do not serve us forever. We know that another has made us and not we ourselves. Through His creative power we have been given life. We are dependent not only on His power to uphold us but on His mercy to forgive us.

In his self-written epitaph, Benjamin Franklin has combined the recognition of the transitoriness of human life with the faith in God who is the source of our hope:

<blockquote>
The Body of
B Franklin Printer,
(Like the Cover of an old Book
Its Contents torn out
And stript of its Lettering and Gilding)
Lies here, Food for Worms,
But the Work shall not be lost;
For it will, (as he believ'd) appear once more,
In a new and more elegant Edition
Revised and corrected,
By the Author.[1]
</blockquote>

At this time we also acclaim the worth of a life faithfully lived. In these moments we spend together, it is fitting that each one should offer his prayer of thanksgiving for the good in the life of the one remembered. Each person can open the book of memory and find there reasons for his own gratitude.

[1] From *Benjamin Franklin* by Carl Van Doren.

Great accomplishments are not necessary to give worth to life. The highest human qualities do not need high station or vast power to come to fruition. Honesty can be exercised in simple transactions. He that is faithful in little is faithful also in much. In the eyes of Jesus, faithfulness is faithfulness whether it characterizes the man in a place of heavy responsibility or the person in some obscure place of duty. To hold our dear ones in grateful remembrance is a fresh reminder that some of God's best gifts to us have come through the people who have entered the intimate circle of our affection and friendship.

The recognition of a life's passing calls also for new dedication on our part. The end of a life on earth summons you and me to consider the ends for which life is to be lived. Those who are followers of Jesus Christ remember that He said: "I am come that they might have life, and that they might have it more abundantly" (John 10:10). Confronted by the fact of death, we again seek for the highest meaning of our human adventure.

The prophet Micah wondered how he could fulfill his highest destiny as a man. He wondered how he could make life good. His severe sense of guilt made him ask whether he ought to sacrifice his firstborn son as an expiation for his sins. To him came this reassuring word: "He hath shewed thee, O man, what is good; and what doth the Lord require of thee, but to do justly, and to love mercy, and to walk humbly with thy God?" (Mic. 6:8).

In these words the prophet has given us some of the main themes to be sounded in the music of a good life. The thoughts and deeds of every day are but variations on these themes.

Similarly, Jesus Christ gave an answer to the man who wanted to know what he had to do to inherit eternal life. This questioner had more in mind than the dimension of life beyond the death of the body. Length of life is meaningless unless the quality of life is worthy. He wanted to know what gave life high significance here and hereafter. Christ held before him the love of God and the love of neighbor as the twin pillars upon which a good life is built: "Thou shalt love the Lord thy God with all thy heart, and with all thy soul, and with all thy strength, and with all thy mind; and thy neighbor as thyself" (Luke 10:27).

In these last offices of faith and love for one who has passed from this life, we dedicate ourselves anew to "the high calling of God in Christ Jesus" (Phil. 3:14). In this resolve we are aware that our best efforts and our best achievements still leave us dependent upon the mercy of a forgiving God. At the end of each day and at the end of an earthly life we entrust our own lives and the lives of our dear ones to God with the Psalmist's words of faith, "Into thine hand I commit my spirit," and with the greater words of assurance of our Saviour, "Father, into thy hands I commend my spirit."

Rolland W. Schloerb

I. PAUL'S PERSUASION

PAUL'S PERSUASION

I am persuaded, that neither death, nor life, . . . shall be able to separate us from the love of God, which is in Christ Jesus our Lord.   ROMANS 8:38-39

The Christian ministry brings grave responsibilities as well as glorious opportunities to those who enter it seriously. We will say nothing to belittle the value of any part of the pastoral office, but again and again it has been found that the greatest testing has come when we have stood in the presence of death.

One thing we quickly discover is that though in one sense death is always the same, it comes in many different forms. There are times when it brings a sense of relief, when, for example, illness has been long and painful, almost intolerable not only to him who suffers but also to those who faithfully minister to him. There are other times when it is as natural as the falling of petals when a flower has done its work: the life has been long and splendid, the passing peaceful, and with gratitude in our hearts we feel that that is what death ought to be. There are other times, however, when everything seems tragic and awful, and dark questions arise in many minds, when, for example, a promising child is killed accidentally or a faithful and much-needed parent is snatched away by war or disease. It is not easy for anyone to be equal to every situation. There was one young minister who was well-known and much in demand who when called to visit a certain house of mourning found himself so inadequate to the occasion that in agony of heart he walked up and down the street before he found courage to knock at the door.

Moreover, for all of us death raises so many of the fundamental problems. We can pass through many stages of life unconcerned. We can even suffer loss and frustration and still feel able to repeat with assurance the doctrines we affirmed when the road was smooth and pleasant. It often happens, however, that death silences us or causes us to protest vehemently. There was Tennyson, to mention one out of many, who in early manhood lost his intimate friend, Arthur Hallam, and in the great elegy, *In Memoriam,* poured out not only

175

his sorrow and sense of loneliness but his doubts and fears. After years of intellectual and emotional conflict he found a stronger and deeper faith, but not all of us are so successful. There are some who find the lilt taken from life: all they can do is to limp their way through to the end.

There are matters here too large for a short address, but let us go a long way back and see how one great soul was shaken and how he survived.

There are reasons for believing that Saul of Tarsus was so deeply troubled by the thought of death that not all the wisdom of Gamaliel could give him relief. We may assume that one of the critical moments of his pilgrimage was the stoning of Stephen when he stood consenting to the terrible deed of violence. It did not take long to silence the solitary martyr, but it was another matter to restore peace in Saul's mind. He turned deliberately to further persecution; he pledged himself to root out the new heresy and bring men of Stephen's faith to a similar end. But even as he put his plan into operation, he himself was being pursued. You know what happened near Damascus and how suddenly he was converted. At that moment he was not only initiated into the Christian fellowship, but he was saved from the fear of death. Not everything was made clear at once. Much adaptation and thought were required before matters were sorted out and seen in their true light. But gradually he became fully persuaded that for those who are in Christ death had no terror. Again and again we find him exclaiming: "O death, where is thy sting? O grave, where is thy victory?" (1 Cor. 15:55).

We can be quite certain that such cries were not mere rhetoric. He was writing as one who had not only thought deeply on such matters, but as one who had often faced danger and even expected a violent end. Moreover, what was the Gospel he preached but a message of crucifixion and resurrection? And when he spoke of such things he meant not only historic events but experiences shared in some measure by all real Christians. He and his fellow believers knew what it was in some degree to be buried with Christ and with Him to rise in life and liberty.

How can we participate in such a faith? Not perhaps by argument. Reason has its place in religion, as elsewhere, but rarely the supreme place. But by dwelling upon the experiences of others and noticing the triumphs of faith through the centuries we may find ourselves persuaded. And as persuasion takes the place of doubt and fear we find ourselves comforted in bereavement, strengthened in tribulation,

and made content even as we move steadily toward our own departure. We find, not escape from reality, but a growing assurance that we
are in the hands of God and that nothing can separate us from His
love and care. Instead, therefore, of saying in bitterness of spirit,
"Let us eat and drink, for tomorrow we die," we find ourselves join-
ing in hymns of praise with those who stand in the apostolic succession.
With the spirit and the understanding, year in and year out, we
join with George Matheson and a greater multitude than man can
number in sentiments like this :

> O Cross, that liftest up my head,
> I dare not ask to fly from Thee;
> I lay in dust life's glory dead,
> And from the ground there blossoms red
> Life that shall endless be.[1]

Frank H. Ballard

196   *THE ETERNAL GOODNESS*

For I am persuaded, that neither death, nor life . . . shall be able to
separate us from the love of God.   ROMANS 8:38-39

Our faith in the immortality of the soul ultimately rests upon the
nature and character of God. "If God be for us, who can be against
us?" (Rom. 8:31). If God is good, then all will be well.

If, however, we are not sure of God, if there is any doubt in our
minds about His nature or uncertainty concerning His character,
then there will be uncertainty. Then we can be sure of nothing, not
even of life itself. Why were we born? Why are we here? And those
who are in doubt concerning life have scant hope of finding a meaning and a purpose concerning death. Uncertainty about God smothers
everything in uncertainty.

But if we *are* sure about the goodness of God, then we are sure
about everything. With even a minimum concept of God's goodness
as being at least up to that of a good man, His integrity to be trusted
merely to the extent we can count upon any real friend, His justice
but matching human justice as we normally measure it, then there
could be no ruthless annihilation of this human spirit which is of His
creation and into which He has forever fixed the instinct for spiritual
survival.

This faith is not reserved for the intellectually elect. It may be as
artless as that of a child who, when he puts his hand into the hand of

[1] From "O Love, that Wilt Not Let Me Go."

his mother, knows without being either able or inclined to prove it that she loves him and that he is safe. We need only a full trust in the goodness of God to know that we shall safely survive the ordeal of that natural change and decay which is called death. Such a faith is the unique contribution of Christianity, for those who believe in Jesus Christ possess the sign and seal of God's essential character. Christ's life was love incarnate, and He said, "He that hath seen me hath seen the Father" (John 14:9).

There will still be mystery, of course, beyond our comprehension. But earth is crammed with mystery, and we shall entrust the mystery of death to that same supreme Mind to which we are so very content to leave the fairer, but equal, mysteries of birth and life. There will still be problems which we cannot solve, but fortified by the overwhelming evidence of our own daily experiences, we must concede that there can be solutions beyond our immediate grasp.

John Greenleaf Whittier was a Quaker. The one emphasis of his faith, which he so beautifully shared with us through his poetry, was the Eternal Goodness. Early in his famous poem by that name is to be found the relatively unfamiliar stanza which is the key to all the others:

> Yet, in the maddening maze of things,
> And tossed by storm and flood,
> To one fixed trust my spirit clings;
> I know that God is good!

Only one trust, but it is fixed—the sure knowledge that God is good! Thus armed, the assurance in the better-known stanzas could not be otherwise:

> I know not where His islands lift
> Their fronded palms in air;
> I only know I cannot drift
> Beyond His love and care.
>
> I know not what the future hath
> Of marvel or surprise,
> Assured alone that life and death
> His mercy underlies.

In the language of Christians there is a word far more appropriate than "deceased' for such an hour as this. When one from our fellowship removes from one church to another, we customarily use the good word "transferred."

Therefore, it now becomes my solemn duty to announce the "transfer" of our beloved friend, with the highest recommendations of *his* pastor, from the Church mortal to the Church triumphant and eternal, located in that City "which hath foundations, whose builder and maker is God" (Heb. 11:10).

H. Hughes Wagner

197   *CERTAINTY OF LIFE IN CHRIST*

For as in Adam all die, even so in Christ shall all be made alive.
1 CORINTHIANS 15:22

The fifteenth chapter of First Corinthians is the greatest essay ever written on eternal life. In it St. Paul rose to heights of inspired understanding. His whole thesis, based on the fact of the resurrection of Christ at the beginning of the chapter, makes the paean of praise possible at the end: "Thanks be to God, which giveth us the victory through our Lord Jesus Christ" (1 Cor. 15:57).

Paul made no effort to evade the fact of death. He was too wise a man for that. Rather, he says, "In Adam all die." Here is the inescapable fact of our mortality. It is "appointed unto men once to die" (Heb. 9:27). To the modern secular mind, death often seems an impertinence. Dean Willard Sperry of Harvard remarked at the funeral service of a famous scholar that many present-day intellectuals resent the fact of death. Rebel as we might, we cannot escape the truth of St. Paul's statement, "In Adam all die."

Death appears an impertinence because of our innate longing for continuation of personality and of the powers and the joys we have known here on earth. The Greeks believed in the natural immortality of man. Man has a right to immortality because of his very humanity. Thomas Wolfe caught this mood:

> Something has spoken in the night . . .
> And told me I shall die, I know not where.
>
> Saying:
>> "To lose the earth you know, for greater knowing:
>> To lose the life you have, for greater life;
>> To leave the friends you loved, for greater loving;
>> To find a land more kind than home, more large
>>   than earth—
>> "—Whereon the pillars of this earth are founded,
>> Toward which the conscience of the world is tending—
>> A wind is rising, and the rivers flow."[1]

[1] From *You Can't Go Home Again*.

St. Paul contrasts the first man, Adam, who gave us our mortality with the second man, Christ, who gives us hope of eternal life. He says that, "Adam became a living being" (r.s.v.). Our human life we have from Adam. But from Adam we also have the fact and the necessity for physical death. The first clause in Paul's statement, "As in Adam all die," is transformed for the Christian by the second, "So also in Christ shall all be made alive." The certainty of death we recognize. Whether it is an impertinence or not we all must face it. As Paul was sure of the certainty of death he was equally as sure of the certainty of life in Christ. In fact, we could say that he was even more sure. Paul based his assurance on the resurrection of Jesus, who was seen by Peter, by the twelve, by more than five hundred, by James, and "last of all he was seen of me also" (1 Cor. 15:8).

The Christian belief in the continuance of personality is not held because of a philosophy about the natural immortality of man. In fact, the Christian does not believe primarily in immortality. He believes in the resurrection. "So in Christ shall all be made alive. But every man in his own order: Christ the firstfruits; afterward they that are Christ's at his coming." The resurrection hope is built on what a modern theologian calls, "Christ *the event.*" "In Christ shall all be made alive." The events connected with the birth, the life, the teachings, the death, and the resurrection of Jesus are all of a piece for those who belong to Christ. These events transformed the life of the Apostle Paul; these events transform our lives today. We do not fear death for we have walked with the Lord of life. Franklin Elmer, Jr., knew this when he wrote:

> Who struggles up the tortuous peaks
> Roams the hills with easy stride.
> Who storms across the widest seas
> Embarks upon a pond with casual mein.
> Who beholds the majesty of God
> Is fearless in the presence of mortality.

St. Paul compares the mystery of the resurrection with the grain of wheat that is planted and dies only to grow into something far more significant and meaningful than it ever knew before. The apostle makes no effort to fill in the details, nor should we. Ignorance of details does not necessarily mean the lack of reality. "It is sown a physical body, it is raised a spiritual body." St. Paul continues, "The first man Adam became a living being: the last Adam Christ became a life-giving spirit." Now there is all the difference in the world between simply living and *giving life* to others. Edwin Arlington Robinson understood that we have to give life for a work really to begin:

> I have lived
> Because the faith within me that is life
> Endures to live, and shall, till soon or late,
> Death, like a friend unseen, shall say to me
> My toil is over and my work begun.

The certainty of death in Adam is far surpassed by the assurance of life in Christ. "Death is swallowed up in victory" (1 Cor. 15:54). So taught the blessed apostle, and so we can close our quest on the note of victory *in Christ*:

> I shall go forth some day
> Forgetting the foolishness of song and rhyming,
> And slowly travel life's road until twilight
> Whispers: "This is the end of earth's journey;
> Your pathway
> Is now up, past the stars;
> Keep on climbing."
>
> With quick intake of breath,
> Eyes wide with wonder at the white gleaming
> Chalice of exquisite revelation . . .
> I shall drink, and drinking know the renascence
> From death,
> And be done with all doubt,
> And all dreaming.[1]

"Thanks be to God who gives us the victory through our Lord Jesus Christ."

Hillyer H. Straton

198   THE SECRET OF LIFE'S RENEWAL

Forgetting what lies behind and straining forward to what lies ahead, I press on toward the goal for the prize of the upward call of God in Christ Jesus.   PHILIPPIANS 3:13-14 (R.S.V.)

What is the secret of life's renewal? The answer is found in Paul's letter to the Christians at Philippi. "I press on"—this is the secret of life's renewal! When we stop pressing on we die mentally and spiritually as well as physically. But so long as we strain forward with God's help we find ourselves continually regenerated.

[1] From "The Final Quest" by John Richard Moreland.

Each Christian is an athlete for God. He must carry the torch in the great relay race which is the story of man's life on this earth. To each one of us is assigned a specified portion of the entire course for which he is especially responsible. This thought of each person's part in the unfolding human story is in itself very challenging, but not until we see it in the full perspective of the Christian faith are we able to grasp its true magnitude. "The upward call of God in Christ Jesus" is the tremendous thing. Even the greatest men and women, those who live the richest and fullest lives, are quite unable to exhaust in fourscore years or more, all that is in God's "upward call." It takes *more than a lifetime* to enter into the full meaning and glory of God's call to us through Christ Jesus. There is a *beyondness* about it which opens our eyes to a world beyond this world and to a life beyond this life.

One of the great reasons for our Christian affirmation in immortality is the fact that there is more to the Christian life than can possibly be achieved in this world. When we look at the earth and see its marvelous complexity, its vastness, and its grandeur, and when we know that human personality is the highest and noblest product of all this development, can we really believe that physical death ends it all?

When we let this question grip our minds, such a conclusion is truly fantastic. Instead of being reasonable, it is utterly unreasonable. It is against the very rationality, the purpose, and the glory of existence. It is far more reasonable to believe that "deep calls unto deep," that God, whom Jesus Christ revealed to us as our Heavenly Father, reaches out in great love and purpose, forgiveness and redemption, to draw us unto Himself if we surrender our minds and hearts to Him and become obedient to His will.

What we call death is not the end but the great new beginning, not tragedy but triumph and fulfillment, if before that great moment by faith in Christ we have begun really to live in Him. Worth-while life here and now depends upon daring trust in God. The life to come depends upon nothing less. Fortunate are those who have learned the secret of life's renewal and "press on toward the goal for the prize of the upward call of God in Christ Jesus."

Frederick A. Roblee

199 *THE REWARD OF FAITH*

For I am now ready to be offered, and the time of my departure is at hand. I have fought a good fight, I have finished my course, I have kept the faith: henceforth there is laid up for me a crown of righteousness, which the Lord, the righteous judge, shall give me at that day: and not to me only, but unto all them also that love his appearing. 2 TIMOTHY 4:6-8

The abiding love of family and friends, the joy of work, and the satisfaction of achievement all contribute to the happiness which life may offer, yet sorrow, pain, trials, and ultimately death is the lot also of each of us. Many times when we are called upon to face unfortunate experiences we feel that our difficulties are particularly our own. We forget that everyone at one time or another is called upon to travel the same road.

Death to a child of God, though necessarily associated with heart-ache and loneliness, is not an experience to be dreaded—but, indeed, to be anticipated. One great witness to this truth is the Apostle Paul, who in calm and patient resignation and without fear awaited the ap-proach of the executioner to his Roman prison cell. Such quiet sur-render may, and verily should, be the experience of every disciple of Jesus when he awaits the approach of death.

This assurance is based on two facts. First, the disciple of Christ has "fought a good fight." In other words, he has faced and battled life's experiences and, within human limitations, has conquered them. Such a satisfaction is the inheritance of each person who has walked the path of Christian life.

With Paul he may also say, "I have finished my course." Like Paul, the disciple of Christ has had a definite conviction of a life purpose. To discover God's purpose for life and to follow the Lord's plan is the privilege and goal for each follower of Jesus. To approach the end of life with the conviction that one has, as best he may, followed his Creator's purpose is to face death with a peaceful, calm assurance, for he may say, with Paul, "I have kept the faith." This is the crowning experience of life. To remain firm in one's trust in Christ, whatever the difficulties along the way, brings victory in the battle of life.

Second, Paul's assurance was also based upon the promises of God. To those who have had a regenerating experience through faith in the crucified and living Christ, who have followed His way of life, and who have obediently carried out His Divine purpose, every promise of our heavenly Father will be fulfilled. "Henceforth there is laid up for me a crown of righteousness."

What is this "crown of righteousness?" In his letter to the church at Philippi Paul tells us: "I count all things but loss for the excellency of the knowledge of Christ Jesus my Lord . . . that I may win Christ" (Phil. 3:8). The one thing above all else he coveted was to be like Christ. From the moment he met Christ on the Damascus road that was his life goal. The deepest desire of his soul is found in his words, "When Christ, who is our life, shall appear, then shall ye also appear with him in glory" (Col. 3:4), and in the words of another, "We know that, when he shall appear, we shall be like him; for we shall see him as he is" (1 John 3:2).

Thrilled at the blessed hope of eternal glory, the apostle writes that this marvelous attainment—likeness to Christ—is the treasured hope of every true follower of the Lord Jesus. "Not to me only, but unto all them also that love his appearing."

So, my friends, though you sorrow, you do not sorrow as those who have no hope. Your loved one has received the "crown of righteousness" and has been transformed into the perfect spiritual character of Jesus. Your dear one has now realized the deepest and holiest of all desires. May your hearts be comforted today and may the peace of God which passeth understanding abide with you.

Herbert Barclay Cross

FOR A PUBLIC SERVANT

200   *PAUL'S LAST WORD AND OURS*

I have fought the good fight, I have finished the race, I have kept the faith. Henceforth there is laid up for me the crown of righteousness, which the Lord, the righteous judge, will award me on that Day, and not only to me but also to all who have loved his appearing.   2 TIMOTHY 4:6-8 (R.S.V.)

At this time, as we honor one who has served *his* church and community with distinction and fidelity, we are made particularly aware of the noble words of the Apostle Paul: "I have fought the good fight, I have finished the race, I have kept the faith. Henceforth there is laid up for me the crown of righteousness, which the Lord, the righteous judge, will award me on that Day, and not only to me but also to all who have loved his appearing."

With these words Paul, having kept the heavenly vision through the years of his pilgrimage, expresses with confidence his expectation that the Lord of Life will acknowledge his faithfulness.

Our *brother* and friend, like Paul, has fought the good fight and kept the faith. And we trust that as a fellow heir with Paul *he* has received the crown of righteousness.

Our *brother* was a *man* of great private faith in our Lord and Saviour. From the hidden resources of prayer and study emerged *his* great public profession which has so long inspired and encouraged us.

There are many whose lives are like opened books, to be read by all men. Someone has said that Martin Luther could conceal nothing from the world, even the scraps of paper tossed into his wastepaper basket have been eagerly studied by inquiring students. But we must not think that the witness and good works of public servants are more important in furthering God's kingdom than your witness and mine.

Before his death, George Fox, the devout Quaker leader, addressed a letter to his friends. After sealing it, he inscribed it with the title, "Not to be opened before the time." In 1691, a year after the death of Fox, the epistle was opened and read at the Friends' Meeting in London. There they found in his last message words of hope and light and an outline of the salient points of his religious faith. His legacy to his followers consisted not in houses and barns, not in costly cathedrals and boisterous power, but in quiet faith and life-giving confidence in the future. And this from a man who for his Christ was eight times imprisoned, constantly ridiculed, hated!

Our *brother* has given us a legacy of faith and good will. How many persons there are who love Christ because *he* loved Christ. How many persons have clung to the promises of the cross because *he* clung to the cross. How great have been not only his last words to us, but his early words and good works!

What would we wish to impart as our last words to our families, our business associates, and our friends? Some of us, I dare say, would leave only the customary last will and testament, written with care and properly recorded. Our last word would be only concerned with financial instructions, perhaps, words representing our wish to bestow our goods in a particular fashion.

And yet, all of us, in spite of ourselves, leave a testimony after our deaths—footsteps for all to see. Some imbed their footprints in wet cement where they harden into stone, never to be forgotten by the world. Others press their feet into mud, and the sun dries the moisture and preserves the marks at least for a season. Others leave their footprints in the sands only, and these marks are swept away by the tide in the night. Yet let us not be deceived. God does not always pay heed to those footprints which the world perceives. Sometimes He knows that what appears to us to be marks only in the sands are actually the footprints that survive all tides and all storms. And He, with His mighty emery wheels of judgment, grinds and obliterates other footprints from the rock where they seemed eternally lodged.

We cannot contemplate death without searching ourselves to determine what we would write down in such a letter to be opened after our deaths. What would we say about the worth of virtue? What would we declare about Christ and His promises? In such a message, some of us would have to confess in shame: "Heed what I have said and not what I have done, for my deeds have not matched my convictions." Others would have to admit a modern form of hypocrisy: "I really had more faith than I permitted anyone to know and had higher thoughts than anyone guessed."

Pondering so weighty a matter, we awaken to the fact that when death comes, as it has to this loved one, it is of little importance where we lived or when, how much we owned or owed. Of supreme significance, rather, is the nature of our living, our working, our playing, our serving, our dying. How desperately it behooves us to say with Paul in his last letter to the world: "I have fought the good fight, I have finished the race, I have kept the faith. Henceforth there is laid up for me the crown of righteousness, which the Lord, the righteous judge, will award me on that Day, and not only to me but also to all who have loved his appearing."

C. Eugene Sill

J. THE MEMORY OF THE JUST

BLESSED MEMORIES

The memory of the just is blessed. PROVERBS 10:7

God has placed in the hand of man two wonderful lamps. One is the lamp of Hope, which leads us forward through the uncertain mists of the future; the other is the lamp of Memory, which takes us by the hand and leads us back through the mists of the past to the happy scenes and experiences of yesterday. By the soft glow of that lamp of Memory we look into those faces which we have loved long since and lost awhile.

How poor would man be without memory? Memory is the only paradise out of which man cannot be cast. It was a false sentiment which Shakespeare put into the mouth of Mark Anthony when he made him say in his oration over the body of the assassinated Caesar:

> The evil that men do lives after them;
> The good is oft interred with their bones.[1]

It is, indeed, true that evil deeds and evil men cast a long and dark shadow. But it is not true that what the good men do is interred with their bones. Nothing is more certain than the blessed influence of a just and godly man. St. John spoke truly in the Apocalypse when he wrote: "Blessed are the dead which die in the Lord from henceforth: Yea, saith the Spirit, that they may rest from their labors; and their works do follow them" (Rev. 14:13).

The memory of the just inspires us to worthy living. Which one of us, having had a godly father or mother, husband or wife, brother or sister, who walked the path of the just and did that which was right in the sight of the Lord, has not felt the uplifting power of their memory and their example? Because they lived worthily, they call upon us to follow in their footsteps.

In the hour of temptation the memory of the just is blessed. How many sermons from personal experience of that truth could be preached today! Many years ago I read *The House of Rosmersholm*

[1] From *Julius Caesar*, Act III, Scene 2.

by Henrik Ibsen, the great Norwegian writer. A rector is dangerously tempted to do evil, but every time he is on the point of yielding to the temptation he looks at the portraits of his godly ancestors which hang on the walls of his home. Each lifts a warning hand and speaks a warning voice to hold him back from transgression. Harriet Beecher Stowe, the author of *Uncle Tom's Cabin*, used to say that it was her brothers' recollections of their mother, and their hope of meeting her in Heaven, that held them back from many a temptation and sin. We Protestants do not say much about guardian angels, although there is some suggestion in the Scriptures concerning the possibility of such a ministry. There is, however, one kind of guardian angel about which we can be certain: that is the saving and guarding and protecting memory of a just and godly father and mother who have gone before us.

The memory of the just is blessed to the soul of man in the time of doubt. When the foundations of life and character are being undermined by doubt, when old beliefs are crumbling, then how often it has been that the memory of the just has called the soul back to faith. It may have been a portrait on the wall, the music of a familiar hymn, a room in the home where prayer was wont to be made, a Bible once caressed by hands that now are dust. But that was enough to bid the spirit of doubt and unbelief to retreat. The stars of faith came out once again.

> And when the fight is fierce, the warfare long,
> Steals on the ear, the distant triumph song,
> And hearts are brave, and arms are strong again.[1]

The memory of the just is blessed in the time of sorrow. In his one chapter letter to his friend Philemon, as beautiful as it is brief, St. Paul tells that he is sending back to Philemon the fugitive slave, Onesimus, who had robbed him and fled from Colosse to Rome, where Paul found him and brought him to Christ. In this letter Paul says to Philemon that he wants him to receive Onesimus back, no longer as a slave, but as a brother beloved, "for perhaps he therefore departed for a season, that thou shouldest receive him for ever" (Philem. 15).

When Paul said that, I think he meant something more than that Philemon, having lost for a time the services of his slave, was now to have him back again as long as he lived. I think Paul was speaking

---

[1] From "Adonais" by Percy Bysshe Shelley.

also of the indissoluble union of Christian hearts, for he says he wants Philemon to receive Onesimus "as a brother beloved." Those words, "departed for a season, that thou shouldest receive him for ever," strike the chord of the great hope of reunion in the life to come, and also of the influence of the departed and blessed dead in this life.

When our loved ones are taken from us, it seems that their passing brings a sorrow which is unalleviable by time or circumstance. Yet how often we discover that their passing into the unseen world, their removal from the uncertainties of this life and "the contagion of the world's slow stain," only adds to their power to strengthen, guide, and comfort us. Jesus said to His disciples in His tender last farewell: "Sorrow hath filled your heart. Nevertheless I tell you the truth; it is expedient for you that I go away: for if I go not away, the Comforter will not come unto you; but if I depart, I will send him unto you" (John 16:6-7). So, although in a different way, we can say that it was wise and necessary that our friends should be taken from us in order that we might know to the full their power to help and guide and comfort us on the path of life.

I have left for the last the supreme illustration of our text, "The memory of the just is blessed." That supreme illustration is our Lord Jesus Christ, who died "the just for the unjust" (1 Peter 3:18), that He might bring us to God. He, above all others, demonstrates the power and the blessing of the memory of the just; and it was He who said, "This do in remembrance of me" (Luke 22:19).

Remember Jesus Christ. Remember His purity, His patience, His compassion. When you feel hurt or wronged by another, remember what Peter said of Jesus, that Peter who himself had done so much to hurt and wrong his Lord: "Leaving us an example, that ye should follow his steps: . . . who, when he was reviled, reviled not again; when he suffered, he threatened not; but committed himself to him that judgeth righteously" (1 Peter 2:21, 23). Above all, remember His death for you on the cross, that your sins might be forgiven, and that you might have Life Everlasting. Make it a personal memory and relationship, as Paul did, when he said, He "loved me, and gave himself for me" (Gal. 2:20). If you do this, then as the days and the years go by, in all your trials and sorrows and struggles you will discover how true it is that the memory of Christ is blessed, and that He is able and willing to bestow upon you that blessing which "maketh rich, and he addeth no sorrow with it" (Prov. 10:22).

Clarence Edward Macartney

202   *THE GARDEN OF BEAUTIFUL MEMORIES*

Surely goodness and mercy shall follow me all the days of my life.
PSALM 23:6

In His infinite wisdom our heavenly Father has bestowed upon us many priceless gifts. How many they are! With the gift of reasoning our Lord has made man "to have dominion over the works of thy hands; thou hast put all things under his feet" (Ps. 8:6). With the gift of appreciation we are kept from being hard, cold, and unresponsive. And with the gift of love our hearts are opened to God and to all of His children.

When we consider God's gifts to man, we marvel at His goodness and mercy which attends all of our days. As we travel along life's pathway we are apt to place greater or lesser value upon these gifts in proportion to the need of the hour. When we seek comfort for our hearts as we pass through the valley of the shadows, how precious God's mercies and goodness become.

At a moment such as this one, the great good gift of memory seems most precious. It is wonderful to walk through the gardens of God when we are bereaved, "to lie down in green pastures," to walk "beside the still waters," and to have our souls restored. And as the hours wear away, how wonderful it will become to walk through the Garden of Beautiful Memories! God helps us to forget the sorrow and the despair and to remember the good and the beautiful. In this garden we are led along the "paths of righteousness" and we feed our souls on God's goodness and mercy.

During the last World War, I was called to see a young mother who had received word that her husband had been killed in the Battle of the Bulge. I went to comfort her in whatever way I could. As I was leaving she turned to a boy, hardly three years old, who was playing in the yard. "That's our only child," she said. "He looks just like Joe." A sob came from her shocked and broken heart. Then a light seemed to illumine her face. "You know," she continued, "Joe will always be alive. As long as little Joe and I keep alive the memory of the things he believed in and stood for, Joe will live. He will never die! Little Joe and I won't let him die."

Since that time I have been constantly reminded that God has given us the precious gift of memory which helps us to keep alive those principles and ideals by which God builds a better world.

I know that the family and friends of the one whose life we honor now will often walk in the Garden of Beautiful Memories. We will remember the things for which *he* stood. We will remember *his* little kindnesses, *his* devotion to his family, and, above all else, *his* love and loyalty to our Lord Jesus Christ whom *he* served faithfully. As we thank God for His goodness in giving us the privilege of loving and being loved by *him*, our souls are filled with the God-given inspiration to keep alive the fires of goodness which burned in *his* heart.

Because God understands the sorrows of our hearts in this hour, He has bestowed upon us the precious gift of memory to sustain us. May we trust that "all things work together for good to them that love God" (Rom. 8:28), and that God's "goodness and mercy shall follow us all the days of our lives."

William A. Tyson, Jr.

203   *THEIR WORKS DO FOLLOW THEM*

And I heard a voice from heaven saying unto me, Write, Blessed are the dead which die in the Lord from henceforth: Yea, saith the Spirit, that they may rest from their labors; and their works do follow them. REVELATION 14:13

"Their works do follow them." It is delightful to think of the perpetuity of all goodness. It is not too much to say that a truly good action, an action done from true love to it, and from a regard to the will and glory of God in it, lasts forever. You are tempted to give an angry look. The memory of Christ restrains you; and you give a kind and loving one; and that glance—though sent forth in a moment of time—will be fixed as in a picture to all eternity. You are on the point of speaking a harsh word, not without provocation; but love, inspired by Christ, conquers, so that you speak a tender one; and that momentary vibration of the air will echo to endless ages and bless your soul in Heaven. The simplest act of self-denial that a child performs, the father's blessing, the mother's prayer, these will repeat themselves ever more in the sounding-board of Heaven, and never die away!

Have we not some shadow of this perpetual influence ever here upon earth? What words and looks, it may be of friends long departed, it may be of ministers, who have been for many years in their graves, still hang about us, and make us better than we otherwise should be! Nor are these influences for good that we have all received only to be traced back to persons of position and prominence in the true Church of God. The humblest have wrought with them; and it may be as ef-

fectually; and the piety that may have little memorial on earth shall
be startled at the wide circle of its influences which it shall meet in
Heaven! I delight to think of the obligation which Christians have
to the obscure and the unknown, to those who were "never heard of
half a mile from home," and of the glorious chapters of celestial history that will then be written when the rich and the poor meet together and the Lord is the Maker of them all!

What a revelation will then be made of the bearing of one Christian
life upon another, largely in proportion to the closeness of the relations between them, but also with a wondrous liberty of grace to find
instruments of the highest good in ways past finding out. We speak
too hastily of the history of the Church as already written, and of
those who shine in its firmament of stars of greater or lesser magnitude. The history of the Church in regard to the influence of its members can only be written in the world of immortality; and what secrets
of domestic, of congregational, and even of world-wide Christian im-
port shall then be unveiled, where there is no fear of jealousy or misunderstanding being aroused, or of sensitive delicacy being offended.

Much of the blessedness of Heaven will arise from these disclosures,
and from the endless bonds which they shall seal! In the light of these
undying soul-relationships the labor of the way shall be forgotten.
Paul may be heard exclaiming, "Blessed be God for my bonds and
scourging in Philippi, which have brought this jailer here with all his
house!" John may be heard exclaiming, "Blessed be my exile in
Patmos; for but for it these visions had never been opened to me, nor
the multitudes cheered and comforted whom they have led hither!"
You may hear all the martyrs exclaiming, "Blessed be God for the
shedding of our blood, from which all these immortal souls have
sprung up as from precious seed!" Then it will be seen how the bitter
tears, and wrestling prayers, and long-deferred hopes of God's saints
have been crowned, and how those at length have been brought home
to God, who were born as it were out of due time!

Many of us have made pilgrimages to the lonely spots—some of the
wildest and most secluded in our country—where our forefathers,
when hunted on moor and mountain, testified for Christ, and for His
sake loved not their lives unto death. Now these solitary wanderers
have shaped our history, have given us our laws and our liberties; and
they are leading the fight, in the heart of our great cities for the
Gospel, the Bible, and the Sabbath; and in the midst of foreign lands,
where new nations are rising, they are stamping their image to the

latest posterity! Such is the perpetuity of moral influences, and of its final disclosure; for there is nothing covered, that shall not be revealed, nor hid that shall not be known!

And with all the other following of the good works of the righteous, let us not forget its influence upon themselves; for what are we but what our works make us? What on earth or what in Heaven? We live in the atmosphere of our own actions, and if we live to God and to Christ, the work tells upon ourselves, more than upon all besides; and the Spirit that prompted it is in us a well of water springing up into everlasting life!

John Cairns

FOR A MEMORIAL SERVICE
OF A SOLDIER KILLED IN ACTION

204   *THE LAST FULL MEASURE OF DEVOTION*

Greater love hath no man than this, that a man lay down his life for his friends.   JOHN 15:13

When taps has sounded over a battlefield cemetery and tired, aching soldiers turn back to their hated task, the same thought fills their minds that fills our minds today. "Why?"

We know that the child who enters this life through the doorway called birth must one day leave through the door marked death. The day and hour remain unknown to us. But we know that sooner or later each one of us will go through the physical experience called death. This thought is not depressing or terrifying to a healthy mind. It is simply one of the limits within which we must live this part of our eternal life.

As Christians we believe that death is the opening of a door in a life that is greater than anything we have known on earth. Even so, at times like these, we sorrow. Jesus wept at the grave of a friend. We do not grieve for the one who has passed over to the other side. We grieve because of our personal loss.

But the question remains, "Why?"

Each one of us must some day lose his earthly life. We are met here in grateful memory of a man who gave his life. He gave it, all that he had, in order that others might live. He hated war, but he hated tyranny even more. He loved his own life, but even more greatly did he love the lives of others. In the defense of our lives, he gave up his own. Jesus said, "Greater love hath no man than this, that a man lay down his life for his friends."

The issue of the struggle which has blackened and blighted the twentieth century is one of freedom. Can ordinary people, people such as you and me, live together with ordinary people in other countries? Or do we need some giant of political power to tell us how to act?

Our fathers developed strength by refusing to bow before any but God. They dreamed of a land—and of a world—in which free men and women might live together under the law, and where they might settle their differences by discussion and vote, not by the club of a secret police. Our fathers did more than dream of such a land; they faithfully worked to make such a dream come true.

There have been many working within and beyond our country to destroy this dream. We have kept it only at an unbelievable cost of human bravery on the battlefield, in the courthouse, in the schoolroom, in the newspaper office, in the home, and in the church of Jesus Christ. Is the dream worth keeping? Is it worth fighting for? We are met in memory of one who answered yes not only with his lips but with his life.

How can we thank him? Would he want us to brood and sorrow over what is past? Or would he want us to carry on the work in which he was engaged?

A soldier's immediate task is victory in battle. But we all know that victory does not solve our problems. At best military victory will bring an opportunity for us to put good will to work in a world that has known more of ill will than of good will.

We know that hatred begets more hatred, that injustice breeds more injustice. Dare we hope that decency and law and kindness will work on a world scale? Only if we hold to such a hope and if we work to turn it into a fact are we showing adequate thankfulness to those who have fought to give us the opportunity. Count no contribution small that brings a measure of comfort, of justice, of freedom to another human being. But count no contribution large enough for you to say that you have done your full share.

As long as any child lives in fear of bombers flying overhead, as long as any man lives in fear of the secret police, as long as any person lives in the valley of the shadow of tyranny, just so long does our task remain unfinished.

This son and brother, this friend whom we have known in the fellowship of church, school, and community life, has finished his part of the task. He has given everything that a human being can give. If

you value what he has done, then make his sacrifice meaningful in
your lives. Now his dreams may become a living portion of your lives.
It is not enough that one such as he should fight for freedom. We
must be worthy of it ourselves, and we must offer it to others. That is
all the thanks we can give to one who gave his last full measure of
devotion that we might have the opportunity.

Andrew W. Blackwood, Jr.

FOR MEMORIAL DAY

205   *ANOTHER DAWN*

I have finished the work which thou hast given me to do. JOHN 17:4

Memorial Day reminds us each year of the perennial problem of
the death of the young. It seems fitting that older people should die.
They have run their course and have found rest. But why should the
brilliant, the purposeful, the zestful be snatched away? Our repeated
"Why?" indicates that we have found no satisfactory answer. There
are, however, some suggestions that we may consider.

Comfort for us comes in remembering that our Lord was still young
when He died on the cross. He was only thirty-three years of age. And
yet He said: "I have finished the work thou hast given me to do. . . .
Father, into thy hands I commend my spirit." His friends were
shocked that He died so young. But could more have been accomplished if He had lived to be seventy? To him, perfection in life was
not a matter of quantity, but of quality. Life can be perfect in quality,
and in that respect finished, no matter at what age we lay it down.

We can also believe that nothing happens to us or to our loved ones
which is outside the circle of God's providence and God's will. "Nothing walks with aimless feet" in our world. The Bible says our times
are in God's hand.

Most of our confusion and suffering comes from our not being able
to comprehend God's plans for us. We are finite, He is infinite. What
we think is the end of the book is only the end of a chapter. He sees
the end from the beginning. We think in terms of only one world
at a time. He thinks in terms of all time.

Was it instinctive faith or just sheer desperation which dictated the
belief in a life beyond the grave? We don't know. But we do know
that our Lord confirmed that belief when He said: "In my Father's
house are many mansions: if it were not so, I would have told you. I
go to prepare a place for you" (John 14:2).

If, then, we believe that life goes on over there, we also know that it must have purpose and progression. And if there is purpose there, it must have people to carry it out.

This is as Elma Dean pictures it in her poem about our soldier dead:

Let them in, Peter, they are very tired;
Give them the couches where the angels sleep.
Let them wake whole again to new dawns fired
With sun, not war. And may their peace be deep.
Remember where the broken bodies lie . . .
And give them things they like. Let them make noise.
God knows how young they were to have to die!
Give swing bands, not gold harps, to these our boys.
Let them love, Peter,—they have had no time—
Girls sweet as meadow wind, with flowering hair . . .
They should have trees and bird song, hills to climb—
The taste of summer in a ripened pear.
Tell them how they are missed. Say not to fear;
It's going to be all right with us down here.

Perhaps, then, one of the salvages of senseless war is the influx of youth into the life and economy over there. It helps to keep earth's balance true, as we face the loss of our beloved young, to think that God in His wisdom needed them there more than here. They being made perfect in a short time, God took them.

There is this, further, that can be said: only those who have passed on are really our own. Nothing can ever again separate them from us. Nothing is our own except our dead. We remember them in that other life, but close to us also as we still carry on here.

Sometimes all of life that is worth living is offered to us in one dramatic, flaming moment, and that seized, we have forgotten ourselves into immortality. What more could Colin Kelly have accomplished, after having driven his plane down to certain death in a deed of valor, even if he had lived to be a hundred? What more could our young war dead have done that would have added to the quality of heroism in their lives than to have surrendered them for a cause?

We died, those bitter winters, believing in a spring.
When all the buds would blossom, and all the bells should ring,
Not for our own doomed selves, but for all tribes of sons unborn—
For us to plough the heavy fields, for them to reap the corn:
We died, unhating, killed and died, that wars at last should cease,
And man, to fuller stature grown, honor us dead with Peace.

Howard J. Chidley

FOR A WOMAN OF ADVANCED YEARS

206   *A FAREWELL OF FAITH*

The righteous shall be in everlasting remembrance. PSALM 112:6

While anticipating this service of love and memory, I found myself wishing that it might follow the pattern set by our Quaker friends. If it did, we would gather quietly with no one person appointed to speak. All would sit in silence, each busy with his own thoughts. It is not hard to imagine what thoughts would engage our minds in such moments of meditation. In varying sequence, they would run somewhat as follows:

A few at least would think first of the great glad gift of life. Never do we appreciate life as much as when we linger in the presence of death. For life's strange power of growth, for the capacity to dare, to dream, and to do, for the ability to love and be loved, we give hearty thanks to Him from whom our spirits came and to whom they will return at the end of our earthly day.

Others, especially those who are older, would dwell on the brevity of life. They would recall that as children the years seemed endlessly long. They are but as yesterday now they have passed, a little more than "a watch in the night" (Ps. 90:4). Even though one has lived beyond the allotted span, life is "soon cut off, and we fly away" (Ps. 90:10). That is why we are admonished to "number our days" (Ps. 90:12). Only the possibility of its rich fullness offsets the brevity of life.

Still others, at times like these, think of their own dear and faithful dead who have made the distant Heaven a home. We all cherish the memory of those who have left us, whose faces we no longer see, whose voices we no longer hear. What tender memories come to us as we think of them! What beautiful recollections arise as we recall their names, those friends and classmates, brothers and sisters, fathers and mothers! They have all helped to make that great cloud of witness of which they are now a living part seem very real.

In due season someone, moved by the spirit, would arise to speak or to pray. If a prayer is offered, it would be addressed to Him before whose face the generations rise and pass away and with whom live the spirits of those who depart in the Lord. Others would express themselves in lines of poetry like the following:

> I only know I cannot drift
> Beyond His love and care[1]

[1] From "The Eternal Goodness" by John Greenleaf Whittier.

or

> I hope to see my Pilot face to face,
> When I have crossed the bar.[1]

Stanzas of old familiar hymns would inevitably become the vehicles
through which some would express themselves. How we cherish such
precious hymns as "Lead, kindly Light," "Rock of Ages," "For all the
saints, who from their labors rest," and "Just as I am, without one
plea."

Quite naturally some would relive their emotions by quoting Scripture: "The Lord shall preserve thy going out and thy coming in from
this time forth, and even for evermore" (Ps. 121:8), and "From everlasting to everlasting, thou art God" (Ps. 90:2). Then, as if in answer
to some inquiry, "We know that if the earthly house of our tabernacle were dissolved, we have a building from God, an house not
made with hands, eternal in the heavens" (2 Cor. 5:1). At last a final
word of confidence in things unseen that endure, "And now abideth
faith, hope, love" (1 Cor. 13:13).

Eventually someone would speak with deep feeling concerning our
friend whose life on earth is ended, but whose life with God goes on.
A friend of earlier years would speak of her strength and energy that
made her seem like Martha in the Bethany home where the Master
often visited. Another friend of later years would refer to her calm,
poise, and serenity that made her seem more like Mary, the sister of
Martha. Then someone would recall some of those

> little nameless, unremembered acts
> of kindness and of love.[2]

Possibly even her children would rise to tell what a blessing she had
been to them and to theirs. The companion of the years might
be heard to thank God for what she had meant to him since the day
long ago when she said, "Whither thou goest, I will go" (Ruth 1:16).
And her pastor might add what she herself had carved on the mantle
in the parlor as a memorial to her mother, "She loved the church."

I would repeat the tribute paid to my own mother at such an hour.
An old friend and neighbor, who had known her for three-fourths of
a century, came to me after her weary and wasted body had been laid
to rest and said, "Hers was a completed life." So had it been, in the
sense that she had rounded out the cycle: a loving child, a devoted

---

[1] From "Crossing the Bar" by Alfred Tennyson.
[2] From "Lines Composed a Few Miles above Tintern Abbey" by William Wordsworth.

daughter, a happy bride, a wonderful mother, and a faithful wife. So has it been with our friend whose gracious life now becomes a radiant memory. Somewhere early in life she mastered the secret that made life rich and beautiful. Unlike the organist who happened on a chord of music that transformed life and then could never find it again, she caught and held the music that has made her life as beautiful as a symphony.

Long ago a poet wrote that little babies came "trailing clouds of glory"[1] as they arrived on this scene of human existence. If this be true, and I think it is, then it is also true that those who precede us for a little time leave behind them another cloud of glory. The nearest parallel I know is that which you have seen in the Western sky after a gorgeous sunset. Long after the sun goes down the sky is lighted with colors that defy description. They make up what many have called the afterglow. For long years to come those who knew and loved our friend will feel the spell of her life. Its afterglow will linger and abide with us forever and a day.

Horace Greeley Smith

FOR A YOUTH

207 *GOD'S JEWELS*

They shall be mine, saith the Lord of hosts, in that day when I make up my jewels. MALACHI 3:17

With mingled emotions and a rich harvest of memories, we meet to honor one whose early passing fills our hearts with profound feelings of sorrow.

We extend the prayerful and loving sympathy of Christian fellowship to you members of *his* family and to you who are *his* friends. It is hard for each of us to appreciate that never again will we have *his* inspiring presence with us in worship.

He would wish our words of tribute to be brief and simple. We have known a good *man* and we have enriched ourselves in *his* friendship. *His* memory is a treasure to last throughout our lives.

The prophet Malachi described the one whom God seeks, a person such as our friend, in these words: "They shall be mine, saith the Lord of hosts, in that day when I make up my jewels." It is not difficult to think that our loved one has been added to God's collection.

Of all jewels, *he* reminded me most of the diamond with its facets

[1] From "Intimations of Immortality" by William Wordsworth.

flashing rich lustre. The love of Jesus reflected in *his* soul and revealed new graces.

His humanity was rich and powerful. It possessed a rare goodness which was illumined again and again by a spontaneous and kindly humor. Amid the daily associations, *he* displayed in Stevenson's phrase, "a bright morning face." *He* lit many fires in empty rooms.

Another facet was *his* efficiency. Despite ill health and the many demands for *his* services in the life of the church and kindred social organizations, always fulfilled with ungrudging willingness, nothing less than the best was *his* ideal.

We will ever remember another superb quality which was particularly *his*, brotherliness. *He* ever found delight in the love of little children, in the aspirations and the confidence of youth, and in the joys of older folk. *He* sought to emulate the example of John Wesley who wrote, "The world is my parish." To *him* the earth had no strangers.

His was a jewel of a life! Nothing seems more fitting than the words of Sir Henry Wotton's hymn:

How happy is he born and taught
    Who serveth not another's will;
Whose armour is his honest thought
    And simple truth his utmost skill!

Whose passions not his masters are,
    Whose soul is still prepared for death,
Not tied unto the world with care
    Of public fame, or private breath;

Who God doth late and early pray
    More of his grace than goods to lend;
And walks with man, from day to day,
    As with a brother and a friend.

Bert Wright

208   *GOD'S GOOD MAN*

Enoch walked with God: and he was not; for God took him.   GENESIS 5:24

Here is a sentence, set like a glowing jewel, in a chapter of matter-of-face genealogy. The record of Enos, Cainan, Mahalaleel, and the others, is given in an uninspiringly repetitive manner. We are told how long each lived and of his children and of his death with the words, ". . . and he died." Nine times over the account runs.

Of the tenth man much the same formula is given before we reach this sentence, "And Enoch walked with God; and he was not; for God took him."

This sentence—in each phrase—applies to our beloved one who is in our remembrance today.

In remembrance we ask, "What sort of *man* was *he?*" That is what people most want to know. Of Enoch and of our loved one, we may reply, *he* "walked with God." He was that kind of *man*.

You will remember how the aged Emerson, his mental powers failing, stood by the grave of his friend, the poet Longfellow, and said, "The gentleman who lies here was a beautiful soul, but I do not remember his name." It does not matter what name or title men may give to our dead, if only they may with sincerity speak like that of them.

And in remembrance we ask, "Will there be those who will miss *him?*" The words used about Enoch, "And he was not," are often used to suggest something mystical about his passing. But do they not seem to reveal in the simplest form possible just this: the utter sense of loss now that he is gone?

In one of the loveliest poems in the English language is a striking parallel. William Wordsworth tells of Lucy, a girl "who dwelt among the untrodden ways . . . a violet by a mossy stone, half-hidden from the eye":

> She lived unknown, and few could know
> When Lucy ceased to be;
> But she is in her grave, and, oh,
> The difference to me![1]

"And, oh, the difference to me!" How much it means, in sheer human pathos, when the voice of *him* whom we have loved is no longer heard to cheer and comfort us. Always there is a gap which cannot be filled by another. And it is just here that God's comfort is most needed— and God is with us to help us and to bid us lift our gaze on high.

And in remembrance we also ask, "Is *his* passing the end of *him?*" Men's lives are a pointer. The direction is all important. It is a terrible thing when men say of a loved one—and say it without the feeling of incongruity—"And that's the end of him" or "He's snuffed out."

In Enoch's case the story does not end that way. He was God's good man. He walked with God. Words of despair will not do. Of Enos,

[1] From "Lucy."

Cainan, and Mahalaleel they may be used; but not of Enoch. The chronicler is certain that Enoch is still with God!

Little children sometimes make the most discerning comments about life's most puzzling moments. Hubert Simpson tells of a small child who explained our text in this manner: "Enoch and God used to take long walks together. And one day they walked further than usual: and God said, 'Enoch, you must be tired; come into My House and rest.' "[1] Can you better that?

Because of the way Enoch lived, his friends believed in a life beyond death. They knew that the direction of his life led not to a grave, but to God.

Generations later a friend said of One greater than Enoch, "It was not possible that he should be holden of [death]" (Acts 2:24). Death could not hold Him, for He had brought to believing men the gift of eternal life. Those who are His are bound in a relationship which death cannot sever. They know His voice. He calleth His own sheep by name. And they go in and out and find pasture. They walk with Him, here and hereafter. Though they be greatly missed, we are sure of their eternal destiny.

Cyril H. Powell

FOR A DEVOUT CHURCHMAN

209   *THE CANDLE OF THE LORD*

The spirit of man is the candle of the Lord.   PROVERBS 20:27

Words are poor tools with which to fashion the appreciation which all our hearts would like to express today. The distance between abstraction and living reality is always great, but never more baffling than when we try to state the meaning conveyed by one who lived intimately with us and gave himself fully to the Lord whom we serve through this church.

I am helped, however, by noting that for all who share the Christian hope, our *brother* touches us today, as he did when he was still with us, at the point where we most need renewal and confirmation in the work of Christian living. In this service, he has given me the words which I bring to you. "The darkness does not blot out the stars; it only makes them shine more brightly." This thought, joined with that of the poet of old who said, "The spirit of man is the candle of

---

[1] From *Altars of Earth.*

the Lord," suggests the ways in which our *brother* let his light shine upon us.

First, he brought to us the light of faith. He believed that the universe is dependable and on the side of the good; that underneath the marshlands of sin and the shifting sands of doubt, there is certainty, foundations unshaken and abiding. He believed in victory beyond defeat; in triumph beyond tragedy; that in spite of shattered human hopes and man's inhumanity to man, there are bright goals ahead worth every ounce of energy one has to give to them. I do not mean that he never saw the darkness, for he did; that he was never discouraged, for he was. But he never failed to see the substance of things hoped for. He weighed the evidence of things not seen. He viewed the unrealized promises from afar and took possession of the future by an act of faith. He looked for a city with foundations whose builder and maker is God.

Second, he brought to us the light of truth. Truthfulness for him was the central fact. But as he saw it, truth involved more than correct ideas and logic. It meant the spirit of honesty and loyalty in personal relations, a basic respect for every man, and the kind of conduct toward others that acknowledged the work of God in every man. Most of all, he knew the one great truth about Christian living, that the life in Christ is living for God in the service of man, not living in the service of one's own reputation.

Third and finally, he brought to us the light of love. In him we saw a playful element sometimes overlooked in our thought about Christian love. The good humor which he had is always the sign of freedom among friends. When people are suspicious and afraid, they do not laugh. He knew also how to use the lighter touch to relax people in conversation and endeavor and how to plant a fruitful thought while they smiled. But more than in any other way, his love for our church was shown by the spirit of utter self-giving which marked his daily work. He grew weary under the load, but he never complained.

In his relations outside of the church, he was equally devoted to the cause of Christ. He enlisted the lives and services of man in the work of the kingdom. Thus love overspends itself but never fails. In testimony of all this, a friend wrote the other day saying, "He was behind every good thing that has happened to me." But for himself, we all know that the source of this sustained devotion was the love of

God. Of this he often witnessed in his recitation of the words of George Matheson which he loved so greatly.

> O Love, that wilt not let me go,
>   I rest my weary soul in Thee;
> I give Thee back the life I owe,
> That in Thine ocean depth its flow
>   May richer, fuller be.

Today the life of our *brother* is richer, fuller, crowned with eternal glory, enshrined forever in the heart of God. We hear the echo of the trumpets which have sounded for him on the other side. We see the lights he has left to guide us in our further journey—the light of faith, the light of truth, the light of love.

Oren H. Baker

FOR A FAITHFUL MINISTER

210　　　*HE LEFT THE WORLD RICHER*

Like Abraham, he went where he was called and was faithful in all things.

Like Moses, he had led the people of God from doubts and fears to confidence for success in the face of many difficulties.

Like Joshua, he loved his country and fought and suffered for its success.

Like Jonathan, he met many a discouraged brother and cheered him by giving him strength from God.

Like David, he sang the church to victory and shouted on the battle of blessed triumph.

Like Isaiah, he constantly pointed the church to brighter days and better things in the future.

Like Daniel, he was true through life to the teachings of his boyhood days.

Like Malachi, he believed in bringing all the tithes into the Lord's storehouse.

Like John the Baptist, he delighted to cry to the multitudes: "Behold the Lamb of God."

Like St. John, he believed with all his soul that Jesus Christ was the Son of God.

Like Peter, he honored the Holy Ghost by teaching the doctrine of the operation of the Divine Spirit upon the souls of men.

Like Paul, he rejoiced that Jesus died for all men and he did his best to let the world know this blessed truth with pen, song, and sermon. He pled with the church to send the gospel to all.

Like Jesus, his Divine Master, whom he followed daily, "he went about doing good."

Like Enoch, "he walked with God, and he was not, for God took him." A blessed and consecrated Christian, he was true to his God, his country, his church, and his fellow man. He sought to inspire others to share his enthusiasm and worked to the very last moment of his busy life for the interest of the unsaved world.

The world is richer because he lived, worked, and died in the faith of the Lord Jesus Christ. When he died there was only one place he could go and that place was Heaven. And there he is today. And it seems to me that I hear him sing, "Worthy the Lamb that was slain for us."

Robert Stephens

FOR A BELOVED PHYSICIAN

211   *A FAITHFUL DISCIPLE*

Luke, the beloved physician . . . greet you.   COLOSSIANS 4:14

When a physician lays down his work it is not like the passing of an ordinary citizen. He has held a peculiar relation in the community. He is not simply a public agent for the transaction of business. He is a public friend. He deals not with the simple external goods of men. He holds the most sacred trusts. Under his hand the strong man lies down upon the scant couch in an unconscious sleep and trusts the thread of life to his careful skill. To him the woman tells her deepest secrets and trusts implicitly to his truth and honor. He watches over our entrance and exit from the world. He is a family friend. The sick one looks impatiently for his coming, and opens the eyes with trust and hope and gratitude into his cheerful thoughtful face. His people feel that they own him; he is subject to their call by day and night. And how many I have heard say during the last few days with that peculiar consciousness of this close relationship, "He was our doctor."

There seemed to come from him something more than his medicine; it was his personality. The patient was better before the drops were administered.

It is no wonder that in the naming of the disciples and early Christian leaders of the New Testament, while they called one the zealot, one the publican, one the son of thunder, Luke, the physician, they called "the beloved." And we realize something of the pathos, yet strength and comfort of the lonely Paul, physically weak and wrecked, when he told how all his followers save one had left him; we could guess who that one was. It was the physician, "Only Luke is with me" (2 Tim. 4:11).

The greatest glory of this hour is that we are paying the tribute of a church and a community not alone to a good doctor, but to a devout and consecrated disciple of the Great Physician. Because of his love of God, his labors among us have been performed with a keen and sensitive awareness of eternal values. And the Great Physician has welcomed our friend, I believe, with the words, "The beloved physician is with me."

Frederick T. Rouse

212 *LOVE CAN NEVER LOSE ITS OWN*

If ye loved me, ye would rejoice, because I said, I go unto the Father. JOHN 14:28

There is no past in real love; it is not memory that keeps love alive, it is love itself which cannot die, and which involves the persistent life of memory, becoming in itself an undersigned guarantee of immortality. God is love and love is God, and therefore such love as has been begotten and welded by the simultaneous passage of hearts through many happy scenes in life, and many happy spiritual experiences in this school of education, is as immortal as God, and such love must strive to teach itself not to mourn overmuch when the embodiment of its object is taken from its sight. It strains and yearns in the track of the loved spirit that has passed into the Paradise of God. It sheds its human tears of "anguish in solution" as it lays the beloved form in the grave; but love, real, Spirit-born love knows nothing of death, and pierces into the other world, and realises the creed of catholic Christendom, "I believe in the Communion of Saints."

Love knows that the beat of the silvery wings which carried Lazarus to Abraham's bosom has borne the dear spirit to the spotless shore

> Where loyal hearts and true
> Stand ever in the light,
> All rapture through and through
> In God's most Holy Sight.

And though we yearn intensely for some realised interchange of thought, though we often look upon the well-known features in some

faithful portrait and say with Cowper as he gazed on the likeness of
his mother

> Oh that those lips had language; Life has passed
> With me but roughly since I heard thee last,[1]

real love will reach beyond the narrow frontier of this world, and in
its inmost rejoice that the dear spirit has gone to the Father.

Thus then I consider that God's manifested ideal of perfect manhood, Jesus Christ, spoke to the hearts of the bereaved for every age
when He said to His disciples, "If ye loved me, ye would rejoice because . . . I go unto the Father." If your love were heavenly, unselfish,
strong enough to look beyond sense and time, you would recognise
that it is not only more glorious for the departing but more expedient
for the bereaved, that the separation should take place. There are
times when we positively long for a dear spirit to be free from a suffering body, and when, with Kingsley, we say:

> Give me the calm strength to wait, to know and feel Thee just—
> 'Tis not the suffering ones who most have need of trust.
> They may have faith in thee, they may have peace within,
> But we who look on their distress are tempted, Lord, to sin.

Then it is "expedient for us" that they should go away.

The sweet unions of this world are but shadows of truer unions
beyond the veil; they are unavoidably marred here on earth by the
atmosphere of the flesh. "If I go not away," said Jesus, "the Comforter
will not come unto you" (John 16:7), and the Comforter was Himself,
set free from limitations, and therefore more really present than when
in the flesh, for there is no division in the threefold nature of God.

Basil Wilberforce

[1] From "On the Receipt of My Mother's Picture."

III. *An Anthology of Funeral Poems*

The personal and intimate nature of the great poems of consolation make them particularly meaningful in the funeral service. Although a poem expresses an experience from the poet's own life, the genius of the gifted poet is such that his words rise above himself and become a witness of the grief and hope of Everyman.

Most pastors do not wish to be continually identified with a small number of poems, "Crossing the Bar," for instance, and two or three others. The breadth of verse suitable for the funeral is so great that he may find individual poems which easily and naturally match the requirement of a particular service.

Certain generally accepted bases for the reading of poems apply to the use of verse at the funeral.

1. A poem should be thoroughly understood by the pastor himself if he is to interpret it effectively. There is little which will contribute as greatly to the understanding of a poem as practice in reading aloud.

2. Poems should be read slowly. Most readers err more in terms of rapid than slow delivery.

3. If the understanding of the poem is to be shared with the congregation and if the beauty of imagery and sound is to be made evident, enunciation should be clear and forceful.

4. The rhythm and rhyme of a poem frequently require a brief pause at the end of each line and usually a pause, however slight, somewhere within each line.

5. The reading of poetry is enhanced by a natural voice and manner. Few poems are written for an "orated" delivery.

Should poems be memorized? Not necessarily, although, of course, some poems may be more beautifully interpreted from the mind than from the notebook. Frequently, however, the memorizing of a poem may result in hesitation or may call more attention to the manner of delivery than to the content of the lines. Anything which detracts from the words and draws attention to the officiating person should be avoided.

The little anthology of poems which follows is divided into two groups: general poems and prayer poems.

A. GENERAL POEMS

213   *THE JOURNEY*

When Death, the angel of our higher dreams,
Shall come, far ranging from the hills of light
He will not catch me unaware; for I
Shall be as now communing with the dawn.
For I shall make all haste to follow him
Along the valley, up the misty slope
Where life lets go and Life at last is born.
There I shall find the dreams that I have lost
On toilsome earth, and they will guide me on,
Beyond the mists unto the farthest height.
I shall not grieve except to pity those
Who cannot hear the songs that I shall hear!

Thomas Curtis Clark

214   *IF I SHOULD SUDDENLY BE CALLED*

If I should suddenly be called to go
    With Death, on some far journey, on a day
    When Life besought me joyously to stay—
Why should I then consider him my foe!
He has appeared so often—now I know
    That he is but the guide upon the way
    To such divine adventures as we may
Not even dream of here on earth below.
Death takes the film of earth-dust from our eyes
    And frees the spirit from its flesh outworn,
That we may journey through the morning skies
    Within the Everlasting Arms upborne,
Till on our new-found vision shall arise
    The glory of our resurrection morn.

Annie Lees Huget

215   *SOME MORNING I SHALL RISE FROM SLEEP*

Some morning I shall rise from sleep,
　When all the house is still and dark.
I shall steal down and find my ship
　By the dim quayside, and embark,

Nor fear the seas nor any wind.
　I have known Fear, but now no more.
The winds shall bear me safe and kind,
　Long-hoped for and long-waited for.

To no strange country shall I come,
　But to mine own delightful land,
With Love to bid me welcome home
　And Love to lead me by the hand.
                          Katherine Tynan Hinkson

216   *SEALED ORDERS*

We bear sealed orders o'er Life's weltered sea,
　Our haven dim and far;
We can but man the helm right cheerily,
　Steer by the brightest star,

And hope that when at last the Great Command
　Is read, we then may hear
Our anchor song, and see the longed-for land
　Lie, known and very near.
                          Richard Burton

217   *'TIS LIFE BEYOND*

I watched a sail until it dropped from sight
Over the rounding sea—a gleam of light,
A last, far-flashed farewell, and, like a thought
Slipt out of mind, it vanished and was not.

Yet, to the helmsman standing at the wheel,
Broad seas still swept beneath the gliding keel;
Disaster? Change? He felt no slightest sign,
Nor dreamed he of that far horizon line.

So may it be, perchance, when, down the tide
Our dear ones vanish. Peacefully they glide
On level seas, nor mark the unknown bound.
We call it death—to them 'tis life beyond.

Author Unknown

218   *BEYOND THE HORIZON*

When men go down to the sea in ships,
'Tis not to the sea they go;
Some isle or pole the mariners' goal,
And thither they sail through calm and gale,
When down to the sea they go.

When souls go down to the sea by ship,
And the dark ship's name is Death,
Why mourn and wail at the vanishing sail?
Though outward bound, God's world is round,
And only a ship is Death.

When I go down to the sea by ship,
And Death unfurls her sail,
Weep not for me, for there will be
A living host on another coast
To beckon and cry, "All hail!"

Robert Freeman

219   *From THE BEYOND*

It seemeth such a little way to me,
Across to that strange country, the Beyond;
And yet, not strange, for it has grown to be
The home of those of whom I am so fond;
They make it seem familiar and most dear,
As journeying friends bring distant countries near.

So close it lies that when my sight is clear
I think I almost see the gleaming strand;
I know, I feel, that those who've gone from here
Come near enough sometimes to touch my hand;
I often think, but for our veiléd eyes,
We should find heaven right about us lies.

❋

And so for me there is no sting to death,
And so the grave has lost its victory;
It is but crossing with abated breath
And white, set face, a little strip of sea,
To find the loved ones waiting on the shore,
More beautiful, more precious than before.

Ella Wheeler Wilcox

220   *ON THE DEATH OF TENNYSON*

No moaning of the bar; sail forth, strong ship,
   Into that gloom which has God's face for a far light.
Not a dirge, but a proud farewell from each fond lip,
   And praise, abounding praise, and fame's faint star light,

Lamping thy tuneful soul to that large noon
   Where thou shalt choir with angels. Words of woe
Are for the unfulfilled, not thee, whose moon
   Of genius sinks full-orbed, glorious, aglow.

No moaning of the bar; musical drifting
   Of Time's waves, turning to the eternal sea,
Death's soft wind all thy gallant canvas lifting,
   And Christ thy Pilot to the peace to be.

Edwin Arnold

221   *JOURNEY'S END*

The spirit shall return unto God who gave it.

We go from God to God—then though
   The way be long,
We shall return to Heaven our home
   At evensong.

We go from God to God—so let
   The space between
Be filled with beauty, conquering
   Things base and mean.

We go from God to God—lo! what
   Transcendent bliss,
To know the journey's end will hold
   Such joy as this!

Evelyn H. Healey

222   *THE GUESTS OF GOD*

From the dust at the weary highway—
From the smart of sorrow's rod,
Into the royal presence—
They are bidden as guests of God.
The veil from their eyes is taken,
Sweet mysteries they are shown,
Their doubts and fears are over
For they know as they are known.

For them there should be rejoicing
And festival array,
As for the bride in her beauty
Whom love hath taken away—
Sweet hours of peaceful waiting
Till the path that we have trod
Shall end at the Father's gateway,
And we are the guests of God.

                                    Mary Frances Butts

223   *From THE KISS OF GOD*

So I looked up to God,
And while I held my breath
I saw Him slowly nod,
And knew—as I had never known aught else,
With certainty sublime and passionate,
Shot through and through
With sheer unutterable bliss.
I knew
There was no death but this
God's kiss.
And then the waking to an everlasting Love.

                            G. A. Studdert-Kennedy

224 *GOD KNOWS*

God knows, not I, the devious ways
Wherein my faltering feet may tread
Before into the light of day
My steps from out this gloom are led;
But since my Lord the path doth see
What matter if 'tis hid from me.

God knows, not I, how sweet accord
Shall grow at length from out this clash
Of earthly discords that jar on
Soul and sense. I hear the crash
But feel and know that on His ear
Break harmony full deep and clear.

His perfect plan I may not grasp
Yet I can trust love infinite
And with my feeble fingers clasp
The Hand which leads mine into light;
My soul upon His errand goes,
The end I know not, *but God knows.*

Author Unknown

225 *THE MYSTERY*

He came and took me by the hand
  Up to a red rose-tree,
He kept His meaning to Himself
  But gave a rose to me.

I did not pray Him to lay bare
  The mystery to me;
Enough the rose was Heaven to smell,
  And His own face to see.

Ralph Hodgson

226   *THE CONCLUSION*

Ever such is Time, that takes in trust
   Our youth, our joys, our all we have,
And pays us but with earth and dust;
   Who, in the dark and silent grave,
When we have wandered all our ways,
Shuts up the story of our days.
But from this earth, this grave, this dust,
My God shall raise me up, I trust!
                      Walter Raleigh

227   *From WHEN ALL IS DONE*

When all is done, and my last word is said,
And ye who loved me murmur, "He is dead,"
Let no one weep, for fear that I should know,
And sorrow too that ye should sorrow so.

                *

When all is done, say not my day is o'er,
And that thro' night I seek a dimmer shore:
Say rather that my morn has just begun,—
I greet the dawn and not a setting sun,
           When all is done.
             Paul Laurence Dunbar

228   *From IF A MAN DIE*

There is a hope, a quiet hope,
   Within my heart instilled,
That if undaunted on I sail,
The guiding star shall never pale,
But shine within my labor's scope,
   Fulfilled!

And there's a tide, a quiet tide,
   Flowing toward a goal,
That sweeps by every humble shore,
And at its fullest ebbs no more,
And on that final swell shall ride,
   My soul!
            J. D. Jones

229   *DAWN*

Out of the dark, the light! O Hearts, remember
The eternal truth God gives us as a sign
That after the dark, as glowing as an ember,
Deep at the core of life, a light will shine:
The light of hope, after the bitter weeping;
The light of peace, after the lengthened pain.
The Christian heart held close within God's keeping
Will find the dark skies brightening again.

The risen Christ is proof of light's returning;
The risen Christ is symbol of the dawn.
O you who have been striving, longing, yearning
To catch the light ahead, move out, move on.
You will find him there among the springtime flowers,
Among the clean winds of a new-born day.
He is the lamp for all our future hours;
He is the light to guide us on our way.
                              Grace Noll Crowell

230   *CHARTLESS*

I never saw a moor,
I never saw the sea;
Yet know I how the heather looks,
And what a wave must be.

I never spoke with God,
Nor visited in heaven;
Yet certain am I of the spot
As if the chart were given.
                         Emily Dickinson

231   *NATURE*

As a fond mother, when the day is o'er,
   Leads by the hand her little child to bed,
   Half willing, half reluctant to be led,
And leave his broken playthings on the floor,

Still gazing at them through the open door,
  Not wholly reassured and comforted
  By promises of others in their stead,
Which, though more splendid, may not please him more;
So nature deals with us, and takes away
  Our playthings one by one, and by the hand
  Leads us to rest so gently, that we go
Scarce knowing if we wish to go or stay,
  Being too full of sleep to understand
  How far the unknown transcends what we know.

Henry Wadsworth Longfellow

232   *From IT IS NOT DEATH TO DIE*

It is not death to die,
  To leave this weary road,
And, midst the brotherhood on high,
  To be at home with God.

It is not death to close
  The eye long dimmed with tears,
And wake in glorious repose,
  To spend eternal years.

It is not death to fling
  Aside this sinful dust,
And rise on strong, exulting wing,
  To live among the just.

Jesus, thou Prince of Life,
  Thy chosen cannot die!
Like Thee, they conquer in the strife,
  To reign with Thee on high.

George Washington Bethune

233   *From THERE IS NO DEATH*

There is no death! The stars go down
  To rise upon some other shore,
And bright in heaven's jeweled crown
  They shine for evermore.

There is no death! the dust we tread
  Shall change beneath the summer showers
To golden grain, or mellow fruit,
  Or rainbow-tinted flowers.

There is no death! An angel form
  Walks o'er the earth with silent tread;
He bears our best loved ones away,
  And then we call them "dead."

Born unto that undying life,
  They leave us but to come again;
With joy we welcome them—the same
  Except in sin and pain.

And ever near us, though unseen,
  The dear immortal spirits tread;
For all the boundless universe
  Is life—there are no dead!
                    John Luckey McCreery

234   *From THERE IS NO DEATH*

There is no death,—
They only truly live
Who pass into the life beyond, and see
This earth is but a school preparative
For larger ministry.

There is no death
To those whose hearts are set
On higher things than this life doth afford;
How shall their passing leave one least regret,
Who go to join their Lord?
                    John Oxenham

235   *WHAT IS DEATH?*

What is death? A little broadening of a ripple
Upon the Eternal shore.
A little loosening of the bands that cripple—
This and nothing more.
What's death? A parting of the cloud above us
Which hides the sun,
A gold vision of the souls that love us
And labor done.
What's death? The opening of a perfect flower;
No watcher sees
The silent spirit, who at twilight hour
The bondman frees.
What's death? God's mercy strange
Uncomprehended;
The undiscovered goal;
The land of promise when the toil
Is ended—
The day-dawn of the soul.

                              Author Unknown

236   *DEATH IS A DOOR*

Death is only an old door
    Set in a garden wall.
On quiet hinges it gives at dusk
    When the late birds call.

Along the lintel are green leaves;
    Beyond, the light lies still;
Very weary and willing feet
    Go over that sill.

There is nothing to trouble any heart,
    Nothing to hurt at all,—
Death is only an old door
    In a garden wall.

                              Nancy Byrd Turner

237   *From TO THE QUEEN*

The Door of Death is made of Gold,
That Mortal Eyes cannot behold;
But, when the Mortal Eyes are clos'd,
And cold and pale the Limbs repos'd,
The Soul awakes; and, wond'ring, sees
In her mild Hand the golden Keys:
The Grave is Heaven's golden Gate,
And rich and poor around it wait.

William Blake

238   *DIVINE RHYTHM*

Clouds, then glory of sunset;
   Darkness, then burst of the morn;
Dearth, then the gentle shower;
   Sacrifice—Truth is born!

The earth-throe, then comes the harvest;
   Silence, and then the word;
Mist, before the full starlight;
   Discord, ere music is heard!

Erring, and then the forgiveness;
   Heart's-ease after the strife;
Passion, and then the refining—
   Death, then the wonder of life!

Henry Meade Bland

239   *MY SOUL AND I*

As treading some long corridor,
   My soul and I together go;
Each day unlocks another door
   To a new room we did not know.

And every night the darkness hides
   My soul from me awhile—but then
No fear nor loneliness abides;
   Hand clasped in hand, we wake again.

So when my soul and I, at last,
  Shall find but one dim portal more,
Shall we, remembering all the past,
  Yet fear to try that other door?
                    Charles Buxton Going

240   *EMANCIPATION*

Why be afraid of Death as though your life were breath!
Death but anoints your eyes with clay. O glad surprise!

Why should you be forlorn? Death only husks the corn.
Why should you fear to meet the thresher of the wheat?

Is sleep a thing to dread? Yet sleeping, you are dead
Till you awake and rise, here, or beyond the skies.

Why should it be a wrench to leave your wooden bench,
Why not with happy shout run home when school is out?

The dear ones left behind! O foolish one and blind.
A day—and you will meet,—a night—and you will greet!

This is the death of Death, to breathe away a breath
And know the end of strife, and taste the deathless life.

And joy without a fear, and smile without a tear,
And work, nor care, nor rest, and find the last the best.
                    Maltbie D. Babcock

241   *PROSPICE*[1]

Fear death?—to feel the fog in my throat,
  The mist in my face,
When the snows begin, and the blasts denote
  I am nearing the place,
The power of the night, the press of the storm,
  The post of the foe;
Where he stands, the Arch Fear in a visible form,
  Yet the strong man must go;

[1] The title means "look forward." The poem was written shortly after his wife's death.

For the journey is done and the summit attained,
   And the barriers fall,
Though a battle's to fight ere the guerdon be gained,
   The reward of it all.
I was ever a fighter, so—one fight more,
   The best and the last!
I would hate that death bandaged my eyes, and forbore,
   And bade me creep past.
No! let me taste the whole of it, fare like my peers
   The heroes of old,
Bear the brunt, in a minute pay glad life's arrears
   Of pain, darkness, and cold.
For sudden the worst turns the best to the brave,
   The black minute's at end,
And the elements' rage, the fiend-voices that rave,
   Shall dwindle, shall blend,
Shall change, shall become first a peace out of pain,
   Then a light, then thy breast,
O thou soul of my soul! I shall clasp thee again,
   And with God be the rest!

                              Robert Browning

242   *DEATH*

      Death stands above me, whispering low
        I know not what into my ear:
      Of his strange language all I know
        Is, there is not a word of fear.
                Walter Savage Landor

243   *From LAST LINES*

    No coward soul is mine,
  No trembler in the world's storm-troubled sphere,
    I see Heaven's glories shine,
  And faith shines equal, arming me from fear.

    O God within my breast,
  Almighty, ever-present Deity!
    Life—that in me has rest,
  As I—undying Life—have power in Thee!

There is not room for Death,
Nor atom that his might could render void:
Thou—*Thou* art Being and Breath,
And what *Thou* art may never be destroyed.

Emily Brontë

244   *A DYING HYMN*

Earth, with its dark and dreadful ills,
  Recedes, and fades away;
Lift up your heads, ye heavenly hills;
  Ye gates of death, give way!

My soul is full of whispered song,
  My blindness is my sight;
The shadows that I feared so long
  Are all alive with light.

The while my pulses faintly beat,
  My faith doth so abound,
I feel grow firm beneath my feet
  The green immortal ground.

That faith to me a courage gives
  Low as the grave, to go:
I know that my Redeemer lives:
  That I shall live, I know.

The palace walls I almost see,
  Where dwells my Lord and King;
O grave, where is thy victory!
  O death, where is thy sting!

Alice Cary

245   *From PARACELSUS*

If I stoop
Into a dark tremendous sea of cloud,
It is but for a time; I press God's lamp
Close to my breast; its splendor, soon or late,
Will pierce the gloom: I shall emerge one day.

Robert Browning

246   *From NOT KNOWING*

So I go on, not knowing,—I would not, if I might;
I would rather walk in the dark with God than go alone in the light;
I would rather walk with Him by faith than walk alone by sight.
Mary Gardner Brainard

247   *FAITH*

The sea was breaking at my feet,
And looking out across the tide,
Where placid waves and heaven meet,
I thought me of the Other Side.

For on the beach on which I stood
Were wastes of sand, and wash, and roar,
Low clouds, and gloom, and solitude,
And wrecks, and ruins—nothing more.

"O tell me if beyond the sea
A heavenly port there is!" I cried,
And back the echoes laughingly
"There is! there is!" replied.
James Whitcomb Riley

248   *HOME*

There lies a little city in the hills;
White are its roofs, dim is each dwelling's door,
And peace with perfect rest its bosom fills.

There the pure mist, the pity of the sea,
Comes as a white, soft hand, and reaches o'er
And touches its still face most tenderly.

Unstirred and calm, amid our shifting years,
Lo! where it lies, far from the clash and roar,
With quiet distance blurred, as if through tears.

O heart that prayest so for God to send
Some loving messenger to go before
And lead the way to where thy longings end,

Be sure, be very sure, that soon will come
His kindest angel, and through that still door
Into the Infinite love will lead thee home.

Edward Rowland Sill

249   *HOME OF THE SOUL*

I will sing you a song of that beautiful land,
    The faraway home of the soul,
Where no storms beat on the glittering strand,
    While the years of eternity roll.

O that home of the soul! In my visions and dreams
    Its bright, jasper walls I can see;
Till I fancy but thinly the veil intervenes
    Between the fair city and me.

Ellen H. Gates

250   *GOD'S TO-MORROW*

The night is very black and grim,
—Our hearts are sick with sorrow,—
But, on the rim of the curtain dim,
A pulsing beam, a tiny gleam,
Whispers of God's To-morrow.

Beyond the night there shines a light,
—Our eyes are dim with sorrow,—
But Faith still clings, and Hope still springs,
And Love still sings of happier things,
For Life is flighting strong new wings
In search of God's To-morrow.

John Oxenham

251   *THE FATHER'S HOUSE*

The Father's house has many rooms,
    And each is fair;
And some are reached through gathered glooms
    By silent stair;
But he keeps house, and makes it home,
Whichever way the children come.

Plenty and peace are everywhere
  His house within;
The rooms are eloquent with prayer,
  The songs begin;
And dear hearts, filled with love, are glad,
Forgetting that they once were sad.

The Father's house is surely thine,
  Therefore why wait?
His lights of love through darkness shine,
  The hour grows late.
Push back the curtain of thy doubt,
And enter—none will cast thee out!

Marianne Farningham
(Mary Anne Hearne)

252   *IN MY FATHER'S HOUSE*

In my Father's house are many mansions.   JOHN 14:2.

No, not cold beneath the grasses,
  Not close-walled within the tomb;
Rather in my father's mansion,
  Living, in another room.

Living, like the one who loves me,
  Like yon child with cheeks abloom,
Out of sight, at desk or schoolbook,
  Busy, in another room.

Nearer than the youth whom fortune
  Beckons where the strange lands loom;
Just behind the hanging curtain,
  Serving in another room.

Shall I doubt my Father's mercy?
  Shall I think of death as doom,
Or the stepping o'er the threshold
  To a bigger, brighter room?

Shall I blame my Father's wisdom?
Shall I sit enswathed in gloom,
When I know my love is happy
Waiting in another room?

Robert Freeman

253　　　*HEAVEN OVERARCHES EARTH AND SEA*

Heaven overarches earth and sea,
　Earth-sadness and sea-bitterness.
Heaven overarches you and me:
A little while and we shall be—
Please God—where there is no more sea
　Nor barren wilderness.

Heaven overarches you and me,
　And all earth's gardens and her graves.
Look up with me, until we see
The day break and the shadows flee.
What though to-night wrecks you and me,
　If so to-morrow saves?

Christina Georgina Rossetti

254　　　　　　　　*BE STILL*

Be still, my soul: the Lord is on thy side;
　Bear patiently the cross of grief or pain;
Leave to thy God to order and provide;
　In every change he faithful will remain.
Be still, my soul: thy best, thy heavenly Friend
Through thorny ways leads to a joyful end.

Be still, my soul: thy God doth undertake
　To guide the future as he has the past.
Thy hope, thy confidence let nothing shake;
　All now mysterious shall be bright at last.
Be still, my soul: the waves and winds still know
His voice who ruled them while he dwelt below.

Be still, my soul: the hour is hastening on
When we shall be forever with the Lord,
When disappointment, grief, and fear are gone,
Sorrow forgot, love's purest joys restored.
Be still, my soul: when change and tears are past,
All safe and blessed we shall meet at last.
Katharina von Schlegel; tr. by Jane L. Borthwick

255   *PEACE, PERFECT PEACE*

Peace, perfect peace, in this dark world of sin?
The blood of Jesus whispers peace within.

Peace, perfect peace, by thronging duties pressed?
To do the will of Jesus, this is rest.

Peace, perfect peace, with sorrows surging round?
On Jesus' bosom naught but calm is found.

Peace, perfect peace, our future all unknown?
Jesus we know, and he is on the throne.

Peace, perfect peace, death shadowing us and ours?
Jesus has vanquished death and all its powers.

It is enough: earth's struggles soon shall cease,
And Jesus call us to heaven's perfect peace.
Edward H. Bickersteth

256   *THE LOVE OF GOD*

God's boundless Love and arching sky
Above us when we wake or sleep,
Above us when we smile or weep,
Above us when we live or die.

God's tireless Love! Beside the cot
Of her sick child the mother sleeps.
The Heavenly Father ever keeps
Unweary watch—He slumbers not.

God's patient Love! Misunderstood
By hearts that suffer in the night.
Doubted—yet waiting till Heaven's light
Shall show how all things work for good.

God's mighty Love! On Calvary's height,
Suffering to save us from our sin,
To bring the Heavenly Kingdom in,
And fill our lives with joy and light.

God's changeless Love! The wandering one
Forsakes, forgets, dishonors; yet,
Repenting, going home, is met
With no reproach—"Welcome, my son!"

God's endless Love! What will it be
When earthly shadows flee away,
For all Eternity's bright day
The unfolding of that Love to see!

Maltbie D. Babcock

257 *IN HEAVENLY LOVE ABIDING*

In heavenly love abiding,
  No change my heart shall fear;
And safe in such confiding,
  For nothing changes here.
The storm may roar without me,
  My heart may low be laid;
But God is round about me,
  And can I be dismayed?

Wherever He may guide me,
  No want shall turn me back;
My Shepherd is beside me,
  And nothing can I lack.
His wisdom ever waketh,
  His sight is never dim;
He knows the way He taketh,
  And I will walk with Him.

Green pastures are before me,
  Which yet I have not seen;
Bright skies will soon be o'er me,
  Where the dark clouds have been.
My hope I cannot measure,
  The path to life is free;
My Saviour has my treasure,
  And He will walk with me.

Anna L. Waring

258   *A ONE HUNDRED FIFTY-FIRST PSALM*

The Lord is my friend, so I shall not be lonely even in a strange land;
He is the Good Angel above my bed, so I shall see the dawn.

Even though I wandered far from His counsel, He did not desert me;
When I arose to return, it was His voice that I heard.

When I beheld the glory of the West at eve, I remembered Him;
The moonrise over the mountains was the trailing of His mantle.

When the storm crashed against the mountain, His almightiness
    pealed forth,
And the gray face of the desert whispered His holy austerity.

As I entered the place of prayer, I was strangely moved;
When I came away, I had said not a word.

Yet, as I kept silence before Him, He understood:
My soul was lifted as though I had seen His face.

When I awoke in the night, He possessed my thought;
And in the morning I turned a moment from my task to speak of Him.

He has traveled further for me than any one; He has done more;
Yet there is no price upon Love, and I cannot repay Him.

When I was at Death's door, He closed it and led me away.
Surely He will be there when I must pass through.

Henry B. Robins

259   *From THE ETERNAL GOODNESS*

Yet, in the maddening maze of things,
    And tossed by storm and flood,
To one fixed trust my spirit clings;
    I know that God is good!

I long for household voices gone,
    For vanished smiles I long,
But God hath led my dear ones on,
    And He can do no wrong.

I know not what the future hath
    Of marvel or surprise,
Assured alone that life and death
    His mercy underlies.

And so beside the Silent Sea
    I wait the muffled oar;
No harm from Him can come to me
    On ocean or on shore.

I know not where His islands lift
    Their fronded palms in air;
I only know I cannot drift
    Beyond His love and care.

And Thou, O Lord! by whom are seen
    Thy creatures as they be,
Forgive me if too close I lean
    My human heart on Thee!
                        John Greenleaf Whittier

260   *GOD*

There is an eye that never sleeps
    Beneath the wing of night;
There is an ear that never shuts
    When sinks the beams of light.

There is an arm that never tires
When human strength gives way;
There is a love that never fails
When earthly loves decay.

That Eye unseen o'erwatcheth all;
That Arm upholds the sky;
That Ear doth hear the sparrows call;
That Love is ever nigh.

James Cowden Wallace

261   *IT CANNOT BE*

It cannot be that He who made
This wondrous world for our delight,
Designed that all its charms should fade
And pass forever from our sight;
That all shall wither and decay,
And know on earth no life but this,
With only one finite survey
Of all its beauty and its bliss.

It cannot be that all the years
Of toil and care and grief we live
Shall find no recompense but tears,
No sweet return that earth can give;
That all that leads us to aspire,
And struggle onward to achieve,
And every unattained desire
Were given only to deceive.

It cannot be that, after all
The mighty conquests of the mind,
Our thoughts shall pass beyond recall
And leave no record here behind;
That all our dreams of love and fame,
And hopes that time has swept away,—
All that enthralled this mortal frame,—
Shall not return some other day.

It cannot be that all the ties
  Of kindred souls and loving hearts
Are broken when this body dies,
  And the immortal mind departs;
That no serener light shall break
  At last upon our mortal eyes,
To guide us as our footsteps make
  The pilgrimage to Paradise.

David Banks Sickels

262   *CHRISTUS CONSOLATOR*

Beside the dead I knelt for prayer,
  And felt a presence as I prayed.
Lo! it was Jesus standing there.
  He smiled: "Be not afraid!"

"Lord, thou hast conquered death, we know;
  Restore again to life," I said,
"This one who died an hour ago."
  He smiled: "*She* is not dead!"

"Asleep then, as thyself didst say;
  Yet thou canst lift the lids that keep
Her prisoned eyes from ours away."
  He smiled: "*She* doth not sleep!"

"Nay, then, tho' haply she doth wake,
  And look upon some fairer dawn,
Restore her to our hearts that ache."
  He smiled: "*She* is not gone!"

"Alas! too well we know our loss,
  Nor hope again our joy to touch,
Until the stream of death we cross."
  He smiled: "There is no such!"

"Yet our beloved seem so far,
  The while we yearn to feel them near,
Albeit with thee we trust they are."
  He smiled: "And I am here!"

"Dear Lord, how shall we know that they
    Still walk unseen with us and thee,
Nor sleep, nor wander far away?"
    He smiled: "Abide in me!"
                                Rossiter W. Raymond

263   *THE UNSEEN BRIDGE*

There is a bridge, whereof the span
Is rooted in the heart of man,
And reaches, without pile or rod,
Unto the Great White Throne of God.

Its traffic is in human sighs,
Fervently wafted to the skies;
'Tis the one pathway from despair,
And it is called the Bridge of Prayer.
                                Gilbert Thomas

264   *COME, YE DISCONSOLATE*

Come, ye disconsolate, where'er ye languish;
    Come to the mercy-seat, fervently kneel:
Here bring your wounded hearts, here tell your anguish;
    Earth has no sorrow that Heaven cannot heal.

Joy of the desolate, light of the straying,
    Hope of the penitent, fadeless and pure,
Here speaks the Comforter, tenderly saying,
    "Earth has no sorrow that Heaven cannot cure."

Here see the Bread of Life; see waters flowing
    Forth from the throne of God, pure from above;
Come to the feast of love; come, ever knowing
    Earth has no sorrow but Heaven can remove.
                                Thomas Moore

265   *ANGEL OF PATIENCE*

To weary hearts, to mourning homes,
God's meekest Angel gently comes:
No power has he to banish pain,
Or give us back our lost again;
And yet in tenderest love, our dear
And Heavenly Father sends him here.

There's quiet in that Angel's glance,
There's rest in his still countenance!
He mocks no grief with idle cheer,
Nor wounds with words the mourner's ear;
But ills and woes he may not cure
He kindly trains us to endure.

Angel of Patience! sent to calm
Our feverish brows with cooling palm;
To lay the storms of hope and fear,
And reconcile life's smile and tear;
The throbs of wounded pride to still,
And make our own our Father's will!

O thou who mournest on thy way,
With longings for the close of day;
He walks with thee, that Angel kind,
And gently whispers, "Be resigned:
Bear up, bear on, the end shall tell
The dear Lord ordereth all things well!"

                         John Greenleaf Whittier

266   *WHEN SORROW COMES*

When sorrow comes, as come it must,
In God a man must put his trust.
There is no power in mortal speech
The anguish of his soul to reach,
No voice, however sweet and low,
Can comfort him or ease the blow.

He cannot from his fellow men
Take strength that will sustain him then.
With all that kindly hands will do,
And all that love may offer, too,
He must believe throughout the test
That God has willed it for the best.

We who would be his friends are dumb;
Words from our lips but feebly come;
We feel, as we extend our hands,
That one Power only understands
And truly knows the reason why
So beautiful a soul must die.

We realize how helpless then
Are all the gifts of mortal men.
No words which we have power to say
Can take the sting of grief away—
That Power which marks the sparrow's fall
Must comfort and sustain us all.

When sorrow comes, as come it must,
In God a man must place his trust.
With all the wealth which he may own,
He cannot meet the test alone,
And only he may stand serene
Who has a faith on which to lean.

Edgar A. Guest

267   *SORROW*

Count each affliction, whether light or grave,
    God's messenger sent down to thee; do thou
    With courtesy receive him: rise and bow;
And, ere his shadow pass thy threshold, crave
Permission first his heavenly feet to lave;
    Then lay before him all thou hast; allow
    No cloud of passion to usurp thy brow,
Or mar thy hospitality; no wave

Of mortal tumult to obliterate
Thy soul's marmoreal calmness. Grief should be
Like joy, majestic, equable, sedate;
Confirming, cleansing, raising, making free;
Strong to consume small troubles; to commend
Great thoughts, grave thoughts, thoughts lasting to the end.

Aubrey Thomas de Vere

268   *WHY SHOULD WE WEEP FOR THOSE WHO DIE*

Why should we weep for those who die?
They fall—their dust returns to dust;
Their souls shall live eternally
Within the mansions of the just.

They die to live—they sink to rise,
They leave this wretched mortal shore;
But brighter suns and bluer skies
Shall smile on them for evermore.

Why should we sorrow for the dead?
Our life on earth is but a span;
They tread the path that all must tread,
They die the common death of man.

The noblest songster of the gale
Must cease, when Winter's frowns appear;
The reddest rose is wan and pale,
When Autumn tints the changing year.

The fairest flower on earth must fade,
The brightest hopes on earth must die:
Why should we mourn that man was made
To droop on earth, but dwell on high?

The soul, th' eternal soul, must reign
In worlds devoid of pain and strife;
Then why should mortal man complain
Of death, which leads to happier life?

Charles Tennyson-Turner

269   *From THE SLEEP*

He giveth his beloved sleep. PSALM 127:2
   Of all the thoughts of God that are
   Borne inward into souls afar,
   Along the Psalmist's music deep,
   Now tell me if that any is,
   For gift or grace, surpassing this:
   "He giveth his belovèd—sleep"?
          Elizabeth Barrett Browning

270   *REQUIEM*

Under the wide and starry sky,
Dig the grave and let me lie.
Glad did I live and gladly die,
   And I laid me down with a will.

This be the verse you grave for me:
Here he lies where he longed to be;
Home is the sailor, home from the sea,
And the hunter home from the hill.
          Robert Louis Stevenson

271   *THE HILLS OF REST*

Beyond the last horizon's rim,
   Beyond adventure's farthest quest,
Somewhere they rise, serene and dim,
   The happy, happy, Hills of Rest.

Upon their sunlit slopes uplift
   The castles we have built in Spain—
While fair amid the summer drift
   Our faded gardens flower again.

Sweet hours we did not live go by
   To soothing note, on scented wing;
In golden-lettered volumes lie
   The songs we tried in vain to sing.

They all are there; the days of dream
    That build the inner lives of men;
The silent, sacred years we deem
    The might be and the might have been.

Some evening when the sky is gold
    I'll follow day into the west;
Nor pause, nor heed, till I behold
    The happy, happy Hills of Rest.

Albert Bigelow Paine

272   *DIRGE*

Calm on the bosom of thy God,
    Fair spirit, rest thee now!
E'en while with ours thy footsteps trod,
    His seal was on thy brow.

Dust, to its narrow house beneath!
    Soul, to its place on high!
They that have seen thy look in death
    No more may fear to die.

Lone are the paths, and sad the bowers,
    Whence thy meek smile is gone;
But oh! a brighter home than ours
    In heaven, is now thine own.

Felicia Dorothea Hemans

273   *From THE HOUR OF PERFECT REST*

There is an hour of peaceful rest
    To mourning wanderers given;
There is a joy for souls distressed,
A balm for every wounded breast,
    'Tis found alone in heaven.

There is a home for weary souls
    By sin and sorrow driven;
When tossed on life's tempestuous shoals,
Where storms arise, and ocean rolls,
    And all is drear but heaven.

There faith lifts up her cheerful eye,
    To brighter prospects given;
And views the tempest passing by,
The evening shadows quickly fly,
    And all serene in heaven.

There fragrant flowers immortal bloom,
    And joys supreme are given;
There rays divine disperse the gloom:
Beyond the confines of the tomb
    Appears the dawn of heaven.

William Bingham Tappan

274 *From ELEGY ON THE DEATH OF DR. CHANNING*

Therefore I cannot think thee wholly gone;
    The better part of thee is with us still;
Thy soul its hampering clay aside hath thrown,
    And only freer wrestles with the Ill.

Thou livest in the life of all good things;
    What words thou spak'st for Freedom shall not die;
Thou sleepest not, for now thy Love hath wings
    To soar where hence thy Hope could hardly fly.

And often, from that other world, on this
    Some gleams from great souls gone before may shine,
To shed on struggling hearts a clearer bliss,
    And clothe the Right with lustre more divine.

James Russell Lowell

275 *FRIENDS BEYOND*

I cannot think of them as dead,
    Who walk with me no more;
Along the path of life I tread—
    They have but gone before.

The Father's House is mansioned fair,
    Beyond my vision dim;
All souls are His, and here or there
    Are living unto Him.

And still their silent ministry
   Within my heart hath place,
As when on earth they walked with me,
   And met me face to face.

Their lives are made forever mine;
   What they to me have been
Hath left henceforth its seal and sign
   Engraven deep within.

Mine are they by an ownership
   Nor time nor death can free;
For God hath given to love to keep
   Its own eternally.

Frederick L. Hosmer

276   *WELL DONE*

Servant of God, well done!
   Rest from thy loved employ:
The battle fought, the victory won,
   Enter thy Master's joy.

The pains of death are past,
   Labor and sorrow cease,
The Life's long warfare closed at last,
   Thy soul is found in peace.

James Montgomery

277   *REST*

   They are at rest.
We may not stir the heaven of their repose
By rude invoking voice, or prayer addrest
   In waywardness to those
Who in the mountain grots of Eden lie,
And hear the fourfold river as it murmurs by.

They hear it sweep
In distance down the dark and savage vale;
But they at rocky bed or current deep
    Shall never more grow pale.
They hear, and meekly muse, as fain to know
How long untired, unspent, that giant stream shall flow

    And soothing sounds
Blend with the neighb'ring waters as they glide;
Posted along the haunted garden's bounds,
    Angelic forms abide,
Echoing, as words of watch, o'er lawn and grove,
The verses of that hymn which seraphs chant above.

                              John Henry Newman

278   *From AFTER DEATH IN ARABIA*

    Farewell, friends! yet not farewell;
    Where I am, ye too shall dwell.
    I am gone before your face,
    A moment's time, a little space.
    When ye come where I have stepped,
    Ye will wonder why ye wept;
    Ye will know, by wise love taught
    That here is all, and there is naught.
    Weep a while, if ye are fain,—
    Sunshine still must follow rain;
    Only not at death,—for death,
    Now I know, is that first breath
    Which our souls draw when we enter
    Life, which is of all life center.

                              Edwin Arnold

279   *From LUCY HOOPER*

Farewell! A little time, and we
    Who knew thee well, and loved thee here,
One after one shall follow thee
    As pilgrims through the gate of fear,
Which opens on eternity.

Yet shall we cherish not the less
    All that is left our hearts meanwhile;
The memory of thy loveliness
    Shall round our weary pathway smile,
Like moonlight when the sun has set,
A sweet and tender radiance yet.
Thoughts of thy clear-eyed sense of duty,
    Thy generous scorn of all things wrong,
The truth, the strength, the graceful beauty
    Which blended in thy song.
All lovely things, by thee beloved,
    Shall whisper to our hearts of thee;
These green hills, where thy childhood roved,
    Yon river winding to the sea,
The sunset light of autumn eves
    Reflecting on the deep, still floods,
Cloud, crimson sky, and trembling leaves
    Of rainbow-tinted woods,
These, in our view, shall henceforth take
A tenderer meaning for thy sake;
And all thou lovedst of earth and sky
Seem sacred to thy memory.
                John Greenleaf Whittier

280   *From AWAY*

I cannot say, and I will not say
That he is dead.—He is just away!

With a cheery smile, and a wave of the hand,
He has wandered into an unknown land.

And left us dreaming how very fair
It needs must be since he lingers there.

And you—O you, who the wildest yearn
For the old-time step and the glad return,—

Think of him faring on, as dear
In the love of There as the love of Here;

Think of him still as the same, I say;
He is not dead—he is just away!

James Whitcomb Riley

281   *TURNING THE CORNER*

I often saw you
When I turned the corner
Into your street.

A while ago I followed you
As you bent to meet the storm
Along the one-way street.

And then you turned the corner
Where the shadows lie,
And I lost sight of you.

And I must still go on,
But when I turn the corner
I hope to see you again.

Arthur B. Rhinow

282   *VERSES WRITTEN IN 1872*

Though he that ever kind and true,
Kept stoutly step by step with you
Your whole long gusty lifetime through
    Be gone awhile before,
Be now a moment gone before,
Yet, doubt not, soon the seasons shall restore
    Your friend to you.

He has but turned a corner; still
He pushes on with right good will,
Thro' mire and marsh, by heuch and hill
    That self-same arduous way,—
That self-same upland hopeful way,
That you and he through many a doubtful day
    Attempted still.

He is not dead, this friend; not dead,
But, in the path we mortals tread,
Got some few, trifling steps ahead,
    And nearer to the end,
So that you, too, once past the bend,
Shall meet again, as face to face, this friend
    You fancy dead.

Push gaily on, strong heart! The while
You travel forward mile by mile,
He loiters with a backward smile
    Till you can overtake,
And strains his eyes, to search his wake,
Or whistling, as he sees you through the brake,
    Waits on a stile.

Robert Louis Stevenson

283   *From SNOW-BOUND*

Yet Love will dream, and Faith will trust,
(Since He who knows our need is just,)
That somehow, somewhere, meet we must.
Alas for him who never sees
The stars shine through his cypress-trees!
Who, hopeless, lays his dead away,
Nor looks to see the breaking day
Across the mournful marble play!
Who hath not learned, in hours of faith,
    The truth to flesh and sense unknown,
That Life is ever lord of Death,
    And Love can never lose its own!

John Greenleaf Whittier

284   *UNION OF FRIENDS*

They that love beyond the World, cannot be separated by it.
Death cannot kill, what never dies.
Nor can Spirits ever be divided that love and live in the same
Divine Principle; the Root and Record of their Friendship.
If Absence be not death, neither is theirs.

Death is but Crossing the World, as Friends do the Seas; they live in one another still.

For they must needs be present, that love and live in that which is omnipresent.

In this Divine Glass, they see Face to Face; and their Converse is Free, as well as pure.

This is the Comfort of Friends, that though they may be said to Die, yet their Friendship and Society are, in the best Sense, ever present, because Immortal.

William Penn

285   *THE DEPARTED*

They cannot wholly pass away,
    How far soe'er above;
Nor we, the lingerers, wholly stay
    Apart from those we love:
For spirits in eternity,
    As shadows in the sun,
Reach backward into time, as we,
    Like lifted clouds, reach on.
        John Banister Tabb

286   *From THEY SOFTLY WALK*

They are not gone who pass
Beyond the clasp of hand,
Out from the strong embrace.
They are but come so close
We need not grope with hands,
Nor look to see, nor try
To catch the sound of feet.
They have put off their shoes
Softly to walk by day
Within our thoughts, to tread
At night our dream-led paths
Of sleep.

They are not lost who find
The sunset gate, the goal
Of all their faithful years.

Not lost are they who reach
The summit of their climb,
The peak above the clouds
And storms. They are not lost
Who find the light of sun
And stars and God.

Hugh Robert Orr

287   *THE VICTOR*

He is not dead. Why should we weep
Because he takes an hour of sleep—

A rest before God's greater morn
Announces a new world is born;

A world where he may do the things
He failed in here; where sorrow's stings

And disappointment yield to joy,
Where cares and fears cannot destroy?

He is not dead. He hurried on
Ahead of us to greet the dawn,

That he might meet the loved who left
Us yesterday. We are bereft—

But weep not—hail him where, afar,
He waits for us on some bright star.

He is not dead. Beyond all strife,
At last he wins the prize of Life.

Thomas Curtis Clark

288   *From A COMRADE RIDES AHEAD*

I would not hold our loss too lightly;
    God knows, and he, how deep the pain;
But, friends, I see still shining brightly
    The brightest link in all our chain
    That links us with a new domain.

*

For friendship binds the worlds together—
    World over there, world over here.
From earth to heaven is the tether
    That brings the earth and heaven near
    And makes them both a bit more dear.

*

Whatever vales we yet may wander,
    What sorrow come, what tempest blow,
We have a friend, a friend out yonder,
    To greet us when we have to go—
    Out yonder someone that we know.

To all eternity he binds us;
    He links the planet and the star;
He rides ahead, the trail he finds us,
    And where he is and where we are
    Will never seem again so far.

Douglas Malloch

289   *THEY NEVER QUITE LEAVE US*

They never quite leave us, our friends who have passed
    Through the shadows of death to the sunlight above;
A thousand sweet memories are holding them fast
    To the places they blessed with their presence and love.
The work which they left and the books which they read
    Speak mutely, though still with an eloquence rare,
And the songs that they sang, the words that they said,
    Yet linger and sigh on the desolate air.
And oft when alone, and oft in the throng,
    Or when evil allures us, or sin draweth nigh,
A whisper comes gently, "Nay, do not the wrong,"
    And we feel that our weakness is pitied on high.

Margaret E. Sangster

290   *IMMORTAL*

How living are the dead!
Enshrined, but not apart,
How safe within the heart
We hold them still—our dead,
Whatever else be fled!

Our constancy is deep
Toward those who lie asleep
Forgetful of the strain and mortal strife
That are so large a part of this, our earthly life.

They are our very own—
From them—from them alone
Nothing can us estrange,
Nor blight autumnal, no, nor wintry change.

The midnight moments keep a place for them
And though we wake to weep
They are beside us still in joy, in pain—
In every crucial hour, they come again
Angelic from above—
Bearing the gifts of blessing and of love
Until the shadowy path, they lonely trod
Becomes for us a bridge,
That upwards leads to God.

Florence Earle Coates

291   *RESURRECTION*

All that springeth from the sod
Tendeth upwards unto God;
All that cometh from the skies
Urging it anon to rise.

Winter's life-delaying breath
Leaveneth the lump of death,
Till the frailest fettered bloom
Moves the earth and bursts the tomb.

Welcome, then, time's threshing-pain
And the furrows where each grain,
Like a Samson, blossom-shorn,
Waits the resurrection morn.

John Banister Tabb

292   *From IN MEMORIAM (XXVII)*

I hold it true, whate'er befall;
I feel it, when I sorrow most;
'Tis better to have loved and lost
Than never to have loved at all.

Alfred Tennyson

293   *From DANIEL WHEELER*

O dearly loved!
And worthy of our love! No more
Thy aged form shall rise before
The hushed and waiting worshipper,
In meek obedience utterance giving
To words of truth, so fresh and living,
That, even to the inward sense,
They bore unquestioned evidence
Of an anointed Messenger!
Or, bowing down thy silver hair
In reverent awfulness of prayer,
The world, its time and sense, shut out,
The brightness of Faith's holy trance
Gathered upon thy countenance,
As if each lingering cloud of doubt,
The cold, dark shadows resting here
In Time's unluminous atmosphere,
Were lifted by an angel's hand,
And through them on thy spiritual eye
Shone down the blessedness on high,
The glory of the Better Land!

John Greenleaf Whittier

294   *TO MY FATHER*

I cannot think that you have gone away,
You loved the earth—and life lit up your eyes,
And flickered in your smile that would surmise
Death as a song, a poem, or a play.
You were reborn afresh with every day,
And baffled fortune in some new disguise.

Ah! can it perish when the body dies,
Such youth, such love, such passion to be gay?
We shall not see you come to us and leave
A conquerer—nor catch on fairy wing
Some slender fancy—nor new wonders weave
Upon the loom of your imagining.
The world is wearier, grown dark to grieve
Her child that was a pilgrim and a king.

Iris Tree

295   *TO MY FATHER*

A giant pine, magnificent and old,
Stood staunch against the sky and all around
Shed beauty, grace, and power. Within its fold
Birds safely reared their young. The velvet ground
Beneath was gentle, and the cooling shade
Gave cheer to passers-by. Its towering arms
A landmark stood, erect and unafraid,
As if to say, "Fear naught from life's alarms."

It fell one day. Where it had dauntless stood
Was loneliness and void. But men who passed
Paid tribute—said, "To know this life was good.
It left its mark on me. Its work stands fast."
And so it lives. Such life no bonds can hold—
This giant pine, magnificent and old.

Georgia Harkness

296   *EPITAPH ON MY FATHER*

O ye, whose cheek the tear of pity stains,
    Draw near with pious rev'rence, and attend!
Here lie the loving husband's dear remains,
    The tender father, and the gen'rous friend.

The pitying heart that felt for human woe,
    The dauntless heart that fear'd no human pride,
The friend of man—to vice alone a foe;
    For "ev'n his failings lean'd to virtue's side."

Robert Burns

297   *MOTHER*

True heart and wise, that with Love's key
Didst open all life's mystery
And buy life's treasure at the price
Of Love's perpetual sacrifice!

The peace that Love finds hid in care;
The strength that love-bourne burdens bear;
The hope that stands with love and faith
Serenely facing life and death!

The blessing that in blessing lies—
These didst thou know, true heart and wise!
Now God hath added, last and best,
The sudden, glad surprise of rest!
                              Rossiter W. Raymond

298   *From THE VICTORS*

(In Memory of My Father and Mother)

They have triumphed who have died;
They have passed the porches wide,
Leading from the House of Night
To the splendid lawns of light.
They have gone on that far road
Leading to their new abode,
And from curtained casements we
Watch their going wistfully.

They have won, for they have read
The bright secrets of the dead;
And they gain the deep unknown,
Hearing Life's strange undertone.
In the race across the days
They are victors; theirs the praise
Theirs the glory and the pride—
They have triumphed, having died!
                              Charles Hanson Towne

299   *THE RESURRECTION AND THE LIFE*

O little friend, I wait on you with praise,
Seeking to celebrate your early days
Of bugle, drum and gallant rocking-horse
Without complaint of tears, without remorse

For why should man regret the silver dawn,
Nor that the sun has set and from the lawn
Slow mist arises as of quiet tears
Shed for the swift futility of years.

At first when you were gone I turned my face
From life and sat upon a lonely place
Apart from men, bewailed but nursed my sorrow
And, loving yesterday, I loathed tomorrow.

Then suddenly you said, "O foolish one,
Awake, there are no dead—I *am* your son!"
And then above my sorrow and my strife
I found the Resurrection and the Life.

Robert Norwood

300   *From* ON THE DEATH OF A FRIEND'S CHILD

Children are God's apostles, day by day
Sent forth to preach of love, and hope, and peace;
Nor hath thy babe his mission left undone.
To me, at least, his going hence hath given
Serener thoughts and nearer to the skies,
And opened a new fountain in my heart
For thee, my friend, and all: and O, if Death
More near approaches meditates, and clasps
Even now some dearer, more reluctant hand,
God, strengthen thou my faith, that I may see
That 'tis thine angel, who, with loving haste,
Unto the service of the inner shrine,
Doth waken thy beloved with a kiss.

James Russell Lowell

301   *From RESIGNATION*

There is no Death! What seems so is transition;
  This life of mortal breath
Is but a suburb of the life elysian,
  Whose portal we call Death.

She is not dead,—the child of our affection,—
  But gone unto that school
Where she no longer needs our poor protection,
  And Christ himself doth rule.

In that great cloister's stillness and seclusion,
  By guardian angels led,
Safe from temptation, safe from sin's pollution,
  She lives, whom we call dead.

Day after day we think what she is doing
  In those bright realms of air;
Year after year her tender steps pursuing,
  Behold her grown more fair.

Thus do we walk with her, and keep unbroken
  The bond which nature gives,
Thinking that our remembrance, though unspoken,
  May reach her where she lives.

Not as a child shall we again behold her;
  For when with raptures wild
In our embraces we again enfold her,
  She will not be a child;

But a fair maiden, in her Father's mansion,
  Clothed with celestial grace;
And beautiful with all the soul's expansion
  Shall we behold her face.
                          Henry Wadsworth Longfellow

302   *From THRENODY*

When Emerson lost his lovely boy, it was as if the sun had been taken out of the skies. April might well bloom and morn break, he thought, for "the hiacinthine boy." Out of the depths of his grief, he wrote to Carlyle: "My son, a perfect little boy of five years and three months, has ended his earthly life. You can never sympathize with me; you can never know how much of me such a young child can take away." His "Threnody" is among the gems of literature; but that "ode of tears" was not all written at one time. The first part came out of a broken heart—too full of tears to understand that God would make them into a spiritual rainbow. But at last the deep Heart said:

> Wilt thou not ope thy heart to know
> What rainbows teach, and sunsets show?
> Verdict which accumulates
> From lengthening scroll of human fates,
> Voice of earth to earth returned,
> Prayers of saints that inly burned,—
> Saying, *What is excellent,*
> *As God lives, is permanent;*
> *Hearts are dust; hearts' loves remain;*
> *Hearts' love will meet thee again.*

>   *Frederick F. Shannon*

303   *From GONE*

> There seems a shadow on the day,
>   Her smile no longer cheers;
> A dimness on the stars at night,
>   Like eyes that look through tears.

> Alone unto our Father's will
>   One thought hath reconciled;
> That He whose love exceedeth ours
>   Hath taken home His child.

> Fold her, O Father! in Thine arms,
>   And let her henceforth be
> A messenger of love between
>   Our human hearts and Thee.

>   *John Greenleaf Whittier*

304 *THE OPEN DOOR*

You, my son,
Have shown me God.
Your kiss upon my cheek
Has made me feel the gentle touch
Of Him who leads us on.
The memory of your smile, when young,
Reveals His face,
And mellowing years come on apace.
And when you went before,
You left the gates of heaven ajar
That I might glimpse,
Approaching from afar,
The glories of His grace.
Hold, son, my hand,
Guide me along the path,
That, coming,
I may stumble not,
Nor roam,
Nor fail to show the way
Which leads us home.

Grace Coolidge

B. PRAYER POEMS

305

LORD! IT IS NOT LIFE TO LIVE

Lord, it is not life to live,
    If Thy presence Thou deny;
Lord! if Thou Thy presence give,
    'Tis no longer death—to die.

Source and Giver of repose,
Singly from Thy smile it flows;
Peace and happiness are Thine,—
Mine they are, if Thou art mine.
    Augustus Montague Toplady

306

From VESTA

O Christ of God! whose life and death
    Our own have reconciled,
Most quietly, most tenderly
    Take home Thy star-named child!

She leans from out our clinging arms
    To rest herself in Thine;
Alone to Thee, dear Lord, can we
    Our well-beloved resign!

O! less for her than for ourselves
    We bow our heads and pray;
Her setting star, like Bethlehem's,
    To Thee shall point the way!
    John Greenleaf Whittier

307

OF MY DEARE SONNE, GERVASE

Deare Lord, receive my Sonne, whose winning love
To me was like a friendship, farre above
The course of nature, or his tender age,

260

Whose lookes could all my bitter griefes assuage;
Let his pure soule ordain'd sev'n yeares to be
In that fraile body, which was part of me,
Remaine my pledge in heav'n, as sent to shew
How to this Port at ev'ry step I goe.

John Beaumont

308   *From I KNOW NO LIFE DIVIDED*

I know no life divided,
    O Lord of life, from thee;
In thee is life provided
    For all mankind and me:
I know no death, O Jesus,
    Because I live in thee;
Thy death it is which frees us
    From death eternally.

If, while on earth I wander,
    My heart is light and blest,
Ah, what shall I be yonder,
    In perfect peace and rest?
O blessèd thought! in dying
    We go to meet the Lord,
Where there shall be no sighing,
    A kingdom our reward.

Karl J. P. Spitta

309   *AFTER WORK*

Lord, when Thou seest that my work is done,
Let me not linger on,
With failing powers,
Adown the weary hours,—
A workless worker in a world of work.
But, with a word,
Just bid me home,
And I will come
Right gladly,—
Yea, right gladly
Will I come.

John Oxenham

310   *AT LAST*

When on my day of life the night is falling,
  And, in the winds from unsunned spaces blown,
I hear far voices out of darkness calling
  My feet to paths unknown,

Thou who hast made my home of life so pleasant,
  Leave not its tenant when its walls decay;
O Love Divine, O Helper ever present,
  Be Thou my strength and stay!

Be near me when all else is from me drifting;
  Earth, sky, home's pictures, days of shade and shine,
And kindly faces to my own uplifting
  The love which answers mine.

I have but Thee, my Father! let Thy spirit
  Be with me then to comfort and uphold;
No gate of pearl, no branch of palm I merit,
  Nor street of shining gold.

Suffice it if—my good and ill unreckoned,
  And both forgiven through Thy abounding grace—
I find myself by hands familiar beckoned
  Unto my fitting place.

Some humble door among Thy many mansions,
  Some sheltering shade where sin and striving cease,
And flows for ever through heaven's green expansions
  The river of Thy peace.

There, from the music round about me stealing,
  I fain would learn the new and holy song,
And find at last, beneath Thy trees of healing,
  The life for which I long.

                  John Greenleaf Whittier

311   *From NEARER HOME*

One sweetly solemn thought
    Comes to me o'er and o'er;
Nearer my home today am I
    Than e'er I've been before.

Nearer my Father's house,
    Where many mansions be;
Nearer, today, the great white throne,
    Nearer the crystal sea.

Nearer the bound of life,
    Where burdens are laid down;
Nearer, to leave the heavy cross
    Nearer to gain the crown.

Father, perfect my trust!
    Strengthen my power of faith!
Nor let me stand, at last, alone
    Upon the shore of death.   *Phoebe Cary*

312   *IN SORROW*

Gently, Lord, oh, gently lead us,
    Pilgrims in this vale of tears,
Through the trials yet decreed us,
    Till our last great change appears.
When temptation's darts assail us,
    When in devious paths we stray,
Let Thy goodness never fail us,
    Lead us in Thy perfect way.

In the hour of pain and anguish,
    In the hour when death draws near,
Suffer not our hearts to languish,
    Suffer not our souls to fear;
And, when mortal life is ended,
    Bid us in Thine arms to rest,
Till, by angel bands attended,
    We awake among the blest.
                    Thomas Hastings

313   *FAITH*

If I could feel my hand, dear Lord, in Thine,
    And surely know
That I was walking in the light divine,
    Through weal or woe;

If I could hear Thy voice in accents sweet
    But plainly say,
To guide my trembling, groping, wandering feet,
    "This is the way."

I would so gladly walk therein, but now
    I cannot see.
Oh, give me, Lord, the faith humbly to bow—
    And trust in Thee!

There is no faith in seeing. Were we led
    Like children here,
And lifted over rock and river bed,
    No care, no fear,

We should be useless in the busy throng,
    Life's work undone,
Lord, make us brave and earnest, true and strong,
    Till heaven is won.

                              Sarah K. Bolton

314   *From FAITH*

My faith looks up to Thee,
Thou Lamb of Calvary,
    Saviour divine!
Now hear me while I pray,
Take all my guilt away,
O let me from this day
    Be wholly Thine!

While life's dark maze I tread,
And griefs around me spread,
    Be Thou my guide;

Bid darkness turn to day,
Wipe sorrow's tears away,
Nor let me ever stray
    From Thee aside.

When ends life's transient dream,
When death's cold, sullen stream
    Shall o'er me roll;
Blest Saviour, then in love,
Fear and distrust remove;
O bear me safe above,
    A ransomed soul!

Ray Palmer

315   *From JESUS, SAVIOUR, PILOT ME*

Jesus, Saviour, pilot me
Over life's tempestuous sea;
Unknown waves before me roll,
Hiding rock and treacherous shoal;
Chart and compass come from thee;
Jesus, Saviour, pilot me.

When at last I near the shore,
And the fearful breakers roar
'Twixt me and the peaceful rest,
Then, while leaning on thy breast,
May I hear thee say to me,
"Fear not, I will pilot thee."

Edward Hopper

316   *From JESUS, LOVER OF MY SOUL*

Jesus, Lover of my soul,
    Let me to Thy bosom fly,
While the nearer waters roll,
    While the tempest still is high:
Hide me, O my Saviour, hide,
    Till the storm of life is past,
Safe into the haven guide,
    O receive my soul at last!

Other refuge have I none,
    Hangs my helpless soul on Thee;
Leave, ah! leave me not alone,
    Still support and comfort me!
All my trust on Thee is stay'd,
    All my help from Thee I bring;
Cover my defenceless head
    With the shadow of Thy wing!
                              Charles Wesley

317   *HYMN OF TRUST*

O Love Divine, that stooped to share
    Our sharpest pang, our bitterest tear,
On Thee we cast each earth-born care,
    We smile at pain while Thou art near!

Though long the weary way we tread,
    And sorrow crown each lingering year,
No path we shun, no darkness dread,
    Our hearts still whispering, Thou art near!

When drooping pleasure turns to grief,
    And trembling faith is changed to fear,
The murmuring wind, the quivering leaf,
    Shall softly tell us, Thou art near!

On Thee we fling our burdening woe,
    O Love Divine, forever dear,
Content to suffer while we know,
    Living and dying, Thou art near!
                        Oliver Wendell Holmes

318   *THE PILLAR OF THE CLOUD*

Lead, kindly Light, amid the encircling gloom;
    Lead Thou me on!
The night is dark, and I am far from home;
    Lead Thou me on!
Keep Thou my feet: I do not ask to see
The distant scene; one step enough for me.

I was not ever thus, nor prayed that Thou
  Shouldst lead me on;
I loved to choose and see my path; but now
  Lead Thou me on!
I loved the garish day, and, spite of fears,
Pride ruled my will: remember not past years.

So long Thy power hath blest me, sure it still
  Will lead me on,
O'er moor and fen, o'er crag and torrent, till
  The night is gone;
And with the morn, those angel faces smile
Which I have loved long since, and lost awhile.

John Henry Newman

319   *FATHER, TO THEE*

Father, to Thee we look in all our sorrow,
  Thou art the fountain whence our healing flows;
Dark though the night, joy cometh with the morrow;
  Safely they rest who in Thy love repose.

When fond hopes fail and skies are dark before us,
  When the vain cares that vex our life increase—
Comes with its calm the thought that Thou art o'er us,
  And we grow quiet, folded in Thy peace.

Naught shall affright us on thy goodness leaning,
  Low in the heart Faith singeth still her song;
Chastened by pain, we learn life's deepest meaning,
  And in our weakness Thou dost make us strong.

Patient, O heart, though heavy be thy sorrows!
  Be not cast down, disquieted in vain;
Yet shalt thou praise Him when these darkened furrows,
  Where now He plougheth, wave with golden grain.

Frederick L. Hosmer

320   *BREATHE ON ME, BREATH OF GOD*

Breathe on me, Breath of God,
    Fill me with life anew,
That I may love what Thou dost love,
    And do what Thou wouldst do.

Breathe on me, Breath of God,
    Until my heart is pure,
Until with Thee I will one will,
    To do or to endure.

Breathe on me, Breath of God,
    Till I am wholly Thine,
Till as this earthly part of me
    Glows with Thy fire divine.

Breathe on me, Breath of God,
    So shall I never die,
But live with Thee the perfect life
    Of Thine eternity.

                                            Edwin Hatch

321   *From IN MEMORIAM (PROEM)*

Strong Son of God, immortal Love,
    Whom we, that have not seen thy face,
    By faith, and faith alone, embrace,
Believing where we cannot prove;

Thine are these orbs of light and shade;
    Thou madest Life in man and brute;
    Thou madest death; and, lo, thy foot
Is on the skull which thou hast made.

Thou wilt not leave us in the dust:
    Thou madest man, he knows not why,
    He thinks he was not made to die;
And thou hast made him: thou art just.

Our little systems have their day;
  They have their day and cease to be;
  They are but broken lights of thee,
And thou, O Lord, art more than they.

We have but faith: we cannot know,
  For knowledge is of things we see;
  And yet we trust it comes from thee,
A beam in darkness: let it grow.

Let knowledge grow from more to more,
  But more of reverence in us dwell;
  That mind and soul, according well,
May make one music as before,

But vaster.

Alfred Tennyson

322   *From HYMN TO THE HOLY SPIRIT*

O, let me hear
Thy self, low voice controlling
My devious steps with intimations clear,
With comforts manifold my heart consoling.

Let that sweet sound
To holy deeds allure me,
With heavenly echoes make my spirit bound,
And of my Home in Paradise assure me.

Come, Holy Dove,
Guide me to yon bright portal,
Where I shall see the Saviour whom I love,
And enter on the joys which are immortal.

Richard Wilton

323   *EVENING*

Softly now the light of day
Fades upon my sight away;
Free from care, from labor free,
Lord, I would commune with Thee:

Thou, whose all-pervading eye,
  Naught escapes, without, within,
Pardon each infirmity,
  Open fault, and secret sin.

Soon, for me, the light of day
Shall for ever pass away;
Then, from sin and sorrow free,
Take me, Lord, to dwell with Thee:

Thou, who, sinless, yet hast known
  All of man's infirmity;
Then, from Thine eternal throne,
  Jesus, look with pitying eye.
                    George Washington Doane

324   *From STILL, STILL WITH THEE*

Still, still with Thee, when purple morning breaketh,
  When the bird waketh, and the shadows flee;
Fairer than morning, lovelier than daylight,
  Dawns the sweet consciousness, I am with Thee!

Alone with Thee, amid the mystic shadows,
  The solemn hush of nature newly born;
Alone with Thee, in breathless adoration,
  In the calm dew and freshness of the morn.

*

When sinks the soul, subdued by toil, to slumber,
  Its closing eyes look up to Thee in prayer;
Sweet the repose beneath Thy wings o'ershading,
  But sweeter still to wake and find Thee there.

So shall it be at last, in that bright morning
  When the soul waketh and life's shadows flee;
Oh, in that hour, fairer than daylight dawning,
  Shall rise the glorious thought—I am still with Thee!
                    Harriet Beecher Stowe

325   *From O GOD, OUR HELP*

O God, our help in ages past,
    Our hope for years to come,
Our shelter from the stormy blast,
    And our eternal home:

Beneath the shadow of Thy Throne
    Thy saints have dwelt secure;
Sufficient is Thine arm alone,
    And our defence is sure.

Before the hills in order stood,
    Or earth received her frame,
From everlasting Thou art God,
    To endless years the same.

Thy word commands our flesh to dust,
    "Return ye sons of men":
All nations rose from earth at first,
    And turn to earth again.

A thousand ages in Thy sight
    Are like an evening gone;
Short as the watch that ends the night
    Before the rising sun.

Time, like an ever-rolling stream,
    Bears all its sons away;
They fly forgotten, as a dream
    Dies at the opening day.

Our God, our help in ages past;
    Our hope for years to come;
Be Thou our guard while troubles last,
    And our eternal home!

                                    Isaac Watts

326   *NOW THE LABORER'S TASK IS O'ER*

Now the laborer's task is o'er;
    Now the battle day is past;
Now upon the farther shore
    Lands the voyager at last.
Father, in Thy gracious keeping
Leave we now Thy servant sleeping.

There the tears of earth are dried;
    There its hidden things are clear;
There the work of life is tried
    By a juster Judge than here.
Father, in Thy gracious keeping
Leave we now Thy servant sleeping.

There the sinful souls, that turn
    To cross their dying eyes,
All the love of Christ shall learn
    At his feet in Paradise.
Father, in Thy gracious keeping
Leave we now Thy servant sleeping.

"Earth to earth, and dust to dust,"
    Calmly now the words we say;
Left behind, we wait in trust
    For the resurrection day.
Father, in Thy gracious keeping
Leave we now Thy servant sleeping.
                                    John Ellerton

327   *From* THE SUPREME SACRIFICE

O valiant Hearts, who to your glory came
Through dust of conflict and through battle-flame;
Tranquil you lie, your knightly virtue proved,
Your memory hallowed in the Land you loved.

Proudly you gathered, rank on rank to war,
As who had heard God's message from afar;
All you had hoped for, all you had you gave
To save Mankind—yourselves you scorned to save.

Splendid you passed, the great surrender made,
Into the light that nevermore shall fade;
Deep your contentment in that blessed abode,
Who wait the last clear trumpet-call of God.

These were His servants, in His steps they trod
Following through death the martyr'd Son of God:
Victor He rose; victorious too shall rise
Those who have drunk His Cup of Sacrifice.

O risen Lord, O Shepherd of our Dead,
Whose cross has brought them and whose staff has led—
In glorious hope their proud sorrowing Land
Commits her children to Thy gracious hand.

John S. Arkwright

IV. A Sheaf of Funeral Prayers

Prayer is the heart of the funeral service. Precious and comforting are the words of the pastor who can lead a bereaved mind to the very throne of God.

The funeral prayer should include thanksgiving for the life, good works, love, and faithfulness of the deceased; petition for the benediction and blessing of God's presence upon those who mourn; and intercession that God's power and love may sustain the family and friends as they return to their homes and tasks without the companionship of him whom they have loved.

There are usually three prayers in the home or church service, the invocation or opening prayer, the pastoral prayer, and the benediction, and two at the committal, the committal prayer and the benediction. Another section of this volume includes Scriptural prayers suitable as benedictions.

The funeral prayers are of two orders: the prepared prayer and the extemporary prayer. There are advantages in the use of either kind. The prepared prayer may at times offer a more distinctive, though admittedly less personal, presentation of the essential ministry of comfort and encouragement to the bereaved. Frequently they represent the finest prayers in the Christian tradition.

In the extemporary prayer the pastor probably enters himself more genuinely into the experience of prayer rather than just leading in prayer. Personal reference and application is also possible. Extemporaneous prayer, however, will seldom meet the need of the hour if it is rambling and inconclusive. The most meaningful prayer will usually require forethought concerning content and pattern.

Many pastors include the Lord's Prayer at either the home service or at the committal. Here the congregation may participate, and the repeating of the well-known phrases may add assurance to a distraught heart.

In the nonliturgical service one prayer at least should probably be extemporaneous and offered in the individual wording and manner of the officiant.

An abundance of the familiar language of Scripture, hymns, and verse usually gives meaning and beauty to the wording of the funeral prayer. Indeed, the funeral prayers of some pastors are almost entirely a paraphrasing of Scriptures of comfort and promise.

The following prayers may be useful for actual use in a funeral or as a source of inspiration for the minister as he prepares his own prayers or prepares himself for a funeral service.

A. PASTORAL PRAYERS

328 Our Heavenly Father, whose nature it is to suffer for us rather than to make us suffer, we seek now the solace of Thy presence. Grant that our vision of Thee may be sufficient to save us from bitterness or recrimination. Make us to know that in every circumstance of life Thou art closer than any other. Awaken in us the realization that Thou art willing and able to share even this loneliness and sorrow which the passing of mortality into immortality means to us who yet must perform the labors of time before entering into the rewards of eternity.

We ask the benediction of Thy presence upon *him* who has gone ahead. Thou knowest *his* human frailties and Thou knowest, too, *his* aspirations and *his* hopes. Enter not into judgment with Thy servants, we beseech thee, for all have fallen short of Thy glory. Bestow, rather, new opportunities of service and new encouragements to growth that both *he* and we may grow more and more in Thy fullness and glory as revealed to us in Christ Jesus our Lord.

We ask the holy flame of Thy love in our hearts that the love which no longer can be bestowed upon one may be given to many, that the affectionate concern binding life with life may be deepened to include all life. Make us more poignantly aware of the beauty of friendship and the dignity of common purposes, and so teach us to toil without haste and without rest for the coming of that day when all men shall love without limit.

Assuage, our Father, the anguish of bereavement, leaving to these who are now learning the deeper meaning of life, cherished memories and nobler ambitions that they, and their children in every generation to the end of time, may follow each other in an uninterrupted succession through the gates of glory. In Christ's name. Amen.

Raymond E. Balcomb

329 O Thou Eternal Father, of old did Thy servant say: "Wherefore comfort one another with these words." So, our Father, we read from Thy word and we would with humility and patience listen to the lessons from the Book of Life.

We bless Thee for the comforting power of words: right words rightly spoken, rightly heard; words rightly written, rightly read. What a marvelous strengthening power we find in hours of perplexity and sorrow in such words!

We remember, O Father, the words of Paul: "And my God shall supply every need of yours according to his riches in glory in Christ." How great is our need; but how much greater is the ministry of Thy glory in Christ Jesus.

We remember, O Father, the words of John: "In Him was life, and the life was the light of men. The light shines in the darkness, but the darkness has not overcome it." We bless Thee that in the valley of the shadow we are not without the witness of Thy light and life.

And we remember, O Father, the words of our Saviour, Jesus Christ, who said: "Let not your hearts be troubled." Our hearts are restless till they find rest in Thee. Our hearts are troubled until we hear Thy word from the precious lips of Him who is the Living Word, the Word made flesh: "I go to prepare a place for you. . . . And I will come again and receive you."

O Father, as we receive the ministry of such words, make our imaginations alive, our mouths faithful, our eyes clear, our ears alert, and our hearts receptive. In Christ's name, Amen.

Ward F. Boyd

330 O God, our Heavenly Father, in our sorrow we turn our tear-stained faces toward Thee and we open our grief-stricken hearts to Thy Holy Spirit. Death has once more crossed our path and has removed from our midst one who is very dear to us. We are left to walk the rest of life's journey without *him*.

O Thou who hast never failed us nor left us helpless and alone, Thou wilt not fail us now. We believe the promise of Thy Son, our Saviour, who said, "I will not leave you comfortless. . . . I will come to you." Come to us now, O Father, with all Thy comforting spirit and power. Whisper to each troubled and sorrowing person these assuring words which Jesus long ago spoke to those who grieved, "I am the resurrection and the *life*. . . . I am the way, the truth, and the *life*. . . . I am come that they might have abundant *life*." Help us, here in the presence of death, to realize that with Thee the last word is not death but *life*.

With grateful hearts we praise Thee and bless Thee, O God of life, that we have been permitted to share life until these moments with *him* whom we now honor and whose memory we shall forever cherish. As we tenderly and lovingly lay *his* body in its final resting place among the flowers and dust of the earth, we trust *his* soul to Thy loving and living care. Help us to keep our faces turned toward Thee, and lead us in Thy paths until our life's journey brings us to Thy throne. Amen.

George W. Bruce

331 O Lord, Thou hast been our dwelling place in all generations. From everlasting to everlasting Thou art God and we are Thy children, creatures of Thy hand, spirit of Thy life. We come to Thee as naturally as children in the evening seek for their earthly parents. Thou art here with us to comfort and strengthen us, and we praise Thee for what Thou art now doing through us.

We remember today Thy servant, our *brother* and friend. How precious *he* has been to all of us! Everything good and fine and true about *him* was a gift from Thee, the reflection of Thy glory even as the moon light is the reflection of the sunshine.

We pray for all who loved *him* and those in turn whom *he* loved. Above them may there be the mantle of Thy love and beneath them, we pray, the sustaining power of Thy everlasting arms. We commit ourselves together to Thy care and rest ourselves in the strength that has hitherto led us on the journey of our lives. Grant unto us to walk this day in dignity and to face the morrow with courage.

We accept the answer Thou hast already given to this prayer we have made. Thou art fulfilling now in us the purposes of Thy holy will as we have been taught through Jesus Christ, our Lord and Saviour. Amen.

Robert W. Burns

332 Almighty and everlasting God, our Heavenly Father, we come to Thee and we would cling to Thee in the hour of our sorrow and loss. Turn us not away with our prayer unanswered and our grief unassuaged!

We know in our deepest hearts, beneath our doubts and our fears, that Thou art great. Give us also the confidence that Thou art good and that Thou "forgivest all our iniquities, healest all our diseases and redeemest our life from destruction!" May we see, in the light of Thy countenance, like a rainbow, the tears of our bereavement and grief. "Weeping may endure for a night but joy cometh in the morning."

Thy hand is upon the helm, upon the tides and the stars. Thou takest delight in the song of the bird and in "the flower in the crannied wall." Thou lovest truth and beauty. Thou hast created us in the midst of tender human relationships, binding us together in the bundle of life with those who love us and whom we love. Now, when the cords of affection have been rudely broken, we turn to Thee for consolation and comfort. "Shall not the Judge of all the earth do right?"

Have compassion upon us, O God! Give us the true perspective of faith in which to view life and all its relationships! Help us to discern invisible realities behind the fleeting shadows of sense and time. In the midst of the overwhelming storm that has shaken us to our foundations, we cry with one of old, "When my heart is overwhelmed, lead me to the Rock that is higher than I!"

Give us a new and abiding sense of Thy fatherly compassion and of our kinship with Thy Son, Jesus Christ, who Himself wept with the sorrow of those whom He loved. Give us His confidence in Thy goodness, and in a life beyond this dying! Kindle afresh our hope, renew our courage, and deepen in our bereaved hearts the consciousness that all shall be well with those who put their trust in Thee. In the name of Jesus Christ, Thy Son and our Saviour, we pray. Amen.

William Hiram Foulkes

333 Almighty God, our refuge and strength, a very present help in time of trouble: in the shadows of this hour, grant us Thy light. We need Thy consolation and Thy strength, O Thou who art the Lord of life and the Conqueror of death. Breathe Thy peace into our hearts and remove from us all fear of death. Help us to see that we are spiritual beings living in a spiritual universe and that while the things that are seen are temporal and pass away, the things that are unseen are real and eternal. Help us to realize anew our life in Christ, a life that death cannot take away and the grave cannot destroy.

We remember before Thee those who are mourning for their dead. May the sense of Thy presence and sympathy minister to their loneliness. Touch their wounded hearts with the healing power of Thy Holy Spirit. Give them strength to carry out Thy will in their lives and help them to take up the duties of life more bravely for the sake of the one whose love they will always cherish. Help us to realize that all Thy children are ever in Thy holy care, that the eternal God is our refuge and underneath are Thy everlasting arms.

God of infinite compassion, bless this sorrowing family. May they experience Thy sustaining grace. Be Thou their stay, their strength and shield, for, through Him who strengthens us, we face life bravely and in death we are more than conquerors. Amen.

George J. Goris

FOR A GODLY FATHER

334 O Thou who art the Lord of life and yet our Father: we give Thee thanks for the gift of life and love Thou didst bestow upon us through Thy Son, our Saviour, Jesus Christ. As Thou didst give to Him the gift of life so hast Thou given to us life and the opportunity to serve in love those who are nearest and dearest in human relationship.

We thank Thee for the revelation of Thyself in the lives of those we know best, and especially for the evidence of Thy presence in the life of this Thy child now recalled to be with Thee. Those who have known him as father thank Thee for his strength and courage in the face of difficulty; for his wisdom and kindly guidance, for the sacrifice that was in his daily living. His friends praise Thee for the friendly and generous spirit that made him loved by young and old; for his sparkling sense of humor that made him always a good companion; for the qualities of goodness that made him share what he had of spiritual and material blessings with all. For all these things and the more personal relationships of the spirit we lift our voices in praise.

Thou hast in Thy providence called him to be with Thee in that larger life beyond the grave. We have shared his life and now we give him back to Thee in the full assurance that this life fulfilled here will find a new expression and will accept new responsibility as Thou dost give them to him.

Give to each of us, our Father, a larger understanding of our relationship to Thee and to all of life. Help us as we contemplate the qualities of righteousness seen in this Thy servant, to catch the challenge of his life and to prepare ourselves by the working out of Thy will for us, that in that day when we shall be called Thou canst say of us, "Well done, thou good and faithful servant, thou hast been faithful over few things, I will make thee ruler of many."

In Christ's name we pray. Amen.

Charles O. Harding

335 O living God, in whom there is no death and in whose sight a thousand years are but as yesterday when it is passed and as a watch in the night, our years are as a tale that is told, and we are as the grass that withered and the flower that fadeth.

Yet Thou art the author of our being, the one whose thought called us into existence and whose purpose awoke in us response to truth and the longing for perfection. Within us, we discover aspirations that can never be satisfied in this world and possibilities for service that this earth's passing years can never fulfill.

We long not for the continuance of mere existence. Life would grow wearisome apart from fellowship with Thee and service in Thy kingdom. We crave freedom to grow into the image of the Christ that Thou hast set before us.

Spiritual hunger lures us toward Thee, making us aware of the immortal nature of our spirits. Deep within us is a sense of our incompleteness, the half-formed purpose, the wavering will, the dim vision, the things we feel yet see but darkly. The completed purpose, the steadfast will, the clearer sight—these we covet, certain that, not in time, but in eternity and by Thy grace can we come to such attainment.

O Thou God of the living, take our lives into Thy keeping and lead our steps along the path that leads toward Home. Amen.

S. Ralph Harlow

336 O God of life, in whom there is no death and in whose presence we are called to live as immortal spirits, our thoughts turn to loved ones whom we greatly miss. Their absence has taken from us a treasure the world cannot restore. Yesterday they were with us; now they are with Thee.

The rocks endure though centuries pass away; the ancient hills look down upon a thousand generations; the stars shone on man in his infancy and will shine beyond his little day.

O Thou who art able to guide the suns in their courses, mold the granite of the mountain ranges, and bring life to birth, Thou wilt not let Thy children pass into endless night, their highest hopes unfulfilled.

Still our human needs fill us with loneliness when our beloved go from our sight into the unknown. Thou hast overcome the grave, O Christ; in Thee death is swallowed up in victory. Ten thousand times ten thousand sing the praises of Him who has opened the gates of the City of God.

Praise be unto God who holdeth our loved ones in His mighty keeping and whose love enfolds them every one. Amen.

S. Ralph Harlow

337 Eternal God, our Heavenly Father,
Whose kindness is loving and whose mercy is tender:
We come to Thee that we may be renewed in faith and hope,
For Thou art the Author of life,
And in Thee we live and move and have our being.
Help us not to throw away our souls in bitterness and hate
Because of the anguish that has come to us.
Help us to face death nobly, to greet the unseen with a cheer,
By answering the prayers our hearts cannot make
Because they do not understand.
May we always feel Thy nearness, be strengthened by Thy spirit,
And go forward bravely wherever duty sends us.
Grant us the assurance that they who trust in Thy will
Shall never know defeat in death or life.
We thank Thee for the life of our friend,
Recalling all in *him* that made others love *him*.
Quiet our vain yearnings with memories
Of *his* tenderness, responding to ours,
Filling our days with gladness and beauty.
We pause in love before the great sacrifice of Thy Son,
Thanking Thee that we have a God who knows the depths of human
   suffering.
We pray that His death on the cross may not be in vain for us,
But that we may worthily live our lives for Him,
Who is the Author and Finisher of our faith, even Jesus the Christ.
Amen.

E. Paul Hovey

338 Eternal Father, who hast in every spoken word and deed manifested the spirit of eternity, be Thou in this time of sorrow a refuge for the bereaved. Let Thy words of eternal life and the uplift of Thine everlasting arms be an assurance which will strengthen their hearts and spirit.

O Thou, who knowest death and life, we pray that these whom we seek to comfort may receive the gift of Thy faith in an eternal to-morrow and that through Thy abiding presence the shadows of death may be turned into the glory of the morning. Put Thou the song of promise again in their hearts.

We do not bid farewell to our loved one in the spirit of finality, our Father, for we have known Thee as one who through Thy Son our Saviour has conquered the grave and made it the way into a new ad-venture of abundant living. So may we pass through this valley of sorrow with peace of heart and an appreciation of Thy divine mercy.

O Thou, who hast called us all into the eternal glory of Christ, lift Thou our hearts unto Thee that we may be strengthened in the faith of immortality and the hope of life everlasting. Teach us again of that divine love from which there is no separation and in which we, too, become more than conquerors, even victors over death and the grave.

And when human words fail to bring comfort in sorrow, great God of the living, let Thy Spirit intercede for them with sighs too deep for words, assuring them that in everything Thou dost work for good with those who love Thee, who are called according to Thy purpose.

We humbly pray these petitions in the name of Christ who ever spoke confidently of life eternal and of the everlasting fellowship with the Father. Amen.

R. M. Lautenschlager

339 Almighty God, unto whom all hearts are open, all desires known, and from whom no secrets are hid: meet, we pray Thee, the deepest needs of our lives in this hour of our desolation. Make us sensitive to the presence of the Divine Comforter in accordance with our Lord's assurance that we will not be left alone.

Strengthen our gratitude for the companionship, the tokens of esteem, and the enriching experiences which the years have brought. In this time of sorrow may we be forever grateful for the many indications of Thy favor resting upon us and upon those whom we cherish. May meditation and memory renew the Divine assurance of Thy love which is the same yesterday, today, and forever. Grant us, we beseech Thee, the faith of the prophets who could see, in approaching the shades of night, the promise of a glorious sunrise.

We thank Thee that the Psalmist could walk through the valley of the shadow of death and fear no evil. We thank Thee that our Lord, when facing death, could confidently commit His life into the Father's hands.

So grant us faith in the dependability of the Divine purpose that we may surrender our beloved into Thy care without fear, knowing that underneath are the everlasting arms and that all things work together for good to them that trust Thee. We pray in the name of Him who is the Lord of life, even Thy Son our Saviour, Jesus Christ. Amen.

Milton A. Marcy

340 O God, we thank Thee for the world in which Thou hast placed us, for the universe whose vastness is revealed in the blue depths of the sky, whose immensities are lit by shining stars beyond the strength of mind to follow. We thank Thee for every sacrament of beauty; for the sweetness of flowers, the solemnity of the stars, the sound of streams and swelling seas; for far-stretching lands and mighty mountains which rest and satisfy the soul, the purity of dawn which calls to holy dedication, the peace of evening which speaks of everlasting rest. May we not fear to make this world for a little while our home, since it is Thy creation and we ourselves are part of it. Help us humbly to learn its laws and trust its mighty powers.

We thank Thee for the world within, deeper than we dare to look, higher than we care to climb; for the great kingdom of the mind and the silent spaces of the soul. Help us not to be afraid of ourselves, since we were made in Thy image, loved by Thee before the worlds began, and fashioned for Thy eternal habitation. May we be brave enough to hear the truth, strong enough to live in the light, glad to yield ourselves to Thee.

We thank Thee for that world brighter and better than all, opened to us in the broken heart of the Saviour; for the universe of love and purity in Him, for the golden sunshine of His smile, the tender grace of His forgiveness, the red renewing rain and crimson flood of His great sacrifice. May we not shrink from its searching and surpassing glory, nor, when this world fades away, fear to commit ourselves to that world which shall be our everlasting home. Amen.

William E. Orchard

341 Father, in whose hands are life and death, and by whose grace and power we are sustained in the hour of adversity and by whose mercy we are spared to love and serve our fellow men in the hours of joy and sorrow: look Thou upon us at this moment in pity and forgiveness. Stand by these dear friends in this hour of need and bereavement. In the name of Thy dear Son Jesus Christ our Lord and Redeemer, be Thou to them today "a hiding place from the wind, a covert from the tempest, rivers of water in a dry place and the shelter of a great rock in a weary land."

We thank Thee, dear Father, for being with us in the joys and successes of life, for the sweet fellowship of home life and the fragrance of beautiful memories of Thy companionship in days of sunshine. We came to Thee in those hours with love and appreciation for Thy goodness. Now that trouble has overtaken us, we come to Thee again with boldness, because Thou hast asked us to come and "pay our vows unto the Lord and call upon him in the day of trouble" with the promise that "I will deliver thee." And Jesus said, "Come unto me all ye that labor and are heavy laden and I will give thee rest." Father, we plead these promises, and know Thou wilt not fail us in this moment of great need.

May these bereaved friends know that "underneath are the everlasting arms," and that as they "walk through the valley of the shadow of death" that Thou art with them and that Thy rod and Thy staff will comfort them.

We thank Thee for this privilege of prayer. Thou dost always answer. We are always happy when Thou dost say yes to our requests. Sometimes Thou must say no. Father, help us to thank Thee when Thou must say no to our desires. In the stern conflict of life against the world, the flesh, and the devil, and against all spiritual and physical exigencies, help us to triumph over them all. Strengthen our courage to conquer. Quiet our tongues in all of our complainings. Calm our souls in every storm. Steady our wills in every testing and uphold us when our feet slip on the pathway of duty.

Since we cannot see tomorrow, help us to place our hands by faith into Thy hand knowing that "no one can pluck us from my Father's hand." Garrison our hearts from all fear; lead us to accept joyfully the conditions of our earthly pilgrimage and may we possess our souls and achieve our ultimate destiny in fellowship with our risen Lord and Redeemer.

Even now we feel Thy presence near us, and Thou dost help us to say with confidence as well as in resignation:

> Thy way, not mine, O Lord,
> However dark it be!
> Lead me by Thine own hand,
> Choose Thou the path for me.

Smooth let it be or rough,
  It will be still the best;
Winding or straight, it leads
  Right onward to Thy rest.

I dare not choose my lot;
  I would not, if I might;
Choose Thou for me, my God;
  So shall I walk aright.

The kingdom that I seek
  Is Thine; so let the way
That leads to it be Thine;
  Else I must surely stray.[1]

We commit, dear Father, our ways and our wills to Thee. Accept us as we consecrate ourselves to Thee, in Christ's name. Amen.

Gordon Palmer

342 O Thou Eternal One, we who are doomed to die lift up our souls to Thee for strength, for death has passed us in the throng of men and touched us, and we know that at some turn of our pathway he stands waiting to take us by the hand and lead us—we know not whither. We praise Thee that to us he is no more an enemy but Thy great angel and our friend, who alone can open for some of us the prison-house of pain and misery and set our feet in the roomy spaces of a larger life. Yet we are but children, afraid of the dark and the unknown, and we dread the parting from the life that is so sweet and from the loved ones who are so dear.

Grant us of Thy mercy a valiant heart, that we may tread the road with head uplifted and a smiling face. May we do our work to the last with a wholesome joy, and love our loves with an added tenderness because the days of love are short. On Thee we cast the heaviest burden that numbs our soul, the gnawing fear for those we love, whom we must leave unsheltered in a selfish world. We trust in Thee, for through all our years Thou hast been our stay. O Thou Father of the fatherless, put thy arm about our little ones! And ere we go, we pray that the days may come when the dying may die unafraid, because men have ceased to prey on the weak, and the great family of the nation enfolds all with its strength and care.

We thank Thee that we have tasted the rich life of humanity. We bless Thee for every hour of life, for all our share in the joys and strivings of our brothers, for the wisdom gained which will be part of

[1] From "Thy Way, Not Mine" by Horatius Bonar.

us forever. If soon we must go, yet through Thee we have lived and our life flows on in the race. By Thy grace, we, too, have helped to shape the future and bring in the better day.

If our spirit droops in loneliness, uphold us by Thy companionship. When all the voices of love grow faint and drift away, Thy everlasting arms will still be there. Thou art the Father of our spirits; from Thee we have come; to Thee we go. We rejoice that in the hours of our purer vision, when the pulse-throb of Thine eternity is strong within us, we know that no pang of mortality can reach our unconquerable soul, and that for those who abide in Thee death is but the gateway to life eternal. Into Thy hands we commend our spirit. Amen.

Walter Rauschenbusch

343 Father of all mercies and God of all comfort, we turn to Thee in our perplexity. In the passing of our loved one, our joy has been turned into sorrow and our fondest hopes have crumbled like ashes. We confess unto Thee our utter loneliness; a sharp feeling of desolation overcomes us as we realize the vast distance which separates us even from our closest friends.

O Lord, Thou art our only refuge. Thou alone art able to reach the deepest regions of our hearts which are left untouched even by the most tender expression of sympathy by our friends. Grant us, we pray Thee, the comfort which shall strengthen us in this hour of crisis and give to us the consolation which shall drive from our hearts the desolation of this hour of need. As we walk through the valley of the shadow of death, let us know that Thou art with us.

Increase our faith which has been deeply shaken by the sudden onslaught of grief. Deepen our trust in Thee so that we may hold fast to Thee even when we may not see clearly the road ahead. Quicken our love to Thee and draw us into a closer relationship to Thee through this fellowship of suffering. Enable us to lift our eyes above the dust of this earth and let us behold more clearly the eternal destiny which Thou hast prepared for all them that love Thee. Lead us in the way everlasting. We pray in the name of Jesus. Amen.

Karl H. A. Rest

344 Almighty Lord and everlasting God, we seek Thy presence to strengthen our faith and to refresh our hearts. Thou knowest, O Lord, the weariness which has overcome us in the strain of sorrow and the stress of grief. We hardly have the strength to press onward, but, we pray Thee, give us the grace we need to carry on courageously. The way ahead seems dark and dreary, but we depend on Thee to send out Thy light and Thy truth to lead us. And whenever the recurring pangs of loneliness threaten to overwhelm us in our grief, give us the assurance that we walk not alone; let us live in the blessed knowledge that thou art with us.

Give us the strength of Thy comfort as we lay hold of the great promises Thou hast revealed to us in the Gospel. Thou hast taught us in Thy Word that the end of life is not death, but more life. Thou dost bid us to lift up our hearts above the things which pass away and to set our affection on the things which endure. Thou hast sent Thy Son into the world to guide us through the bewildering complexities of this life and, at last, to bring us to our eternal home.

We thank Thee, O Lord, for the assurance which Thou hast given to us that where Thou art in glory there shall Thy servants be also. Though the passing of our loved one has caused us much sorrow, we praise Thee for all the grace Thou hast bestowed upon him through the course of his life. Thy goodness and mercy have followed him all the days of his life. And now, having received him in glory, we thank Thee for this tie which binds us all the more closely to Thee and to Thine everlasting kingdom. In Jesus' name. Amen.

Karl H. A. Rest

345 Our Heavenly Father, in the solemn stillness of this hour, we raise our hearts unto Thee and acknowledge Thee as the sovereign Lord of life and death. Into Thine almighty hand do we commend the spirit of our departed friend, confident that all is well with them who are entrusted to Thy loving care.

O Lord, be Thou near unto all those who are touched by sorrow and weighed down by grief. Grant unto them, we implore Thee, the comfort which shall strengthen them, the consolation which shall banish all desolation from their hearts, the grace which shall fortify them in all the difficulties of life, the love which shall hold them securely in Thy fellowship, and the peace which shall give rest to their distraught and anguished hearts.

We thank Thee, O holy and most merciful Saviour, that Thou hast led the way through suffering and death, opening up to us the portals of new life, eternal life. We praise Thee for the light of eternity which breaks over death and the grave, proclaiming good tidings of the Home which Thou hast prepared for all who love and trust Thee.

In the solemn earnestness of this hour, help us to consecrate our lives more fully to Thee so that we may live more bravely, follow Thee more closely, and love Thee more faithfully. And then at last, grant us Thy peace. All this we ask in the name of Jesus Christ, our Lord. Amen.

Karl H. A. Rest

346 Hear our prayer, O Lord, and give ear to our cry, as we lay the concerns of our hearts before Thy throne of grace. Thou knowest us better than we know ourselves. Thou knowest the sorrow which has befallen us and Thou art aware of the grief which has assailed us. We look to Thee for the healing of hearts which are wounded by grief and broken in sorrow.

O Lord, Thou art our refuge in all generations and in Thy presence we find our only security. Through this affliction draw our hearts closer to Thy great father-heart of love. May this sorrow serve as a discipline to train our eyes more steadfastly upon Thee who art Lord over all. Even as our joy is turned into sorrow, so Thou art able to turn our sorrow into joy, as we again receive Thy Divine assurance of the eternal destiny which Thou hast prepared for the faithful. May we hear again the promise of life eternal, given us by our Saviour and Redeemer: "I am the resurrection and the life, he that believeth on me, though he die, yet shall he live; and whosoever liveth and believeth on me shall never die."

O God, we thank Thee for the precious heritage of our Christian faith. Through it our troubled hearts find rest even in sorrow. As we commend our loved ones in Thy keeping, we are confident that they rest safely who in Thy love repose. The passing of every faithful spirit from time to eternity brings us more closely to the fellowship of the saints in light. Hear us for Thy great mercies' sake. Amen.

Karl H. A. Rest

347 Our Father, Thou who art the giver of every good and perfect gift: in this hour of sorrow we lift our eyes unto Thy eternal hills from whence cometh our help. We know that our help cometh from the Lord who made the heaven and the earth.

Thou hast seen fit in Thine infinite wisdom and great love to call unto Thyself the blessed spirit of this loved one. We earnestly pray that *he* may be numbered with the redeemed of God and that this may be for *him* an hour of great rejoicing among those who have entered upon their eternal inheritance.

Sustain and strengthen us with the continued presence of Thy Divine grace, Thy strength being made perfect in the weakness which is so evident in all of us. Help us to see through the eyes of faith that all things work together for good and that any suffering of the present moment is not worthy to be compared with the glory that shall be revealed in us.

Comfort, we beseech Thee, this family and their friends and in the days that lie ahead, make their path as the dawning light which shall shine more and more unto the perfect day. Amen.

C. E. Seymour

348 Our Father God, we thank Thee for life and all that makes life sweet and worth the living. We thank Thee for the pleasant world Thou hast given us to live in, and the good comrades and true that are ours. We thank Thee that Thou hast set us in families and hast bound us together both by ties of blood and the bonds of friendship. We thank Thee for father love and mother love, for the love of husband and wife, and brother and sister and little children. We thank Thee for the great friends who have come to us to strengthen our spirits and enlarge our vision. We thank Thee that all human hearts are so kind, that love lights more fires than hate extinguishes, and that the world grows better as the earth grows old. It is good to be alive, our Father, and we thank Thee for the joy of living.

We thank Thee, too, for death. Our bodies were not made to last forever; they grow tired and worn. And we thank Thee that when our work is done, and the day is spent, we may fare homeward and be with Thee, freed from all limitations and weaknesses of the body. We thank Thee that our times are in Thy hands, that we have not the ordering of our lives but live and move in Thee whose wisdom is love and whose love is wisdom.

We thank Thee that every one of us is of concern to Thee, that Thou hast a stake in us, that Thou hast given us work to do and dost add our hearts and brains to the working capital of Thy providence. We thank Thee that Thou dost not let us live in vain if we live at our best. We thank Thee that though we seem to fail the forces of evil are the weaker because of our seemingly ineffectual blow, and the forces of good stronger because we have dreamed and hoped and dared.

We thank Thee for this life which has come to its final change. May it still be to us all an inspiration and guide. May we remember to do *him* honor by being more like *him,* and to show our love for *him* by doing the things *he* loved the best, and our gratitude for *him* by being the kind of men and women in which *he* always took pride. May all we who loved *him* keep in mind that we have more to love and serve because *he* is not here. May we be gentler, kinder, more thoughtful of others and more eager to help and serve for thus only can the world be compensated for *his* loss. May all his friends be braver men and more gracious women and so prove that *he* lived not in vain.

We give back to nature only that which is natural, to the grave only that which the grave can hold. To Thee, Father of us all, we give back a glowing, childlike spirit. *He* was so in love with life we can imagine how *he* has burst into that larger, fuller life of the great beyond. At *his* going out from our hearing and sight we give *him* a hail and a cheer. Give *him* a joyous entrance, O Lord of Life, and all ye brave spirits who have gone before! We pray in the name of our Lord and Saviour Jesus Christ, whose we are and whom we serve. Amen.   *Paul Moore Strayer*

349 O Thou eternal, loving, Heavenly Father, who art ever mindful of the pain and grief of Thy children, who art ever ready to comfort those who turn to Thee for help: we pray for those servants who mourn this day. By the might of Thy Holy Spirit lead them that they may not sorrow as those without hope. Fill them with Thy comforting love so that they may be able to say in their hearts, even as Jesus Christ said in Gethsemane, "Thy will be done."

Give us the assurance that Thou wilt permit no trial greater than our strength to bear. May we in all things acknowledge Thy watch care over us. In this faith may we return to the duties of life, resolved that nothing will ever separate us from the love of Christ Jesus our Lord.

Throughout all the changes of life, may we fix our minds upon whatsoever things are true, whatsoever things are pure, whatsoever things are lovely, whatsoever things are of good report, that wherein there is virtue, wherein there is praise, may we think and do these things; believing in Thy mercy and in Thy everlasting goodness.

Being rooted in Thy love, may we so pass the waves of this troublous world that we may be fit to abide in that world beyond whose borders there are no tears and whose ways are peace. In the name of Jesus Christ our Lord we pray. Amen.

F. Fagan Thompson

350 Our Heavenly Father, we who have come to know Thy love during the years of our earthly pilgrimage, come to Thee in this present sorrow and seek Thy aid.

We realize that it is not within human power to understand all that happens as one progresses toward eternity. We cannot understand the mystery of death. Yet, our Father, we do know that Thou art an all-wise and all-understanding God. Because of our faith in Thee, we have the assurance that all things work together for good to them that love Thee.

Grant that none will become bitter and hardened by these experiences of life. Let us realize anew that Thou art the Creator, Director, and Sustainer of all life. Let our minds and hearts be filled with love for Thee and Thy cause in the world. May we realize that passage through this world is necessary for the privilege of dwelling among Thy saints in the world to come.

Even in sorrow we look to Thee with thankfulness. Especially are we thankful for the life Thou hast given. Though we knew *him* for what has seemed too short a period, we feel that because of *him* both we and our world have been blessed. We thank Thee for Thy love which has bestowed upon us the privilege of *his* love.

Grant Thy blessings upon this family. May each member be provided with the strength and comfort which is needed to sustain him in this hour of sorrow. Let each look to Thee in perfect faith and receive Thy kind and gracious and bounteous ministrations.

This we pray in the name of Jesus Christ. Amen.

William A. Tyson, Jr.

351 Our Heavenly Father, we come to Thee as Thy children who trust without bitterness or rebelliousness because our hearts are filled with gratitude for the blessings brought to us through the life of our loved one who has gone to be with Thee.

We thank Thee for life with all its mystery and its apparent contradictions, far beyond our power to comprehend or to explain to one another, yet sweet and precious to each of us.

And now we praise Thee in tenderest gratefulness for the life of this Thy servant. We thank Thee for the blessed remembrance of *his* parents, for those with whom *he* grew up in the old home, for childhood playmates and school friends, and for the companions of the years. We thank Thee for all who have been kind and good to *him,* whose influences have strengthened and uplifted *him.* And even more, we thank Thee for those in whom Thy servant has had the privilege of investing the best and noblest thoughts and days of *his* own heart and life.

We remember before Thee what Thy Son our Saviour hath done for us upon His cross, and that by His resurrection He did indeed open the Kingdom of Heaven forever unto all who believe and trust and obey. In His name we pray. Amen.

Ralph Walker

352   O God, our Father, keep us from bitterness in bereavement. Save us from cold rebellion when loved ones leave us to face alone life's grim realities. Turn away from our minds all that would lessen our feeling of dependence on Thee. Teach us that where knowledge fails us faith will find a way and when sight is dim hope will bring to view the bright horizon.

From Thee, Eternal Spirit, we have come into this realm of time and space. To Thee, in Thine own way, we shall return. This present life of ours is but a dome of many-colored glass that stains the white radiance of eternity. When the fires of earthly existence burn low and the end of all things would seem to be dust and ashes, wilt Thou make strong our faith and clear our hope in the life that cannot be destroyed.

Through the centuries men have found and been found of Thee. In Christ Jesus this triumphant experience has become our richest treasure. In our Saviour humanity has faced the incredible gift of God in eternal love, the love that spells out to weak mortals the precious syllables suggesting wondrous immortality, the love that sustains the human spirit when surrounded by ruin and decay, the love that brings to our aid the Comforter in hours of utter loneliness.

May our sense of loss serve to make us more aware of Thy nearness. Through suffering let us discover the depth and the warmth of Thy fellowship with all who taste the cup of sorrow. When this life's music falls into tormenting discord for us, wilt Thou give us to hear heavenly harmonies that can awaken in us an ecstasy beyond all earthly joys and a conviction that our own life's melody cannot be shattered by the end of earthly living.

So shall we enter into that blessed experience the blind preacher-poet had made his own when he wrote:

> O Love, that wilt not let me go,
> I rest my weary soul in Thee;
> I give Thee back the life I owe,
> That in Thine ocean depth its flow
> May richer, fuller be.

We pray in the name of Jesus Christ, who hast revealed to us eternal love and has taught us how we may share that love. Amen.

Thomas Wearing

B. BRIEF PRAYERS

353 Almighty God who art our refuge and strength, a very present help in time of trouble: grant us Thy light to shine through the shadows of this hour. Comfort the hearts that are heavy with sorrow, and have compassion upon our weakness. Give us the vision of the eternal realities, and solace us with the hope of larger life beyond; through Jesus Christ our Lord. Amen.

Book of Church Services

354 Our Heavenly Father, we rejoice in the blessed communion of all Thy saints, wherein Thou givest us also to have part. We remember before Thee all who have departed this life in Thy faith and love, and especially those most dear to us. We thank Thee for our present fellowship with them, for our common hope, and for the promise of future joy. O, let the cloud of witnesses, the innumerable company of those who have gone before, and entered into rest, be to us for an example of Godly life, and even now may we be refreshed with their joy; that so with patience we may run the race that yet remains before us, looking unto Jesus, the Author and Finisher of our faith, and obtain an entrance into the everlasting kingdom, the glorious assembly of the saints, and with them ever worship and adore Thy glorious name, world without end. Amen.

Book of Prayer

355 O God of all the living, we thank thee for the happy memory of those whom thou hast called out of this transitory life into the eternal joy of Thy presence. Thine they were upon the earth, as we are Thine; and Thine are they and we in differing experience still. Though our eyes cannot see them and our ears are deaf to their remembered voices, we bless Thee that they are never absent from Thy loving care. We thank Thee for their lives of earthly service, for the happy days we spent in their companionship, the example of their faith and patience, the teaching of their words and deeds, and for their share in Heaven's new opportunities of service. We confess to Thee our neglects and transgressions, our coldness and misapprehension, while they lived upon the earth, which we may no more confess to them. Our hearts have rest, knowing that Thy love changeth not and that they see Thy face with unobstructed vision. Help us so to live that they may welcome us with joy when thou shalt call us to Thyself at last; through Jesus Christ our Lord. Amen.

356   Almighty God, Lord of the storm and of the calm, the vexed sea and the quiet haven, of day and of night, of life and of death: grant unto us so to have our hearts stayed upon Thy faithfulness, Thine unchangingness and love, that, whatsoever betide us, however black the cloud or dark the night, with quiet faith and trusting in Thee, we may look upon Thee with untroubled eye, and walking in lowliness toward Thee, and in lovingness toward one another, abide all storms and troubles of this mortal life, beseeching Thee that they may turn to the soul's true good. We ask it for Thy mercy's sake, shown in Jesus Christ our Lord. Amen.

George Dawson

357   Our Father, unto Thee, in the light of our Saviour's blessed life, we would lift our souls. We thank Thee for that true light shining in our world with still increasing brightness. We thank Thee for all who have walked therein, and especially for those near to us and dear, in whose lives we have seen this excellent glory and beauty. May we know that in the body and out of the body they are with Thee, and that when these earthly days come to an end, it is not that our service of Thee and of one another may cease, but that it may begin anew. Make us glad in all who have peacefully died. Lift us into light and love and purity and blessedness, and give us at last our portion with those who have trusted in Thee and sought, in small things as in great, in things temporal and things eternal, to do Thy holy will. Amen.

Rufus Ellis

358   Almighty God, our Heavenly Father, who hast of Thine infinite goodness ordained that the order of our life should be disquieted by many trials of heart and spirit, and who didst decree that Thy well-beloved Son should be disciplined in the same way of hardship and pain: grant unto us, we pray Thee, in all our necessities, to repose entire confidence in Thee, to feel the assurance of Thy present love, and to walk with Thee by faith, though not by sight. May no perplexity create in us an impatient spirit, no temptation lead us into sin, no sorrow hide Thy loving will from us. But do Thou so increase in us all spiritual gifts, that our very trials may lead us toward a perfect and regenerate life, and, in the days of our mortal pilgrimage, we may be sustained by a strength that is greater than our own. Through Jesus Christ our Lord. Amen.

Henry W. Foote

359   O holy and loving Father, whose mercies are from everlasting to everlasting, we thank Thee that Thy children can flee for refuge in their afflictions to the blessed certainty of Thy love. From every grief that burdens our spirits, from the sense of solitude and loss, from the doubt and fainting of the soul in its trouble, we turn to Thee. Thou knowest our frame and Thou rememberest that we are dust. Be Thou our strength and deliverer. In our great need be Thou our helper. Pour Thy consolations into our hearts, and let the gospel of Thy beloved Son minister comfort and peace to our souls. Amen.

Henry W. Foote

360   Almighty God, our Heavenly Father, who hast given us in Thy Son Jesus Christ a fountain of life, which, springing up within us, can make all things new: we thank Thee for the deeper meaning which He gives to life—for the quickened sense of duty, the faith under sorrow, the immortal hopes, which we owe to Him. In the power of His Spirit, may our griefs be transformed into consolations, our infirmities into strength to do well, our sins into repentance, our fainting and halting spirits into an heavenly mind, and, finally, the doubts, the discouragements, the trials of this earthly life into the full assurance and unclouded bliss of an eternal life with Thee, through the same Jesus Christ our Lord. Amen.

Henry W. Foote

361   Almighty and merciful God, who art the strength of the weak, the refreshment of the weary, the comfort of the sad, the help of the tempted, the life of the dying, the God of patience and of all consolation: Thou knowest full well the inner weakness of our nature, how we tremble and quiver before pain, and cannot bear the cross without Thy divine help and support. Help us, O eternal and pitying God, to possess our souls in patience, to maintain unshaken hope in Thee, to keep that childlike trust which feels a Father's heart hidden beneath the cross. So shall we be strengthened

with power according to Thy glorious might in all patience and long-suffering. So shall we be enabled to endure pain and temptation and in the very depth of our suffering to praise Thee with joyful hearts. Amen.[1]

Johann Habermann

362 O Thou Lord of all worlds, we bless Thy name for all those who have entered into their rest, and reached the Promised Land where Thou art seen face to face. Give us grace to follow in their footsteps, as they followed in the footsteps of Thy Holy Son. Encourage our wavering hearts by their example, and help us to see in them the memorials of Thy redeeming grace, the pledges of the heavenly might in which the weak are made strong. Keep alive in us the memory of those dear to ourselves, whom Thou hast called out of this world, and make it powerful to subdue within us every selfish and unworthy thought. Grant that every remembrance which turns our hearts from things seen to things unseen may lead us always upward to Thee, till we too come to the eternal rest which Thou hast prepared for Thy people; through Jesus Christ our Lord. Amen.

F. J. A. Hort

363 O Lord, our Heavenly Father, without whom all purposes are frustrate, all efforts are vain, grant us the assistance of the Holy Spirit, that we may not sorrow as those without hope, but may now return to the duties of our present life with humble confidence in Thy protection, and so govern our thoughts and actions that no business or work may ever withdraw our minds from Thee, but that in the changes of this life we may fix our hearts upon the reward which Thou hast promised to them that serve Thee, and that whatever things are true, whatever things are honest, whatever things are just, whatever things are pure, whatever things are lovely, whatever things are of good report, wherein there is virtue, wherein there is praise, we may think upon and do, and obtain mercy, consolation, and everlasting happiness. Grant this, O Lord, for the sake of Jesus Christ. Amen.

Samuel Johnson

364 O Thou, before whose face the generations rise and pass away, the strength of those who labor and suffer, the repose of those whose memory we would honor: we rejoice in the communion of

[1] Adapted.

saints; we bless Thy name for all Thy servants who have fought the good fight, who have finished their course in faith, and do now rest from their labors; and we beseech Thee to grant us grace to follow their good examples and to carry on the work which they began. May we all hear the call to nobler living which sounds in our ears as we remember those who gave their best to make life stronger and more beautiful; through Jesus Christ our Lord. Amen.

James Dalton Morrison

365 O Thou who hast created us for Thyself and made us in the image of Thine own eternity, we thank Thee for the hope of a new life beyond. We rejoice that our loved ones, now separated from our sight, have not perished but are at home with Thee forevermore. Although their going from us has brought a deep sense of loss and loneliness, we would not call them back from the goodly land into which they have entered. Only do Thou fortify us who remain against those hours when the shadows deepen, and the way grows hard, and life has lost its radiance. Help us in our dark days to believe that the sun still shines, and to walk with Thee by faith, until at last the light shall break upon us and we shall no longer see as in a mirror darkly, but face to face; through Jesus Christ our Saviour. Amen.

James Dalton Morrison

366 Our Heavenly Father, we turn to Thee in our great need, asking for light in our darkness and deliverance from our doubts and fears. Whether we live or die, we are in Thy loving care; and the shadow that darkens our path is but the close approaching, over-brooding shadow of Thy nearer presence. To Thine unfailing love we commit the beloved soul of our departed. We thank Thee for the gracious memories which gather about this life, for kindly deeds and thoughts, for the love freely given and the love modestly received, and now at last for quiet release from the burden of the flesh and entrance into the peace reserved for those who love Thee.

Sanctify this sorrow to us who mourn, that we may be comforted. Sustain us in our bereavement, and confirm our faith by tranquilizing memories and confident hopes, that the great words may be spoken again: "Let not your heart be troubled; my peace I leave with you; I go to prepare a place for you"; through Jesus Christ our Lord. Amen.

Francis Greenwood Peabody

V. Professional Conduct

A pastor's role at the time of death becomes significant insofar as he relates his responsibilities to the needs of the family of the deceased, to his church polity and fellow pastors, to local customs and practice, to the funeral director, and to fraternal and military groups who may request participation.

I

The most important concern of the pastor relates to the family of the deceased. The death and burial of a loved one is particularly personal and intimate. The occasion requires a genuine and sincere relationship between mourner and pastor.

The pastor is in frequent contact with the sick and aged of his parish. He is, therefore, easily reached when death comes. When notified of a death of a parishioner, he may wish to visit the home at an early hour. His visit will usually be brief. He may offer appropriate words of faith and consolation and may join the family in prayer.

He will wait for a telephone call from the funeral director before volunteering advice in regard to funeral plans. When the funeral director notifies him that the family wishes him to officiate at the service, he will confirm the mechanics of date and hour or request alterations if important previous commitments are involved. Agreement among pastor, director, and family will precede all funeral notices to the general public.

The pastor may then speak with members of the family concerning specific requests about the contents of the funeral service. A family will usually leave details to the pastor, but at times may ask for the inclusion of materials especially meaningful to members of the family group. The pastor will recognize any special request, except when the request actually conflicts with the policies of the church organization he represents.

The friendly considerations of a pastor may do more to bring spiritual and mental poise to the mourner than any amount of assistance by neighbors and friends. A prayer at the home before the service, a firm handclasp before and after the service, a sincere offer of help and comfort on behalf of church friends may not only endear a pastor to a parishioner but may well represent that deep need of the bereaved for human understanding and spiritual fortitude.

Those families who are not actively associated with a church will, of course, require a pastor's leadership at a funeral. Here the pastor may well demonstrate to a family that their life has been incomplete without contact with people of faith. Many families have moved from a funeral into church membership through the good offices of a pastor who represented the ministry of the church at its very best.

To avoid a suggestion that the nonchurch family deserves less respect and thoughtfulness is always highly desirable. A pastor may well suggest to certain of his church leaders that they share his ministry through visitation and the offering of assistance.

There is no generally accepted policy concerning the acceptance by a pastor of a fee for his services. Some ministers feel that funerals are within the scope of the pastoral work they are expected to perform when called to a parish. Other ministers feel that special services require additional effort and ought to offer an additional financial consideration. If the mortician and the florist are paid, why should the pastor be omitted? Frequently in smaller churches a pastor may actually depend upon fees from weddings and funerals. Then, too, many parishioners are adamant in their insistence that their pastor's services be financially recognized.

Certain conclusions seem evident. Local custom ought to determine a pastor's practice. If he would rather not be paid for funerals, he might make this known early in his ministry. If he wishes to recognize a natural desire of parishioners to offer remuneration he may make it clear that all fees will be turned over to such and such a work of the church or community. At any rate, a pastor's practice should be scrupulously consistent.

When local practice requires the payment of a fee, it is often less embarrassing if the mortician bills the family for this along with other items. The mortician may then offer a check to the pastor who will dispose of the fee as need or inclination dictates.

The minister will never ask for a fee and will be disinclined to speak of a failure to receive a fee.

There is general agreement that a fee is accepted when a pastor officiates at the funeral of a person outside of his parish or when he is required to meet certain travel or other expenses in regard to the fulfillment of his responsibilities.

II

Individual churches and denominations make certain requirements of the pastor. Church tradition should be followed, for the pastor officiates as a representative of the larger group.

Not infrequently a bereaved family may wish that a former pastor or other clergyman officiate or participate in the funeral service.

Basic professional ethics should not be violated. The family in a local parish should directly or through the funeral director approach the incumbent when another minister is to participate. This ought always to precede the invitation to the nonresident clergyman. This will avoid or minimize possible irritation and ruffled feelings.

A local pastor should, despite his personal attitudes, accede to the family request. His Christian spirit must outshine pride and vanity.

A nonresident pastor has certain obligations to the incumbent. He does his brother pastor an injustice when he does not recognize these obligations. If he is asked to assume the entire responsibility for the service, he will surely wish to suggest that the incumbent share the service with him. He may even insist that the incumbent preside and that he read the scripture or offer a prayer.

In most instances the incumbent will be the individual to minister to the family in the weeks following the actual funeral. To lose complete contact with the family at the time of the funeral may be unfortunate.

The local pastor, if he is aware of a particularly intimate relationship between another clergyman and the family of the deceased, will, in many cases, offer to refrain from participation.

When the incumbent and a second pastor share in the funeral service, the local pastor will usually open and close the service and may frequently assume full responsibility at the committal. Whatever arrangements are made, both men should be fully aware of the responsibilities of each. A typed order of service may eliminate confusion.

III

What should be a pastor's attitude toward local customs and procedures which are foreign and sometimes unappealing to him? Will he override the desires of the family and community practice? Not if he has wisdom and tact.

A new pastor in a community, for instance, may not approve of the large sums of money expended for floral displays. He may well be right in believing that a more permanent memorial would be appropriate. He will not overlook, however, the fact that for many persons, both donors and bereaved, flowers represent a sincere expression of sentiment. He may suggest from time to time that church friends would fittingly honor the dead through donations to this or that need in the church building or program. If his suggestions are made without bearing to a particular funeral, his words will in time bear fruit.

Most ministers have individual peeves and constructive ideas for the improvement in beauty and meaning of the traditional service. They will, bit by bit, persuade their people of the validity of their ideas, but they will not flaunt their opinions in regard to a service so saturated with sentiment and mingled emotion.

A new minister in the community may be briefed on local customs by a church leader, his official board, or a representative funeral director. If this is done at an early time in his pastorate, he will avoid unnecessary confusion at an hour of emergency.

Local custom ought to have precedence over an individual pastor's inclinations, for local custom will continue to prevail after he has moved on to other charges. But the pastor need not permanently submit to customs he dislikes when through persuasion he may lead his people to appreciate significant changes.

IV

Too many ministers have chastised the mortician's profession from pulpit or lecture platform or have rushed into print with words of condemnation. Many church people, having little or no contact with members of the profession, have false concepts concerning the work of the funeral director.

This is extremely unfortunate, for the minister and the family of the deceased must work harmoniously with the funeral director if the plan and performance of the funeral is to be executed with a maximum of ease and good will.

Occasionally, of course, a minister will run into a quack or profiteer among the morticians with whom he must necessarily be associated. But this, however, is rare and beyond the experience of most clergymen.

When unprofessional conduct is evident in a mortician's relation with members of a parish, the pastor should generally avoid becoming personally involved. The wise pastor will present whatever information he may have to members of his church board and leave it to them to approach the unethical mortician or to counsel with church members. The pastor will wish to be alert for subtle and secondary motives on the part of persons who may complain concerning the conduct of a criticized funeral director.

Few ministers, fortunately, will ever need to face such a situation, for funeral directors, individually and collectively, maintain a high standard of professional ethics. Most of them are Christian gentlemen and active supporters of the work of the church. Most of them consider themselves to be public servants.

Both pastor and people should realize that the mortician is required to maintain varied services and conveniences which represent substantial financial outlay.

Technically the pastor's responsibility at a funeral includes matters spiritual and the funeral director's duties involve physical arrangements. The pastor should avoid offering his people suggestions concerning the choice of a mortician or advice about expenses. If such counsel is requested by a parishioner, the pastor would do well to refer the party to a disinterested layman. To openly prefer one funeral director or another may bring unfortunate results to all involved.

Most morticians welcome suggestions by clergymen concerning the ability of less fortunate parishioners to pay for expensive services.

The pastor should speak with the mortician concerning his arrangements for *each* service and he will make the work of the mortician easier if he briefs him concerning the length and content of each worship service.

V

From time to time a pastor will share the funeral service with representatives of a fraternal group. Most fraternal organizations have a prescribed ritual, a copy of which is available on request.

The pastor will recognize the significance and meaning of a request by a fraternal group for participation. Frequently a fraternal service will be held in the lodge rooms or at the home or funeral parlor at a time preceding the final rites. When participation in the final rites is desired, however, the pastor will wish to have a clear understanding about the details of the fraternal ritual so that there will be no misunderstanding. Usually the pastor of the deceased presides at the opening and closing of both the service in the home, funeral parlor or church and at the grave.

Considerable effort may be necessary to understand the requirements of a particular fraternal organization on the occasion of a pastor's first participation in a joint service. An order of service and a few notes on essentials, if filed in his study, will make later co-operation with the particular group easier.

The pastor will also recognize the right of a family to request a military funeral. He will acquaint himself with the elaborate ritual recommended by the War Department in its Bulletin No. 21-39, "Conduct of a Military Funeral," issued September, 1947, and available to ministers on request. He will arrange with members of military organizations to participate in or to supplement the military service in a manner consistent with both the ritual of the military or veteran group and of the church he represents.

Only on a rare occasion will the pastor find officials of fraternal and military groups unwilling to co-operate with what the pastor considers to be the minimum requirements of the church.

Indexes

Sources

The sources for reprinted prose materials follow. The numerals at the left refer to item numbers.

122 *The Strong Name.* N. Y.: Scribner's, 1941, pp. 248 ff.
124 Quoted in Stanley I. Stuber and Thomas Curtis Clark, eds., *Treasury of the Christian Faith.* N. Y.: Association Press, 1949, p. 353.
126 Quoted in Jacob Helder, ed., *Greatest Thoughts on Immortality.* N. Y.: Richard R. Smith, 1930, pp. 21 ff.
127 *Great Pulpit Masters.* Westwood, N. J.: Revell, 1951, VIII, 147 f.
129 *Experience Worketh Hope.* N. Y.: Scribner's, 1945, pp. 198 ff.
131 *Moments on the Mount.* N. Y.: A. C. Armstrong & Son, 1901, pp. 113 ff.
132 *Faith and Freedom.* Boston: Geo. H. Ellis, 1881, pp. 270 f.
136 *The Secret of the Lord.* London: Hodder and Stoughton, 1910, pp. 195 f.
140 *Facing Life with Christ.* New York and Nashville: Abingdon-Cokesbury, 1940, pp. 174 ff.
141 Quoted in William L. Stidger, ed., *If I Had Only One Sermon to Preach on Immortality.* Harper, 1929, pp. 181 ff.
142 *The Vigil of God.* London: Epworth Press, 1943, pp. 45 ff.
149 *City Temple Sermons.* N. Y.: Revell, 1903, pp. 156 ff.
152 *Foosteps in the Path of Life,* London: Hodder and Stoughton, 1909, pp. 150 ff.
153 *Moments on the Mount.* N. Y.: A. C. Armstrong & Son, 1901, pp. 46 f.
155 *In His Image.* N. Y.: Revell, 1922, pp. 32 f.
158 *Last Sheaves.* London: Hodder and Stoughton, 1903, pp. 91 ff.
161 Quoted in *The Light Shines Through.* New York and Nashville: Abingdon-Cokesbury, 1930, pp. 123 f.
162 *The Gate of Life.* London: Longmans, Green, 1935, pp. 1 f.
163 Quoted in Eric Parker, ed., *A Book of Comfort.* Harper, 1944, pp. 123 ff.
168 *Sermons, Third Series.* N. Y.: J. B. Ford & Co., 1872, pp. 405 ff. (Abbreviated)
170 *Sermons.* London: Swan Sonnenschein & Co., 1902, pp. 124 f.
171 *From Skepticism to Faith.* Harper, 1934, pp. 118 ff.
174 *The Way Everlasting.* London: Hodder and Stoughton, 1911, pp. 177, 183 f. 186 ff.
175 Quoted in Sydney Strong, ed., *We Believe in Immortality.* N. Y.: Coward-McCann, 1929, pp. 148 ff.
176 *The Gates of New Life.* N. Y.: Scribner's, 1940, pp. 166 ff.
178 *The Listening Heart.* N. Y.: Revell, 1907, pp. 208 f.
179 *Sermons, Seventh Series.* N. Y.: Dutton, 1895, pp. 274 ff.
180 Quoted in *The Light Shines Through.* New York and Nashville: Abingdon-Cokesbury, 1930, p. 131 ff.
188 *The Shepherd Psalm.* N. Y.: Revell, 1895, pp. 65 ff.
203 *Christ, the Morning Star.* London: Hodder and Stoughton, 1892, pp. 172 ff.

210 Quoted in F. M. Barton, ed., *One Thousand Thoughts for Memorial Addresses.* N. Y.: Doran, n.d., pp. 111 f.
211 *Ibid.,* pp. 505 f.
212 *The Power That Worketh in Us.* London: Elliott Stock, 1910, pp. 148 ff.
302 *Sermons for Days We Observe.* N. Y.: Doran, 1922, pp. 191 f.
332 Quoted in Herbert Hewitt Stroup, *A Symphony of Prayer.* Phila.: Judson Press, 1944, pp. 23 f.
335-336 *Prayers for Times Like These.* N. Y.: Association Press, 1942, pp. 103 f.
340 *The Temple.* N. Y.: E. P. Dutton & Co., p. 155.
342 *Prayers of the Social Awakening.* Boston: Pilgrim Press, 1909, pp. 91 ff.
348 *A Sheaf of Prayers.* Rochester: Third Presbyterian Church, 1926, pp. 66 f.
355 Quoted in John S. Suter, comp., *Devotional Offices for General Use.* N. Y.: Century, 1928, pp. 111 f.
363 Quoted in Elton Trueblood, ed., *Doctor Johnson's Prayers.* N. Y.: Harper, 1947, pp. 47 f.
364 Quoted in James Dalton Morrison, ed., *Let Not Your Heart Be Troubled,* N. Y.: Harper, 1938, p. 17.
365 *Ibid.,* p. 19.

Names of Contributors

References to contributors of sermons and prayers are listed according to item numbers. The letter "s" following the item number indicates sermon and "p" indicates prayer.

BAINBRIDGE, WARREN S. (First Methodist Church, Boulder, Colo.) **189s**

BAKER, OREN H. (Colgate-Rochester Divinity School, Rochester, N. Y.) **209s**

BALCOMB, RAYMOND E. (Sellwood Methodist Church, Portland, Ore.) **328p**

BALLARD, FRANK H. (formerly of Hampstead Garden Suburb Free Church, London) **195s**

BASSETT, WALLACE (Cliff Street Baptist Church, Dallas, Texas) **128s**

BEECHER, HENRY WARD (1813-1887) **124s, 168s**

BERGER, DAVID I. (The Theological Seminary, University of Dubuque, Dubuque, Iowa) **167s**

BLACKWOOD, ANDREW W., JR. (Northminster Presbyterian Church, Columbus, Ohio) **204s**

BLACKWOOD, JAMES R. (Westminster Presbyterian Church, Wooster, Ohio) **59s**

BLOCKER, SIMON (Western Theological Seminary, Reformed Church of America, Holland, Mich.) **138s**

BOWIE, WALTER RUSSELL (The Protestant Episcopal Theological Seminary in Virginia, Alexandria, Va.) **126s**

BOYD, WARD F. (Southminster Presbyterian Church, Mission, Kansas) **329p**

BRAGG, WALLACE S. (Highway Mission Tabernacle, Assembly of God, Philadelphia, Pa.) **159s**

BROOKE, STOPFORD A. (1832-1916) **132s**

BROOKS, PHILLIPS (1835-1893) **25p, 179s**

BROOKS, WILLIAM E. (formerly of First Presbyterian Church, Morgantown, W. Va.) **133s**

BRUCE, GEORGE W. (formerly of Gresham Methodist Church, Gresham, Ore.) **330p**

BRYAN, WILLIAM JENNINGS (1860-1925) **155s**

BURNS, ROBERT W. (Peachtree Christian Church, Atlanta, Ga.) **331p**

CAIRNS, JOHN (1818-1892) **203s**

CAMPBELL, R. J. (Chichester Cathedral, England) **149s**

CARISS, J. CALVERT (North Street Congregational Church, Kingston, Jamaica) **150s**

CHIDLEY, HOWARD J. (First Congregational Church, Winchester, Mass.) **205s**

CLARK, GLENN (Macalester College, St. Paul, Minn.) **82p**

CLOW, W. M. (1853-1930) **136s**

COURT, FRANK A. (St. Paul Methodist Church, Lincoln, Neb.) **157s**

CROSS, HERBERT BARCLAY (formerly of Judson Memorial Baptist Church, Nashville, Tenn.) **199s**

DAWSON, GEORGE (1821-1876) **356p**

DENNEY, JAMES (1856-1917) **174s**

Poetry Index

Titles are listed in italics to distinguish them from first line references. When a title is similar to the first words of the opening line of a poem, only the first line reference is listed. Item numbers are given.

318

Textual Index

This cross-index of the texts of the funeral sermons in this volume are listed according to item numbers.

Classification Index

The references listed here concern particular classifications. Listing is made according to item numbers.

Topical Index

This cross-index of significant sermon themes and topics lists references according to sermon numbers.